More praise for *Yes, Your Teen is Crazy!*

"Dr. Bradley's excellent book should be required reading for every parent of teenagers. Often funny, sometimes heart-wrenching, and always wise, Dr. Bradley 'tells it like it is.' His book is an invaluable guide for parents in the throes of adolescence."

Virginia Smith Harvey, Ph.D.
Associate Professor, University of Massachusetts Boston
Author of *Effective Supervision in School Psychology*

"Teens *are* crazy! And as parents, we're crazy about our teens. Dr. Bradley's book helps us make sense of it all."

Mark Victor Hansen
Co-creator, #1 *New York Times* best-selling series
Chicken Soup for the Soul®

"Contemporary adolescence is a wild roller coaster ride for most parents. Dr. Bradley's book gives you the skills, strength, and wisdom you need to keep your relationship with your teen on track through the ups and downs of the terrifying, exhausting, yet exhilarating ride."

Charles Schrader, Ph.D.
Director, Juvenile Forensic Unit
Norristown State Hospital, Norristown, Pennsylvania

Mr. William E. Glenn
73 N Main St
Glen Ellyn, IL 60137

"Dr. Bradley tackles the big issues facing teens in today's society with humanism and respect. Offering clear guidelines for parents puzzled by adolescent behavior, his book is rich with stories of families who share the whys and hows of their own experiences."

Claudia K. Berenson, M.D.
Child Psychiatrist and Associate Professor
of Psychiatry & Pediatrics, University of New Mexico

"Insightful, entertaining, truthful, and at times poignant, Dr. Bradley's book is a necessary and wonderful guide for parents of teens."

Anthony F. Chunn, Ph.D.
CEO, CORA Services, Inc., a child and family resource center

"I have worked with thousands of teenagers and applaud this book. It is worth your time. It combines expert advice with old-fashioned values. Dr. Bradley is a wise old owl."

Father Val J. Peter, JCD, STD
Executive Director, Girls and Boys Town

"Dr. Bradley's wise and witty book is a must-read for any parent, professional, or youth development agency whose goal is 'building strong men and women—one kid at a time.'"

Phillip Jackson
President and CEO, Boys and Girls Clubs of Chicago

YES, YOUR TEEN IS CRAZY!

Yes,
Your Teen is Crazy!

Loving Your Kid Without Losing Your Mind

Michael J. Bradley, Ed.D.

HARBOR PRESS
GIG HARBOR, WASHINGTON

Library of Congress Cataloging-in-Publication Data

Bradley, Michael J., 1951-
    Yes, your teen is crazy! loving your kid without losing
your mind / Michael J. Bradley.
      p. cm.
    Includes index.
    ISBN 0-936197-44-7 (alk. paper)
      1. Parent and teenager. 2. Teenagers. 3. Adolescent
psychology. 4. Parenting. I. Title.

HQ799.15.B73 2003
649'.125—dc21   00-050591
                                          CIP

YES, YOUR TEEN IS CRAZY!
Loving Your Kid Without Losing Your Mind

Printed in the United States of America
Paperback   10   9   8   7   6

Harbor Press and the Nautilus shell logo
are registered trademarks of Harbor Press, Inc.

Harbor Press, Inc.
P.O. Box 1656
Gig Harbor, WA 98335

www.harborpress.com

To Sarah, for her joy when I am sad

To Ross, for his courage when I am scared

To Cindy, for her vision when I am blind

Thanks guys.

৩

Visit Dr. Bradley on the Internet at
www.docmikebradley.com

TABLE OF CONTENTS

FOREWORD

WHEN I FIRST HEARD the title, *Yes, Your Teen Is Crazy!* I thought, "Oh, no, not another book that bashes teens." However, by the time I put the book down, I was delighted with how well the concepts resonated with my perspectives as a neuroscientist, a child and adolescent psychiatrist, and a parent. The remarkable book you are about to read incorporates recent research on teen brain development with practical, sound advice for parents in a humorous and informed way.

My role as a scientist is to study the relationship between genes, the brain, and behavior during different stages of development. The brain forms first by greatly overproducing the number of brain cells and connections, and then all of these brain cells and connections fight it out for survival. For quite some time, scientists have known that these processes occurred in the womb, but when we recently started following brain growth in individual children, we were surprised to find a second wave of overproduction and elimination of brain cells that occurred throughout childhood and the teen years.

These dynamic changes in teen brain development coincide with a time of enormous creativity, passion, courage, and experimentation. They also coincide with a time of inconsistencies, missteps, and sometimes baffling behavior as teens struggle to find their unique place in the world, become self-sufficient, and test physical, cognitive, and emotional limits.

While the biology of the teen brain probably hasn't changed much in the last few thousand years, the environment has changed tremendously. Teens today are faced with a dizzying array of choices, more potent and addictive drugs, and, through media and the Internet, far greater exposure to sexual material. Stone Age impulses now have Computer Age temptations.

From my perspective as a practicing child and adolescent psychiatrist, I applaud Dr. Bradley's masterful job at helping parents sort out those behaviors that are a part of normal teen life from those behaviors that may reflect a psychiatric illness. He correctly encourages you to seek help from mental health professionals when symptoms of depression, anxiety, obsessive compulsive disorder, or other disorders are discovered.

Finally, as a parent of four teenagers-in-training, I found Dr. Bradley's pragmatic and concise problem-solving strategies of common adolescent dilemmas must reading for the new millennium parent. Throughout this highly entertaining and imminently useful book, Dr. Bradley will empower you not only to survive the teen years, but to enjoy and cherish the incredible journey from childhood to adulthood.

Jay N. Giedd, M.D.
Chief, Brain Imaging Unit
Child Psychiatry Branch
National Institute of Mental Health

ACKNOWLEDGMENTS

So many people have touched this work in so many powerful ways it seems inadequate to simply name them. But thanks to Bonnie Arena, Pete Bradley, Tony Chunn, Joe Ducette, Matti Gershenfeld, Barry Kayes, Michael McCarthy, Susan Paige, John Riley, Chuck Schrader, Ginny Smith-Harvey, and Gene Stivers. These people will see their own wisdom in these pages.

Thanks to the team that brought this book into being. To Harry Lynn, my publisher, for taking on such a risk and providing his steadfast determination and support. To my fairy godmother, Debby Young. As an editor she not only embodies the iron fist in the velvet glove, but she has a magical knack for nurturing neurotic psychologists through dark tunnels.

Thanks to my son, Ross, who graciously sacrificed far too many missed catches, swims, bike rides, and cloud watchings without ever once complaining.

Most of all, thanks to my wife, Cindy. For all of those countless months when she worked all day at her lab, worked all evening alone with our kids and then somehow always found the grace and patience to sit and listen attentively to my endless late night worries, frustrations, and fears. She is the best person I will ever know.

INTRODUCTION

Your defining act of love for your child will not be the 2:00 A.M. feedings, the sleepless, fretful night spent beside him in the hospital, or the second job you took to pay for college. Your zenith will occur in the face of a withering blast of frightening rage from your adolescent, in allowing no rage from yourself in response. Your finest moment may well be your darkest. And you will be a parent.

IN YOUR HANDS you hold a survival guide for parents facing the tests of raising a new-millennium adolescent. Like talking with a brother who is a shrink, this book empathizes with your pain, explains just what the heck is going on, and provides clear, well-researched recommendations on courses of action. The tone is as soft and humorous as possible to help shell-shocked parents regain a perspective on which to rebuild competence and confidence, two essential qualities for surviving your kid's adolescence.

The startling news offered here is groundbreaking research that is finally proving with science what you've come to suspect through your pain: *Your kid is crazy.* What used to be a sad, quiet joke between Mom and Dad is now becoming accepted more and more as neurological fact. *Adolescents are temporarily brain-damaged.* The implications of this are enormous, and those implications are what this three-part book is about.

Part One describes adolescents. I'll show you what we recently learned about your kid's brain that rocked the adolescent treatment community. This data will help you avoid personalizing your kid's insane behaviors by proving to you that he's not a bad person, he's just brain-challenged. This part is quite fascinating.

Part One goes on to show you how that misfiring brain interacts with the dangerous world we've built around your temporarily disabled child. Did you know that your kid can actually make the case that we adults are the ones telling her to have sex, do drugs, and rock 'n roll (a popular general term used by kids that refers to aggressive and violent acting-out behaviors)? This part is quite terrifying.

In Part Two of the book, you'll learn what this new research says about your behavior. These brain imagings of your kid's head tell us that your parenting training is obsolete—that being what you thought was a good parent actually can create problems for your at-risk kid. We adults must now rethink who we are as parents in light of the new data.

Part Three will teach you how this new information rewrites the old book on how to raise that brain-damaged teen in our value-damaged world. The old rules of parenting adolescents just don't work in this new millennium because *rules* don't work anymore. Today you need *skills* to deal with the insanity that rages both inside your child's brain and outside, in his world.

But the truly wonderful side to the new research is that it gives you a neurological window of opportunity with your child that we never knew existed. Contrary to what we used to believe, the brain development game is not over by adolescence. *You can rewire that head.* Mother Nature believes in second chances; however, that second-chance rewiring can either be miraculous or disastrous. You get to choose by parenting with either obsolete rules or with newfound skills. This is truly exciting stuff, but it comes at a price.

Be forewarned that this is not another "how-to" book. Cookbook approaches to working with difficult adolescents work just about as well as counseling a teenager without working with the parents. As Rocky the Squirrel used to warn Bullwinkle, "That trick never works." And it never will work, my dear parent, *because you are still the most influential force in your adolescent's life.* Yes, that baggy-pantsed, many-colored, multi-pierced creature who elects root canal over being seen in the mall within 10 linear feet of you is nonetheless largely living his life in relation to who you are, for better *and* for worse. Thus, for your child to change, your relationship must change. For this to happen, you must change. That is the first step.

WAIT! Before you angrily toss this book back onto the shelf, stay with me for one more minute. This is *not* about parents being bad people. On the contrary, parents by definition are usually wonderful people. In fact, some of my best friends are parents. Typically, they're hard-working, self-sacrificing, caring, and loving folks. Those with tough adolescents are usually also exhausted, angry, isolated, and terrified. They're just as any one of us would be if someone stuck a scalpel in our hand and told us to perform brain surgery with no medical training—and on our own child, no less. Overly dramatic metaphor? Not to those who have stayed up all night agonizing over how a certain decision would affect their child's life.

You see, it's simply the *training* that you lack, not the heart. If you didn't give a damn, you wouldn't be reading this book, but I'm afraid the training is more involved than just giving advice. It requires our understanding that as parents we are the stage upon which our children will act out their conflicts. We have to go along on their ride, and accept that our teens will confront us with ourselves, rubbing our noses in our own shortcomings. Thus we must be open to difficult self-examination and disclosure. Easy to say. Tough to do.

To make it a little easier, this book teaches with stories. The names in the stories are fictitious, but the circumstances are based on real situations from my patient files. I share them with you to try to ease your pain and sense of isolation.

Just like trauma survivors, parents of adolescents in crisis are very slow to discuss their experiences with "civilians." They've had too many instances where they shared a horror story only to see that infuriating look of pompous disbelief on the faces of those who have had the good fortune of never ducking bullets in a trench. Those judgmental eyes often betray that maddening secret disdain: "I would *never* allow *my* child to act like that."

Parents in crisis first scan the faces of their audience looking for the gray hairs, the facial worry lines, and the knowing, judgment-free nods that tell them *you understand* their pain. Only then can they begin to open up.

The stories are that connection for you. These vignettes are comforting, powerful, and profound, and they signal a safe haven from the societal judgments and self-recriminations that parents often bear. When faced with a crisis, you first need to feel that you are in a safe place. Then, and only then, will you be able to listen to see if there are better ways of dealing with your child. There can be no safer place than in the company of all those parents of adolescents who preceded you. This book is that safe place.

In that light, understand that this book belongs to the many parents and kids who have struggled with the issues we'll visit. The families I've worked with over the past 27 years inspired me to write this book. Many offered to have their stories told without anonymity so that other parents might benefit. These people are the true authors of this work. As you read you will come to see their failings, their wisdom, their tenacity, and most of all their courage. For in sharing their own vulnerabilities and mistakes, they give us the great gift of perhaps not sharing their pain.

Finally, three warnings. First, try to keep in mind those individual differences that make the human race so interesting. These apply to you and to your kid, too. The adolescent issues I address represent the major new trends of parenting teenagers today. Your situation will vary according to your child's and your own uniqueness. Use what I present here as basic examples to shape what works for your particular situation.

Second, the subject matter and language used here are strong and I'm sure offensive to many. If this book were a CD I wouldn't let my nine-year-old play it. But this reflects the reality of the adolescent world, and like it or not, it is part of their language and culture. To edit out the upsetting material means to lose the true context of the experiences. Therefore, all of the dialogue is quoted accurately.

Finally, some may find this book flippant and insensitive. That's because it *is* flippant and insensitive. It sometimes treats serious, painful, and terrifying subjects with comedy and irreverence. For example, calling teenagers "crazy" may alarm or offend some of you who have dealt first-hand with true mental illness, especially in your own families (as I have). And if you haven't dealt with true mental illness, it might make you a bit uncomfortable or defensive to use the word "crazy" to describe your child. But for 27 years, "crazy" has been the word I've heard over and over again used by wide-eyed, ashen-faced parents struggling to explain inexplicable teenage behavior. So throughout this book, I'm going to use your language to explain your kid's behavior. Remember, he's not insane; he's just crazy.

In both my work and this book, I often choose to be flip *just because* this subject matter can be so serious, painful, and terrifying. I've found humor to be our last defense against chaos, allowing us to push back the darkness, keeping it from infecting our souls.

If I offend or shock you, I really do apologize. I'm not a fan of shock jocks myself, but I'm afraid that being offended and shocked are prerequisites for parenting adolescents in the new millennium.

Fasten your seat belt. We're going in.

Part One

YOUR CHILD:
THE NEW-MILLENNIUM ADOLESCENT

CHAPTERS 1 THROUGH 5 turn floodlights on the foggy swamp of contemporary adolescence to see what nasty stuff hides out in there. Dark swamps are mainly scary because our frightened minds fill in all the black areas with monsters much more frightening than daylight reveals. For sure, there are some very scary things there, and many terrible things lurk there today that never did before, but that doesn't mean our kids can't survive the journey. And it doesn't mean that we're powerless to help our children navigate in safety.

It does mean, however, that before deciding how to gird ourselves in Part Two of this book—the parent preparation—we need to first learn about the swamp itself to see what exists there, which noises are threats, which are normal, where we can safely step, how we measure progress, and when to get the heck out.

And most of all, we need to begin to believe that it is possible to survive the swamp of adolescence as a loving family. It really can be done.

Chapter 1

THE ADOLESCENT BRAIN

Michael's mom sat in my office sobbing, repeatedly attempting to reason with her raging and verbally vicious adolescent son. After watching his endless bullying and her tormented begging for too long, I sent him out of the room, turned to her and said, "Why are you talking to him like he makes sense?" "What do you mean?" she sobbed. I gave her the same shrugging "Duh" gesture her son had just used a dozen times and I almost yelled, "He's nuts! You can't talk to crazy people like they make sense." Her eyes and mouth flew open, astonished at my insensitivity. Slowly her wrenching sobs transformed into chuckling, softly at first, then building to a crescendo of raucous laughter that rang off the walls. "Oh, God," she howled, "How I needed to laugh like that! It feels wonderful. You're right. Michael is nuts. And I'm nuts to sit here and talk with him like that."

In our final session several months later, she reminded me of that exchange. "That," she said, "was the beginning of our healing."

MICHAEL'S PERFORMANCE illustrates a lot about contemporary adolescents, which we'll examine shortly. My own performance illustrates much about us as responding adults. While we address this fully in Part Two, let me jump ahead for a minute to help you see the importance of training, which starts with this chapter, as you learn about your kid's brain. And training, after all, is what this book is about.

That cool, controlled psychologist was working hard to restrain an old rule-based urge to eviscerate Michael. This keeping-cool stuff is not as easy as it looks. Part of me wanted to make him cry really hard for daring to be disrespectful to both me and his terrified mother. I wanted badly to physically intimidate him, to jack him up against the wall and scream, "JUST WHO THE HELL DO YOU THINK YOU ARE?" My alternate response came from years of retraining and experience focusing on unlearning my old rules (what I saw my father do) as much as learning new skills.

Parenting an adolescent in today's world is much the same as flying a jet aircraft or performing brain surgery. Any training you received 30 years ago is not only useless, it can actually impair your ability to perform well. Neurosurgeons and pilots constantly upgrade their skills, replacing outmoded thinking with new training that reflects contemporary realities.

No one questions this evolutionary process of learning, except when we talk of parenting. With a near-religious fervor, we often enshrine (and thus cripple) parenting as something sacred and beyond our routine functioning. We love to support the romantic delusion that, unlike surgery, we should intuitively and permanently know how to parent adolescents based on how we were raised, either by doing just what our parents did or the exact opposite, but always as some form of *reaction* to what we experienced decades ago. We attribute the problems of our children to liberalism, conservatism, godlessness, godfulness, evolutionism, creationism—anything that seems to make sense, except the quiet notion that contemporary parenting is a *complex set of learned skills, many of which seem counterintuitive to us*. It's not religion and it sure ain't politics. And it can be learned from good and bad sources, so we must constantly question and upgrade our learning.

Successfully parenting an adolescent in today's world requires levels of skill, endurance, wisdom, and strength that make piloting an aircraft pale in comparison. No joke. Most of all, parenting an adolescent requires training much more personally intense than any pilot can imagine. Simply having a conversation with your contemporary adolescent child can require special skills never before required. What you learned 30 years ago might have worked 30 years ago. You were trained on a Boeing 707. Do you really think you can safely fly the Concorde? Are you sure you can safely raise that 15-year-old? With the right retraining, the answer is yes!

The first step in this retraining is to learn how your kid's brain works. Besides being informative, this will give us an excuse to get a little revenge, and gossip about the nutcase upstairs—the one lying in a sea of pizza boxes and dirty clothes, playing air guitar with his toes and listening to earphone music (music?) that you can actually hear out in the hall because it's so incredibly loud and/or because either he and/or you kicked in his door last week. [Author's note: Throughout this book, whenever I use the word "music," I follow it with a question mark. This is my passive-aggressive way of striking back at my very funny, very sarcastic son whose questionable taste in music (music?) differs from my own excellent taste.]

You may have recently lost your sense of humor regarding your kid, so here's a travel-worn "more truth than humor" story that psychologists have told for years:

Parent: "I want you to evaluate my 13-year-old son."

Doctor: "OK. He's suffering from a transient psychosis with an intermittent rage disorder, punctuated by episodic radical mood swings, but his prognosis is good for a full recovery."

Parent: "What does all that mean?"

Doctor: "He's 13."

Parent: "How can you say all that without even meeting him?"

Doctor: "He's 13."

Who would have thought this tired old joke would turn out to be a dead-on prophecy?

Technically Speaking, They're Crazy

Up until now, psychologists had a lot of great-sounding theories to explain why adolescents tend to act so crazy at times. We believed that all that risk-taking, judgment-impaired, aggressive, and oppositional behavior was a function of early childhood experiences, peer pressure, the hormonal effects of puberty, and, most hurtful of all for too many mothers and fathers, poor parenting. No one thought that massive structural changes in teenagers' brains were largely to blame. We had no clue that their brains were changing.

The textbooks now being used state that brain development races in early childhood, and then calms to a slow but steady pace toward adulthood. Based on studies of brain volume, or size, science tells us that 95 percent of the brain develops in a child by about age five. From this fact, came all of the popular and now useless thinking that the first few years of life were the most critical for your kid—that in early childhood her skills, personality, and everything else get fixed in place, or "hard-wired," as researchers like to say. Up until now, we believed that after those "critical" early years, changing those hard-wired brain components was either difficult or impossible. That's why in the movies the psychologist always says, "So tell me about Johnny's early childhood."

But our science was terribly flawed. While it is true that 95 percent of the brain is developed by age five, *the most advanced parts of the brain don't complete their development until adolescence is pretty much over.*

How We Found Out

Two very recent ground-breaking studies have come together to blow apart our old view of the adolescent brain and provide us with astonishing insights into your kid's head that offer explanations for crazy teen behavior and revolutionize our thinking about how to best help our children survive these difficult times.

Starting in 1991, Dr. Jay Giedd, chief of brain imaging at the Child Psychiatry Branch of the National Institute of Mental Health (NIMH), started taking pictures of kids' brains over a nine-year span. He was curious to know to what extent children's crazy behavior is willful, and to what extent it is beyond their control. He and his colleagues at UCLA and McGill University in Canada used magnetic resonance imaging (MRI) to study exactly how a child's brain grows from ages 3 to 18. They studied almost 1,000 "normal" kids (including two of Dr. Giedd's children) at intervals ranging from two weeks to four years. What they found was nothing short of astonishing, and it completely rewrote our understanding of the adolescent brain.

First, contrary to previous thinking that the brain is completely developed by age five, they saw that throughout the teen years and into the twenties, substantial growth occurs in a brain structure called the corpus callosum. The corpus callosum is a set of nerves that connects all the parts of the brain that must work together to function efficiently, as in making good decisions. This set of "wires" is critical to things like intelligence, consciousness, and self-awareness. This initial finding was revolutionary enough, but these researchers weren't finished.

With amazement, they also found that the prefrontal cortex of the brain goes through a wild growth spurt that coincides with the onset of adolescence. In fact, they found that this part of the brain does the bulk of its maturation between the ages of 12 and 20. The prefrontal cortex is where the most sophisticated of our abilities reside. Emotional control, impulse restraint, and rational decision-making are all gifts to us from our prefrontal cortex, gifts your kid hasn't yet received. Perhaps Dr. Karl Pribram, director of the Center for Brain Research and Informational Sciences at Radford University in Virginia, described it best when he said, "The prefrontal cortex is the seat of civilization."

At about the same time, Dr. Deborah Yurgelun-Todd a neuropsychologist at McLean Hospital in Belmont, Massachusetts, ran a fascinating study that dove-tailed perfectly with Dr. Giedd's findings. Again using magnetic resonance imaging (MRI), Dr. Yurgelun-Todd first showed how adults use two different brain parts to make sophisticated judgments such as interpreting social signals. In her research, she showed a group of adults pictures of faces contorted in fear and then asked them to interpret the emotion the faces conveyed. As the adults responded, she found that both the prefrontal cortex and the brain's limbic system worked to process the task. The limbic system is a kind of primal emotion center that deals with emotions like rage and fear. Once the limbic system is aroused, the prefrontal cortex can process or moderate the reactions or impulses of the limbic system. Using this two-step process, the adults all recognized fear in the faces shown to them in the pictures.

When Dr. Yurgelun-Todd tried this with teens, however, many were unable to process the pictures correctly. She found that the pictures aroused the teens' limbic systems, but *their prefrontal cortexes were not working*. In other words, the teens were moved by the pictures, but were unable to figure out what they meant.

What This Means to You

So what do these studies offer you? Well, we have good news and bad news.

The good news is that positive things such as sports, music, school achievement, responsibility, and social consciousness can be hard-wired into that expanding adolescent brain. You may owe God, Mother

Nature, fate, or whomever you choose a nice dinner out because he, she, or it designed your child to get a second chance at life. All of that new growth in the prefrontal cortex is available for use by your kid. The old view that there is little room for change in your child by the time he is a teen is wrong.

The bad news is that you may want to curse God, Mother Nature, or fate because this second-chance brain programming can be used toward negative things, too. If the teen years are filled with rage, dysfunction, and alienation, they may be "set in stone" in our kids' heads. The old thinking that the brain game is over by age five is wrong. The most critical years for your young adolescent are likely yet to be.

The good *and* bad news is that, first, this wild brain development may create new, unpredictable thought pathways, wherein action thoughts can outrace judgment capabilities just as they did in early childhood. Second, teens may be neurologically handicapped in recognizing and processing social emotions such as anger and fear. This is bad news since it shows the monumental obstacles confronting our adolescents as they try to grow up. The good part is that these behaviors are not character flaws or signs of an evil nature. In adolescent children, the maddening behavior is just the result of mixed-up wiring that will straighten out in time if, if, and only if we adults respond not with raging, hurtful punishments, but with carefully crafted responses intended to calmly but firmly teach brain-challenged children to become functional adults.

Remember 12 years ago when your teen was a toddler and you walked in to find him sitting in the cat box munching on some very scary litter? Remember last week when your teen used the pressure washer to clean your car, stripping off about $500 worth of paint before she realized this was not such a good idea? Do the words *impulsive* and *poor judgment* come to mind? Can you draw that 2-year-old face onto that 12-year-old body? Learn this trick well, because we're going to use it a lot. Both that toddler and adolescent brain at times are unstable, dysfunctional, and completely unpredictable. They both have just developed a bunch of brain circuits that may fire off unexpectedly. Also, they both have neurologically deficient controls to moderate these impulses and to understand the likely outcomes of their actions. In the science of mental health, we have a word for that. We call it crazy.

This book is going to answer the question that is probably running through your head right now: *So what can I do as a parent to get this brain-challenged teen through to adulthood alive, functional, and, dare I say, happy?* First, though, let's point out some evidence that whoever designed teenagers certainly had a sense of humor.

Mother Nature's timing of this adolescent brain growth is either lousy or great depending on the day you've had with your kid. On the positive side, his impulsiveness and risk-taking are critical to his growing up and becoming his own person. This will ultimately help him form the adult personality needed to tackle the challenges that lie ahead. The negative side is that his brain is going wild just as he's seeing himself as an adult, deserving of all the grown-up privileges of autonomy, independent decision-making, and self-regulation.

Common Adolescent Disorders

It is this aspect of teen brain dysfunction that explains the following bewildering displays you may have witnessed with your own child. These stories are actual events from my case notes and illustrate that what looks so uniquely insane, enraging, and terrifying about your child turns out to be pretty commonplace stuff. Your neighbors will never admit that their kid does any of this because they're afraid you'll think their kid is nuts. And you'd be right.

The "disorder" joke-titles are intended to get you to smile through your pain, a skill no family should be without. My son just completed a family coat-of-arms for a school project and his motto is "Keep your sense of humor." Smart kid.

Here are some common adolescent "mental disorders":

♦ *The Shepherdus Germanus Seizure Syndrome:*
Following her arrest for deliberately driving Dad's Range Rover over 10 grand-worth of new landscaping in front of the private school at which she consistently achieved excellence, Susan's parents asked her the dumbest question you can think of: "Why?"

That was the same dumb question Ronald's parents asked when he decided to push the big plastic gas can up the driveway with the lawn tractor, blade running, causing the can to rupture, spraying flaming gas everywhere. (Ronald escaped with singed pride, but the tractor was toast.)

When asked "why," both children seizured in the manner you've likely seen by now with your own adolescent. Eyes wide open, head slightly tilted, tongue hanging out, and slow drooling with nonresponsiveness. This is very much like the look you get asking your German Shepherd puppy, "Why?"

No joke, both the puppy and the adolescent rarely know the "why" of their bizarre actions. We grownups always want to find out what the deep-rooted psychological causes might be for our kids' craziness. Some will spend a lot of money on therapy to sit and speculate in long, complex discussions searching for obscure, unconscious conflicts justifying the aberrant behavior. In turn, we psychologists can expound for hours on great-sounding psychosocial models that neatly explain away the apparent madness of a teenager.

The more likely and mundane truth is that there usually is no deep, mysterious psychological explanation for *occasional* episodes of adolescent insanity. It's just the wiring. Usually your kid is at least as amazed as you are at her behavior. She's just responding to weird, brain dysfunction-based, irresistible impulses to do irrational things. She's losing a race in which her brain impulses outrun her judgment. Frontal lobe stuff. She honestly wishes she knew the answer to "why," for life would then be much easier for her. She usually doesn't know why, and life usually isn't easier. We call this being nuts.

Frequently being asked "why" by parents, and just as frequently not knowing the answer, can lead to another teenage "disorder." Again, the behavior I describe is quite real, as you know all too well. The "disorder" titles are comic relief.

◆ *Aphasia Whenus Iwannus:*
Common to adolescence, this sudden loss of speech appears without warning. It may occur in conjunction with a total but temporary hearing loss. Interestingly, this hearing loss seems most pronounced with sounds that mimic parental voices asking questions about chores or homework. This disability often miraculously improves upon hearing a mechanical voice say, "You've got mail."

Jokes aside, adolescents do feel that they have the option of choosing not to respond to certain parental questions. Parents typically find this a maddening display of arrogance, but it is more often tied to their kid's self-confusion. The silence is frequently a signal that the child can't explain something even to herself, so she doesn't even bother trying since parents may only hammer her more.

◆ *Maturationnus Erraticus:*
   John's dad told me his story slowly, as if afraid of some terrible diagnostic pronouncement. "This morning is a good example of what I mean. My 16-year-old son approached me with his baby sister's 'Tinky Winky' doll under his arm. I had actually watched him play with this thing for the preceding 30 minutes. He competed nicely, but nevertheless competed with his sister for possession of the toy. He then came over to me and asked for the car keys to go pick up his girlfriend. When I asked him where they were going, he exploded: 'YOU ALWAYS TREAT ME LIKE I'M A KID!' As he yelled, he was shaking Tinky Winky in my face. I have to tell you, sometimes I feel nuts myself. I laughed, felt sad, and got mad all at the same time. I didn't know that was possible. My son had no idea why I thought any of this was odd."

Also described as the "Six or Sixteen Syndrome," most adolescents display this behavior to some degree, with maddening results for everyone, especially for the adolescent. He is trapped between the two worlds of childhood and adulthood, and can't find his way out. Like a science fiction character, he finds himself existing in two separate dimensions at the same time, with two completely different sets of rules, expectations, needs, and fears. In one afternoon he might find himself playing Wiffle Ball, having sex, playing with his old army soldiers, and trying to decide if his friend is right about heroin being harmless if you just snort it. This could make anyone nuts, even with good brain wiring, and this level of stress can lead to the onset of this next "more-truth-than-humor" disease.

◆ *Moodus Elevatoris Irrationnus:*
   Fourteen-year-old Harrison, according to his father, bugged Dad relentlessly for three weeks to go the seashore. The morning they were leaving, Harrison was up at 5:00 A.M. (a miracle in itself) packing and pushing everyone to get ready. He ran upstairs to grab one last thing, and never came down. "I'm not going," he finally

screamed out his window as the family kept calling him. "I hate the shore. Why do you always make me go there?"

These out-of-the-blue mood swings can set land-speed records, causing parents to wish their kid had a digital forehead readout to indicate what floor he's on at a particular moment. It looks uniquely crazy. Turns out it's just commonly crazy.

All of these temporary "mental disorders" are normal experiences common to adolescence. One could well argue that most big kids are nuts based on demonstrable brain dysfunction alone, without even taking into consideration the terrible moral-psychological-physical issues they are wrestling with—sex, religion, drugs, sex, power, identity, sex, self-image, sex, violence, sex, and sex (more on this in Chapter 2). Further, their days are typically saturated with messages that loudly and publicly delineate their failures and worthlessness. It ain't easy being a teen.

It starts with the opening of his eyes "WHY CAN'T YOU GET UP ON TIME?" carries into morning "WHY CAN'T YOU RAISE YOUR HAND?" evolves through the afternoon "WHY CAN'T YOU FIELD GROUNDERS TO YOUR LEFT?" and continues into the evening "WHY CAN'T YOU MAKE ENOUGH MONEY TO TAKE ME TO THE 'FLAMING PUKES' CONCERT?" As the day ends he drifts off to sleep hearing that sweet adolescent lullaby, "PIGS COULDN'T STAND TO LIVE IN YOUR ROOM."

So be a little understanding. These are often terrible times for your kid. He is probably brain-challenged, overwhelmed with irresolvable conflicts, and forced to constantly see mostly his failures. Your daughter is nuts and she's scared of not looking right, sounding right, or even thinking right. As such, she requires special handling. Just trying to have a little conversation with a teen caught in the crush of adolescent mental dysfunction can be an art form.

Recognizing the Pain and Confusion

Adrienne stared coldly at her mom in my waiting room, pretending she couldn't hear her mother's repeated pleas to go into my office. She calmly studied her mom's tense smile, searching for her next target.

With a snicker, she found it. She realized her mom was secretly praying not to have yet another humiliating scene in front of a stranger, namely me. "Don't think you're HOT SH. . . 'cause you got me here, MOTHER. I'm not saying a f'ng thing to this SHRINK." She fired her last words towards me, and then turned her head away.

"And what the hell are YOU staring at?" she snapped without even looking at me, as if addressing the wall. For a second, I didn't realize she was talking to me. "Sorry," I responded, "I get told a lot by teenagers that I've got this bad habit of staring. It drives them nuts." "OTHER kids come here?" she snorted incredulously. "I don't believe it! Your music SUCKS!" I nodded. "I've been told that too. You should hear my son do his jokes on my music. He's a riot." She looked away, as if tiring of punching a big marshmallow. Then she boxed herself in: "Well, I ain't goin' into your office. I'm sittin' right here and there's nothin' you can do about it." "OK by me," I shrugged while pulling up a chair. "Mom, why don't you go down the street and grab some coffee for an hour? We'll be fine."

Watching the door close behind her mother, Adrienne looked almost vulnerable. I had to somehow meet her at her level to connect. I went with the "we're both adults, so you choose" tack. "Look, Adrienne, I can't tell your mom anything you tell me anyway, unless it's something that could kill you or someone else, so you're in charge here. You can talk, sing, curse, say nothing, whatever. But my next client likes to come in early, so would you rather say nothing out here with strangers or say nothing in my office with me?" I unconsciously held my breath for my gambit, then exhaled too loudly as she slowly got up and walked to my office door. She quickly turned with exasperation and yelled, "NOW WHAT?" She was used to hearing adults sigh a lot behind her. "Nothing," I laughed, "I just get nervous meeting new people." Looking away, she may have grinned.

Adrienne was perplexed. To regain control, she wouldn't sit down in my office, choosing instead to slowly cruise the room while she defiantly clutched the intake form she had filled out.

"You were in the army?" she asked politely, looking at my mementos. I nodded. With precisely the same "polite" voice she asked, "Did you kill any babies?" I held my response for dramatic effect. I can play, too. "Not recently, although my kids tempt me from time to time." Without any reaction she continued her search of my walls.

Unwittingly she was getting ensnared. "These your kids?" she asked. "Is that the boy who always busts on you?" "That's him," and with obvious love I added, "Doesn't he look like a real wiseass?" Now she turned on me. "Speaking of wiseass, here's your F'ING FORM," she snarled, tossing the intake sheet at me. I stooped to pick it up.

It felt like the bottom of the ninth inning, two on, two out, full count. She must be bringing her heat. Under the heading "Name" she had scrawled "SCREW YOU!!!" She fixed her gaze on me to see how her fastball would do. "Scroo Yu," I read aloud. I looked up at her, held her eyes, and deadpanned. "That's an Asian name, right?"

She stared. She smiled. She laughed. She lost. She won. We had connected.

Adrienne is a wonderful example of how crazy adolescents can be. Whenever I'm debating the premise of this book with colleagues, I often ask them to describe to me how they handle talking with a difficult teenager. Try this exercise yourself.

Think about how you prepare to talk to your kid when he's in a crazy phase. Do you feel at ease talking fully and openly about your thoughts and questions? Or do you find yourself carefully editing your words so you don't set your kid off? Have you had that horrific experience known only to stand-up comics and parents of teens, where you get on a roll only to completely lose your audience by one slightly ill-timed punch line? Are your toe, neck, or stomach muscles sore from all that secret nervous tensing your muscles do after a 10-minute chat with your teen? Does giving those reminders about homework/chore/dinner with grandmom feel like a walk through an Albanian minefield?

Learning how to verbally approach adolescents today is the same rigorous baptism-by-fire known to rookie cops and new workers at mental hospitals. You can't just say what you think because many of the people you work with are mentally ill and cannot handle normal conversation. After a while, you get better at developing a style, but you always know that you have to carefully handle these folks with a trained verbal and emotional discipline. You can't just be natural with your troubled teen. That's because he's nuts.

I'll train you in Parts Two and Three on teen-speak because you do need to learn how to verbally engage your child without getting clawed.

But the very idea of having to learn to talk to your own kid can be tough to get used to.

"Britanny is MY OWN CHILD, for God's sake. I created her inside my womb, carried her, gave birth to her, nursed her, raised her, left an abusive man for her, and struggled just to survive. We've been close for 14 years, with no secrets, ever. SHE IS MY BLOOD AND MY LIFE. AND NOW YOU HAVE THE NERVE TO TELL ME HOW I HAVE TO TALK TO MY OWN CHILD?" As her anger cooled into sadness, her tears overcame her for a moment. Then Tia paused, sighed, and continued in a quiet voice. "I'm sorry. I already knew that I needed to come here and have someone like you teach me how to talk with my own child. That breaks my heart and it makes me hate you. Can you understand that?" "Yes," I answered, "I can understand that. I would hate me too."

I wasn't kidding. The whole concept of having to go and see a stranger or read a book to learn how to be with your own child is disheartening and infuriating. It can make you hate both the shrink and your kid, but try hard to remember that you already have the important parts of parenting mastered: the love, the commitment, and the willingness to get disheartened and infuriated. A therapist, or this book, only acts as a mechanic suggesting how to connect all that good stuff you bring to the relationship.

As infuriating as your kid can be, for now try to remember that it's much worse to be stuck in that adolescent body that yells at you every time you try to talk. As I said, don't talk to crazy people like they make sense. Here, this means don't personalize her outrageous behavior and react as if it came from someone sane. Your child doesn't qualify as sane for now, and that's not a happy way to be.

Being truly mentally ill is perhaps the worst experience we can endure. Think of watching yourself out of control, reacting to things you know aren't real, yet somehow *are* real. Real mental illness robs us of our soul, in a hideously painful fashion.

Adolescence, at times, is a kind of mental illness. That raging child you love, who seems to be delighting in her torment of you, is often in just that kind of terrible pain. She is fighting for her soul, and she can't let anyone know, least of all, her Uncle Louie, who loves to constantly tell her, "These are the best years of your life, kiddo. It's all downhill from here." Thanks so much, Uncle Louie.

By the way, are you feeling a strange, familiar connection with my words, beyond what you see in your kid? I'll tell you why. It's "déjà vu all over again." You probably experienced this yourself as an adolescent. I surely did. *We were all the same way.* Since we've begun to keep such records, researchers have found that, psychologically speaking, teenagers are very consistent creatures from generation to generation. Yet a romantic myth has somehow evolved that today's kids are so different from the way we were in our day—that as teenagers we were more responsible, less violent, less sex-driven, more spiritual, and so on.

What confusing nonsense this is. Our research shows adolescent personality to be amazingly similar over time-comparison studies, which now makes sense in light of our new adolescent brain research. I can remember a number of kids I grew up with who certainly would have been involved with guns and explosives if these had been available to them. Do you recall many adolescent males in your day that would have turned down the opportunity to have sex, protected or not? And just how responsible were your driving habits?

So if kids are essentially the same as we were, why do they seem so particularly crazy these days? Two reasons.

The first reason is a very subtle yet immensely powerful societal change that's been slowly progressing for decades. It's best summarized by saying that we've somehow come to view adolescents as if they were adults and not children. From the kid's perspective, this wish is nothing new. Teenagers of all generations have lobbied for adult privileges with the swaggering assurances that they can handle "it." The fact is that they cannot handle "it" *and they know this.* They cannot handle the dangerous pressures confronting them without some structure from their parents, yet they'll go to war over imposed parental structure.

Paradoxically, kids will tell me how scary it is to be in situations where their peers are in full control without adult supervision, such as parties (no, you can't leave him home alone for the weekend). They really want competent adults to be in charge; at the same time, they'll challenge any adult who tries to be in charge. They'll share with me, as their shrink, all of these conflicting feelings, but never tell you as their parent. Don't take it personally. It's just that you represent the other side of the privilege bargaining table, so there's no way they can give you such information. You'd probably respond by setting appropriate limits or something crazy like that.

For now, know that all teens have always wanted to be treated like adults. What's new is that we've somehow signed onto this disastrous notion that they *are* adults, capable of handling "it" completely solo. It's not working. Teens left on their own as small adults not only screw up big-time, they become depressed and rageful in the bargain.

Our current society of adolescents supports the warning on my son's favorite T-shirt: "Never underestimate the power of stupid people in large groups." With loving apologies to my kid, I must ironically note that adolescents today are powerful because we've allowed them to become that way, stupid because they're brain-challenged, and seriously at-risk because of the second reason they look so scary: The world we've created around them is truly insane. But, unlike your child, it won't get better on its own.

Take three deep breaths and continue on to Chapter 2. How's your seat belt?

Chapter 2

YOUR ADOLESCENT'S WORLD:
SEX, DRUGS, AND ROCK 'N ROLL
LIKE YOU NEVER SAW

IN MOST WAYS, kids are pretty much the same as they've always been. Nuts. But in most ways, the world around them is incomprehensibly different. And also nuts. We've created a world dripping with sex, drugs, and violence and plunked our temporarily insane children in the middle of it. Our wonderful economy has also provided unprecedented quick-path avenues of easy access to these things. It is an adolescent world different from the one you recall.

When your son tells you that you "don't understand," trust him. You don't. Neither do I. He lives in a culture foreign to both of us but with one big commonality: Adolescents do value and respect honesty. So in return for my being straight-up with them, some teenagers have granted me a visa to tour their worlds a bit. Let me tell you what I've seen.

Drugs: A Short-Term Antidote for the Pain

Satan keeps his end of contracts, at least where drugs are concerned. Drugs do what they promise, and a lot more, particularly for teenagers. They are very effective and very efficient ways of changing reality. They're certainly much more proficient than any therapy or prescribed medication that I know. When parents ask me why their child does drugs, I often ask them why she *shouldn't* do drugs.

Remember the discussion in Chapter 1 of the intense and chronic pain that adolescence presents for troubled kids? Drugs are excellent antidotes for that pain. If you, as a competent, rational adult, had a searing toothache with no foreseeable relief, would you respect my admonition to "tough it out" without painkillers that might be addicting, or would you not give a damn about the long-term consequences of drug use, focusing instead only on numbing that terrible pain?

I'd pick Door Number 2. And before you tell me that my metaphor is inappropriate, please remember back to your darkest adolescent day, when the future looked most bleak and long-term consequences were irrelevant because you felt little potential or desire to survive. Remember how scary this time can be. Now, tell me once again, why *shouldn't* your kid do drugs?

The first truly frightening fact you need to confront is that drug use often *does* make major sense in the context of the adolescent world. Drugs can serve so many purposes so well. They change painful emotional realities, make uncool kids cool, provide friends, enable identity development, help rebel against authority, spotlight adult hypocrisy, and do many other wonderful things for your kid, at least in the short term. In the long term, they can kill her.

"Buddy has been depressed ever since his friend Sherry died. They were doing shots with a group of friends celebrating someone's sixteenth birthday. These are good kids, Dr. Bradley. They don't do drugs. We knew they were drinking occasionally, but that's no big deal these days, as I'm sure you know. I guess they didn't keep track of how many [shots] they did, but Sherry ended up having convulsions and inhaling her vomit..." Mom's voice trailed off, overwhelmed at the horrible scene that Buddy had witnessed. When Mom found her composure, she lost her perspective: "It's so hard to believe that Sherry's gone. It's not like these kids do drugs."

ALCOHOL IS *the* DRUG

Believe it or not, your child stands a radically better chance of dying from booze than from marijuana, heroin, cocaine, and hallucinogens *combined*. So why is it that we adults much prefer to find our child drunk on alcohol than stoned on marijuana? Do you drink? Are you wearing blinders? Billy's parents did both.

"We'd caught Billy with marijuana paraphernalia three times. He's only

16. It really terrifies us. He obviously isn't listening to us anymore. He adores his Uncle Bobby, so I asked my brother to take my son out to talk with him about the dangers of drug use. I think it may have worked. We haven't had a drug incident in a few months now, so doctor, why did you call us in?"

"I'm breaking confidentiality with your son, since he's doing something that may be life-threatening, and has refused to tell you himself," I intoned quietly. "He's drinking to a potentially fatal extent on his weekend sleepovers. He needs immediate drug treatment." I couldn't help but ask, "Did you know that Uncle Bobby took your son to a bar for that antidrug conversation, and that they drank together?" Mom looked at Dad. Dad stared at the floor. He knew. Dad, by the way, smelled of beer.

Our national hand-wringing over "drug" (non-alcohol) use among our children becomes laughable in the face of statistics that cite our intense and clandestine love affair with booze. We simply flat-out refuse to admit that alcohol really is a drug, let alone an extremely dangerous one. Want some numbers? Be sure now, because you may look a little differently at that beer in your hand.

In this country last year, for every loser who died as a result of a "drug-related" event (including AIDS fatalities caused by drugs), there were at least *15* "good citizens" who quite legally drank themselves to death. Alcohol factors into *50 percent* of this nation's homicides, suicides, and driving fatalities. *Eighteen million* Americans currently suffer health problems related to drinking.

The numbers in your kid's world run like this: When the Federal Department of Health and Human Services last asked in 1999, *over half* of our seventh through twelfth graders said they drink. *Twenty percent* noted they drink weekly, with 8 percent admitting to binge drinking (five or more shots in a row) more than once in the preceding month. Annually, *45,000* of our teen children get their bodies broken in booze-related driving accidents. And every year we bury *10,000* of our sons and daughters who drink very well and drive very badly. These numbers make the "drug" body count pale in comparison. Last year we lost far more of our children to alcohol poisoning and drunk driving than were stolen from us by heroin, cocaine, ecstasy, accidents, and illness *combined*—so somebody, please explain to me how alcohol is not a dangerous drug!

We don't have a National Booze Czar, or a War on Wine. We actually tax, hawk, and profit from this particular drug in ways that might draw the envious admiration of the worst opium lord in the world. Picture a foreign gangster desperately holed-up in his hideout, with attacking drug-agent helicopters hovering overhead. He glances at his satellite TV and catches a famous American commercial. Incredulously he watches soft, fuzzy, winter camera shots of Christmas-adorned sleighs. They're carrying loving, devoted, drug-bearing, red-blooded American families to warm gatherings to celebrate a joyous day, using nonmedicinal, reality-altering substances that are fully government approved. "This holiday message brought to you by your local connection. We urge you to do your drug responsibly. Have a safe, wonderful day."

Is this a great country or what?

This irony does not escape your kid. The National Institutes of Health celebrated the new millennium by releasing a chilling study that shows one out of every four children in our nation sees family alcoholism and alcohol abuse while growing up. Do we really even see this irony ourselves? We'd better, for if we are disabled by a blindness to our true national epidemic drug, we put our kids at great risk.

One of the most powerful universal truths about adolescents is their zero-tolerance policy for adult hypocrisy. They just go wild (and oppositional) in the face of "Do as I say, not as I do." Having a glassy-eyed, beer-breathed conversation with your child about the evils of marijuana is an excellent way to promote the drug's attractiveness. And having a double standard concerning your kid's use of beer versus marijuana is to make yourself ridiculous in his eyes, for he knows the science of drugs much better than you do. Kids have laughed at our antimarijuana propaganda, which, by default, promotes the great American lie that alcohol is not really a drug. They've also seen the unbiased research that proves that alcohol, in so many ways, *is a deadlier drug* than marijuana. If you don't believe this yourself, read the literature. Quickly. Because your child is watching and reacting to what you do. Your double standard puts him at risk. Before I show you how, I need to explain a few other adolescent cultural differences.

THE NEW-MILLENNIUM DRUGS: STRONGER AND MORE POWERFUL THAN EVER

Marijuana and heroin are not the same drugs they were years ago. In fairness to the pushers, we should rename them, since comparing the drugs of your day with those of today is like comparing a 1975 Corvette with a new one. Today's model is dramatically better and shares only a name with its predecessor.

Marijuana potency has increased radically due to innovations in production. Heroin "purity" rates have increased by factors of *four to nine*, and as a tribute to the efficiency of capitalism, many drugs are much cheaper (relatively speaking) than they were in 1975, so when you hear the "Dosages" used by kids, you need to understand that the drugs you knew (and/or used) that were "10 milligrams" might now be "90 milligrams." They work much better and cause much more damage.

These gains in potency coincide with a frightening reclassification by many adolescents of what technically constitutes "doing drugs." Our own blindness in seeing alcohol as a drug is ultimately responsible here. Here's how it works.

Alcohol (the true horror) is viewed by kids as only slightly more dangerous than caffeinated coffee. It's certainly not a drug. After all, everybody's parents drink, and some drink a whole lot. Many adults drink weekly, even daily, and many parents don't really view drinking as all that bad for adolescents, as long as they don't drive. This is particularly true if the teenager in question is male (you know, "rights of passage," "boys will be boys," "at least he won't end up pregnant," and so on). Therefore, it follows that if alcohol is not a drug, then marijuana cannot be a drug, since according to objective medical and psychological research, *marijuana poses fewer risks than alcohol.*

Be clear that I'm not espousing the virtues of marijuana, by any means. In Chapter 14 we'll talk about the terrible problems all drugs present for our kids, especially marijuana. My point here is that we *grownups* have created this dangerous adolescent paradox that marijuana is OK, and we've done this out of our prejudice against one drug, and out of our blindness towards another. And we expect our kids to listen to us like we make sense?

"I've talked to my daughter Sarina about drugs since preschool. I always felt she was truthfully swearing that she didn't do drugs. Last week her high school principal called and told me she had admitted to being a member of a group they had caught that smoked-up daily before school for almost a year. Incredible! Eight months of daily marijuana use and she doesn't do drugs! When I confronted her, she denied lying to me. With full conviction, my 15-year-old daughter stared me straight in the eye and said, 'MMOOOOMMM, weed is not a drug. It's just like drinking alcohol. Everybody knows that.' Then I felt really confused, like I forgot which way was up. I didn't know what to say. Is it true that marijuana really is not considered a drug anymore?"

There was a puzzle piece missing here. I asked, "Mrs. Young, is alcohol really not considered a drug anymore?"

Mom shifted uneasily in her seat. "Well, alcohol isn't, you know, so bad as using drugs. No one thinks that alcohol is a drug. I mean everyone—mostly—drinks, right? And when she's 21, she'll just drink anyway, so what's so wrong with letting her occasionally drink in my basement with her friends? It's not like we let her do drugs. This way we know where she is, and know she's safe. We even buy it for her so she's not breaking any law." Mrs. Young's eyes begged me to say something, but she needed to hear what she had just said. She had.

Tears flooded her eyes. "Oh my God! We did this, didn't we? But Sarina swore to us that if we let her drink, she wouldn't do drugs. We were so scared of her doing drugs we thought we were helping her. Her grandmother warned me we were making a deal with the Devil." Grandmom knew the Devil when she saw him.

Once we parents hand out a pass to our adolescents on any type of drug, particularly alcohol, we open up Pandora's box. Where would you like to draw the line? Two beers? Six beers? Understand that drug use with teens is just like speeding. If you post 55 miles per hour, everybody pushes to 65. The threshold keeps getting pushed back. This point is made well by the same conversation I have with a different kid once a month:

"So, if alcohol is OK, and grass is safer than booze, then what's the big deal? And if my parents lie to me about marijuana, then maybe they're lying about cocaine and heroin. Hmmmm. . ."

Sex: Too Much + Too Soon = Too Late

It's arguable that, just as we did with heroin purity rates, we may have raised the "potency" impact of sex by 900 percent—as if sex for adolescents needed any tweaking. But before we talk about your kid, let's journey back to your own adolescent sexual experiences. Remember those days? Can you say *obsession?* The adolescent sexuality struggles of your day were overwhelming enough. Today we've gone over the edge.

On its own, teenage sex represents a terrible confluence of volatile developmental and emotional issues simply waiting for a match to ignite them. These "vapors" include new and powerful hormonal rushes, peer acceptance needs, rebelliousness, curiosity, nurturing, intimacy, desires to please (female), desires to dominate (male)—this list could go on for two pages. Remember how sexually preoccupied you were? Good. We can skip the rest of the list.

Now let's add a couple of ingredients to this mix and look at your teenager's sexual struggles.

We have pretty much presented a world to our kids that is saturated by sex. From 1999 to 2000, we increased television "family-hour" sexual references by *74 percent.* This could not have been easy to do. As a society, we've "ratcheted down" the sexualizing of kids to such young ages that they simply don't possess the emotional or rational maturity to process this information in a healthy way (as if they can when they're 17). Six-year-olds now commonly have a detailed fund of knowledge about specific sexual functions that can set off shock waves and alarm bells in the adult community. For example, when Tony's mom told me what her first grader had said, I was pretty sure he hadn't learned it watching Sesame Street.

> "The school staff is convinced that my six-year-old Tony must have been sexually abused. He's been grabbing at girls' private parts and saying terrible things. They tell me that he must have been exposed to these things somehow."
>
> "What things?" she forced me to ask.
>
> "I can't even say it to you, doctor, so I wrote it down." Her shaking hand held a napkin on which she had written her first grader's words to those sweet, angelic six-year-old girls: "Suck my sweet thang, babeee." I silently wondered why this phrasing and even accent

sounded so familiar to me. "There's no way he's ever heard this at home," Mom continued. "We even religiously police his television watching to be sure he's not seeing crazy stuff."

When I brought Tony alone into the room, I started doing the possible sexual assault interview, but nothing fit, either with Tony or in the constellation of behavior that Mom and the school reported. Tony freely admitted saying and doing these outrageous things. "So where'd you hear this stuff, Tony?" I finally asked, like a buddy. He leaned forward. "It's kinda a secret," he confided. "I'm not supposed to tell. When we go to my cousin's house, we're not allowed to watch *South Park* 'cause it's a bad show, so my cousin tapes it late at night when his parents don't know. We watch it until a grownup starts comin' down the stairs to see what we're watching. Then my cousin turns on the other video player with a good movie in it." Admiring their collective genius, it suddenly hit me where I'd heard that phrase before.

As a joke, one of my adolescent clients who thought I was hopelessly unhip used to leave *South Park* sound bites on my phone machine. He always said I needed to know more about kids if I was supposed to help them, "...so at the tone please leave your message for Dr. Bradley. Thank you." Beeeeeep. "Suck my sweet thang, babeee."

This mental sexualization of too-young children coincides with a scary physical change in our kids. In an intriguing coincidence that gives me a bad feeling, the National Association for Pediatric Endocrinologists recently revised their guidelines regarding early puberty initiation. What we used to call "precocious puberty" ain't precocious anymore. Puberty initiation for Anglo girls at age seven and African American girls at age six is now considered normal and not evidence of dysfunction. We don't know why, but girls are commonly beginning physical maturation before seven and eight years of age, and this is now seen as normal due to its prevalence and lack of associated dysfunction. You read that right. *Six- and seven-year-olds.* The melding of this tender-age mental conditioning with this new physical development in first graders sets the stage for some new-age recess games, such as the one that brought Brianna to me.

Brianna was mad. This six-year-old genuinely felt the principal was unfairly making a big deal out of nothing. "The boys play stupid games all the time, and they don't get sent to a doctor!" "What games do they play?" I asked. "Stupid hitting games, like Wrestlemania and stuff." "And what game were you and your friends playing?" "Stripper," she answered with those innocent blue eyes, "Me and Gina and Charlene were dancing and taking off our clothes, and making the boys pick which one of us they wanted." I could not bring myself to ask this child what she meant by "wanted."

INTIMACY AND SEX: A WARPED VIEW

All of this early sexualizing raises a gnawing fear in those of us who are familiar with substance abuse research. This data has shown that the earlier drug experimentation occurs, the greater the odds of developing drug dependency or addiction. In a potentially powerful noncoincidence, early and frequent sexual activity among adolescents has also risen dramatically. Nationally, in 1998, 17 percent of seventh and eighth graders had sexual intercourse. This number increases with age to 50 percent of the girls between 15 and 18, and 60 percent of the boys. Over a million teenage girls become pregnant every year.

Perhaps predictably, boys in general say they have no regrets about having sex. Yet those of us who work with adolescents see subtle and possibly profound damage to these boys who are often more sexually active at 15 than you were at 25. They seem to turn emotionally cold and cynical, as if they've visited places they weren't ready to see. I fear these boys often become emotionally arrested and unable to be truly emotionally intimate with women. They come to believe that through sex they've experienced the ultimate in being part of a couple. While it's great fun, it actually gets old for them. Since they're emotionally incapable of having intimate relationships (they're crazy and immature), they become frozen in space, thinking that impersonal sex is the end point of sexuality. Many of these boys become cold and sad, frequently engaging in wild passion and devoid of any real passion.

But many of these girls don't enjoy the experience. One study showed that 11 percent of the girls regretted having sex, and over 60 percent admitted to mixed feelings. Girls (and women) value emotional intimacy over physical intimacy. Interestingly and frighteningly, girls now cite peer pressure as the greatest factor in their decision to have sex. Their peers' opinions are twice as powerful as the old "pressure from boys." This finding runs so frighteningly contrary to what we believe to be healthy female sexual function that we really have no idea where it may lead.

The other newly researched factors that are involved in a girl's decision about whether or not to have sex have to do with family influences. Parents who value good academic performance typically have teens who postpone sex. Demanding, unaffectionate mothers often have daughters who have sex early and often. Girls from single-parent households are also likely to become involved in sex early. Girls from two-parent families with emotionally and physically distant moms and dads often look for love in sex. They rarely find it, but they keep on looking—and the more they look, the less they find.

In short, we adults have presented our kids with a world that has acculturated sex to an unprecedented level—one where boys now have sex as casually as they used to get a kiss, and where the greatest motivation for girls to have intercourse is to *earn the esteem of their peers* (gee, I thought that's why the boys used to do it). The impact of this insanity for both boys and girls at the very time that their brains are undergoing massive neurological rewiring (see Chapter 1) is so potentially staggering that we are holding our breath to see what the long-term consequences might be. We may be hard-wiring warped views of intimacy and sex into their vulnerable heads. For kids like Karen, *Love Story* is just a stupid old movie.

> Karen ran down the list of her drugs with me. This 17-year-old was in way over her head. The hair on my neck was starting to rise. The pattern looked almost suicidal, as if she might be hoping to die. She spoke dispassionately with the thousand-yard stare of a combat soldier. "And I also do ecstasy a couple of times a month." "Why ecstasy?" I asked. She gave me that "he's a dinosaur" look. "For the sex, of course. I've got a sex problem. I, like, sometimes can't get it on with guys at parties."
>
> Once in a while, a client will say something that makes me pause, groping for some sensitive, objective, noncontaminating question to figure out what the heck the person is saying. This was such a moment. "Karen, do you think you're supposed to...sorry, strike that question. How often do you have sex with guys at parties?" She looked upset with the question. "Just like my friends, maybe a couple times a week.

Some weeks none. Why? You think I'm a whore or something?" "Do you want to be having sex like that?" I asked. At least she had some life in her eyes now. She was mad. "What's wrong with that?" she snapped. "Maybe nothing," I deflected. "I just wanted to know how you felt about it." Her anger slowly melted into tears. Then she cried and cried and cried...

If you're thinking that Karen's predicament and that of her generation represents a lack of morals and ethics on their part, I won't argue. I can't. It's not my field. I'll leave that question to the religious leaders and politicians. I will, however, remind you that these kids are really confused, just like we were. Not morally corrupt and ethically bankrupt. Just nuts. They simply don't have the neurological tools to make good decisions about such things, particularly in the face of the incessant sexual bombardment we adults rain on their heads. These kids didn't write the shows, create the ads, or produce the music. That's on us.

So let's get this straight. We're going to constantly stimulate these brain-damaged people sexually, leave them unsupervised and under-loved, and then act shocked and appalled that they're having sex? Give me a break. What would you have done? Remember, their world is very different from the world you knew as a teenager.

And while we're chatting about bombarding brain-challenged children with dangerous messages, let's look at that other point of saturation we've achieved in what your kid refers to as rock 'n roll.

Rock 'n Roll: A World of Violence and Aggression

Rock 'n roll is the term kids use to encapsulate all of the other forms of adolescent acting-out behaviors. These include criminal acts, fighting, and suicide, all tied commonly by aggression and violence. The news media seems to portray the adolescent world as one of nonstop violence. Actually, in one respect it's much less violent than your world was. In another, it's much more deadly.

A weird paradox has developed in your kid's world regarding violence and aggression that is critical to understanding the contemporary adolescent culture. The good news, disbelieved by most parents, is that according to our statistics, the overall frequency of youth violence has *plummeted.* According to the Centers for Disease Control (CDC), over-all rates of school violence have actually *decreased* by 25 percent since 1993. The number of violence-related school deaths has dropped over *50 percent.* The FBI says that in the early 1970s, *twice* as many kids under the age of 13 years committed murder than in 1999.

But everybody believes the opposite to be true. Most parents and students consistently report that they believe juvenile violence is wildly escalating and most report being much more fearful. Both our schools and our laws are treating kids like deranged, homicidal maniacs suc-cumbing to some mysterious violence virus. The horrific battlefield pic-tures of Columbine High are, blessedly, a less and less frequent occurrence in our media. Yet an overwhelming feeling of fear pervades, and prompts us to install metal detectors in our schools, to suspend kids for minor shoving matches, and to sentence psychologically sick, violent juveniles to adult prisons (more on this later). Are we all just reacting hysterically to overpublicized rage events? Not necessarily.

The bad news is that there appears to be a boiling down of aggres-sion and violence among many adolescents to a leaner, meaner, and more pervasive form not seen previously. This has become accultur-ated into your kid's world in a variety of ways. It's very apparent in the lovers' spats, arguments with parents, and adolescent fighting rules that have been rewritten since your day.

Options to resolve lovers' spats have changed. A recent study of 2,300 adolescents from urban and suburban public and private schools (uniforms offer no protection) found that fully one-third of the kids felt violence to a female is deserved if a girl "disses" (yells at or insults) her boyfriend. They went on to quote the unwritten teen code that an appropriate punishment for a "steady" girl seen talking to another boy is a shove or slap from her boyfriend. This is different from your world. Earlier generations of kids held that violence towards females was con-sidered cowardly. It probably occurred, but it wasn't publicly approved. Now for many kids it's a sign of "true love."

Similarly, the parent versus adolescent fight rules have been revised. Teens have argued loudly with parents since the dawn of time—but not quite like Jesse's kid. Last year, this frightened 39-year-old single mom from a small town in Pennsylvania went to court to obtain a Protection From Abuse (PFA) order. A family member had threatened to burn down her house and to "take us out in body bags." That horrifying threat was not from a drunk, raging ex-husband; that promise was from her son.

What once would have set off titters of laughter has now become a routine sight in courtrooms around the country: terrified parents of adolescents obtaining legal protection against the threats and assaults of their own children. Jesse's request became the sixth PFA granted to parents by that one judge in five months. "They [the parents] have tried everything else," said the judge. "Their children are either assaulting them or their siblings. They're out of control." Even professional veterans of adolescent wars are scratching their heads over this new rage phenomenon—but then again, a fight ain't what it used to be, either.

Years ago a "fight" meant two combatants who used their fists to try to settle a score. Like an exaggerated rugby match, they'd whack at each other until either one went down, or, more commonly, both got too tired to swing anymore. Then, by some unwritten yet strict rule, the match was declared over. Rarely did animosity extend beyond the game clock. Busted noses and lips seemed to be the worst of it. The loser often still won status by simply showing his willingness to make a stand.

Use of weapons or ganging-up on an opponent usually brought disaster for the aggressor. Win or lose, he'd be seen as the real loser, often socially shunned for his blasphemous disregard of the rules. Sometimes a weapons-user would get roughed up by the onlookers for being a cowardly punk. Guns in fights were definitely not cool. These fight rules are changing.

The basic adolescent instinct toward aggression certainly existed previously, but its context may have now changed in a frightening way, where savage gang attacks are not only often sanctioned by teenage onlookers as acceptable, but prized as *entertainment*. And if you are one of those parents who thinks this scary, dark violence exists only in our cities, let me tell you about Eddie. This middle-class, suburban kid will probably think twice before being a Good Samaritan again.

Dad's news clippings told the story of a son who was attacked by four older and larger kids. Eddie managed to fend off one attacker and tried to run. The cheering crowd of 20 students who came to watch the fun apparently felt they hadn't gotten their money's worth. They formed a circle keeping Eddie in the "ring" so the death match could continue.

As Eddie begged for help on his knees, his attackers used TV wrestling elbow swings and kicks to beat Eddie's head into a bloody mash. Undeterred by having an unconscious victim, the attempted murder continued until a neighbor on this nice suburban street pushed his way into the center of the ring to stop the carnage. He was booed by the crowd.

Even the judge who handled the trial, who was no stranger to cases of violence, was clearly at a loss to understand what happened. When she asked one of the attackers for an explanation, he offered that he had heard that Eddie may have said something about the attacker's mother. The truth was that two days before the attack, Eddie had called a teacher to stop one of the assailants from beating up another smaller kid at school. After hearing this, the judge stared for a moment and then said, "All of the testimony I've heard does not explain the hatred, the level of violence here. He nearly died. This was a repeated series of violent acts. That viciousness I don't understand. I don't think there's a rational explanation for this behavior."

These incidents happen every day—in small towns, big towns, cities, and suburbs. While they occur less frequently than in the past, when they do happen, they occur with an edge of rage that might be new. Some psychologists theorize that the reduced fight numbers may reflect the fact that many kids have become much more fearful of physical confrontations and now avoid them at all costs.

While conducting a conflict-resolution program at an elementary school, I asked the upper-grade boys to write down what the goal was in a physical fight with a peer. Forty percent cited causing serious physical injury (hopefully requiring a trip to the hospital) and half of those said that weapons were OK to use in pursuit of that goal. They explained that this was important to discourage the revenge posse they could expect to hunt them down if they only won the fight without seriously injuring their opponent. Winning to these children meant disabling your enemy and infusing fear into the onlookers as well. Incidentally, the elementary school where I conducted this program was a private, suburban institution. This is not to say that these kids would actually commit such horrors, but it is scary to hear how our culture has made an impact on their views of aggression and violence. They see their world as the OK Corral. Guns are becoming acceptable.

Before you become judgmental about teens, think for a moment.

Given the fight rules of today's teen, would you, as a bullied adolescent, have ever considered carrying a gun just in case? Many do. From 1984 to 1994, the death-by-gun rate among teenagers increased fourfold before the homicide rate began to decline mid-decade. Last year, it was estimated that more than 100,000 of our children took guns to school. One kid in 20 admits to having carried a gun to someplace other than school. A 2000 CDC study found that over 17 percent of our kids traveled with various armaments in any given month.

Many psychologists who work with adolescents are as shocked as you are about the number of recent school shootings. We're shocked that the number is so *small* in light of the availability of weapons and the emotional volatility of adolescents. This low number is a tribute to the self-control of our brain-challenged teens, but not to our adult efforts to reduce our kids' exposure to violence. As we've done with sex, we are also saturating our youth with violence.

How many times have you seen fight/assault scenes like Eddie's? If your answer is "lots of times," and you haven't served time in a penitentiary, then you've watched this on TV and movie screens. A lot. Studies of the ironically named "family-hours" on television have found that violent references have increased by 60 percent from 1997 to 1999. I'm sure I don't have to tell you about the movies, CDs, and video games.

Many researchers think they know why the rage factor is worsening, but they just can't prove it yet. We may be redefining adolescent violence as a less frequent but more brutal phenomenon by desensitizing our kids to aggression, but researchers have yet to find scientifically accepted *proof* that these exposures absolutely cause increased aggression. This missing "smoking gun" (pun intended) is due more to the tremendous difficulty of this type of research than to the question itself. Scores of studies show strong correlations between this profitable media fetish and increased child preoccupation with violence, but a *correlation* is different from *cause-and-effect proof*. A correlation just means that these things happen together. Cause-and-effect proof means one makes the other happen.

It's kind of like the confusion surrounding cigarette smoking years ago. We knew it was killing people, but we just could not scientifically prove it. Using this argument as skillfully and unethically as the cigarette makers of yesteryear, the entertainment industry experts insist there is no connection between screen violence and the real thing. Oh, OK. Sure.

Even young children say that screen violence affects them. In the same conflict-resolution seminar that I mentioned earlier, I asked the upper-grade kids if they thought video games, CDs, and TV shows affected their tendency to be aggressive. They all looked at me in amazement that I was the one being paid to do that seminar. "YES!" they all declared in one voice. One student asked, "How can a kid see that stuff all his life and *not* get affected?"

But exclusively blaming the media for our cultural fetish with violence is like blaming the mirror for your weight problem. The media and the mirror both coldly reflect who we are and what we like. Both can contribute to our lust for blood in glorifying violence, but in the end we decide what is real and what is an illusion for our children through our actions. Our kids are learning that the violence we adults present to them in their movies, games, and CDs is the *reality,* not the illusion.

This reality is reinforced by another paradox of youth violence, this one involving kids as the victims. While our juvenile crime rate is declining, those same CDC statistics point out that our nation leads the world in murdered children. Of the world's 26 wealthiest countries, we lose more of our kids to homicide than the other 25 *combined.* Our tendency toward violence exists throughout our society. It is not restricted to adolescents, but they've become our focus and often our scapegoats. We parents who scream at the violence in the media are far too often the same ones who scream at, demean, and hit our children. In a child's mind, just how do we distinguish that "irresponsible" media violence from our "responsible" parental violence of hurting a child to make her stop hurting her brother?

And after relentlessly pounding aggressive, rage-based behavior vignettes into children's neurologically deficient brains 24 hours a day, where do we find the nerve to act so astounded when Johnny pays back his tormentor with a shotgun? I believe we should be thankfully puzzled that so few do.

Adolescent Suicide: The Ultimate in Rock 'n Roll

Adolescent suicide, something almost unknown in the 1960s, has exploded into your kid's world—a 400 percent increase in the last 40 years, with the greatest increase occuring over the last two decades among kids 10 to 14 years old. The Centers for Disease Control (CDC) reported that in 1999, over 19 percent of our teenage children either attempted suicide or had a serious plan to kill themselves. Look at your daughter's sleepover gang. Two of those 10 children came close. Suicide has become a stylized violence ritual, a kind of "X-treme" game of chicken played by disenfranchised, temporarily brain-damaged kids. Often romanticized as victims of desperation, many suiciders elicit little sympathy from psychologists who work with all of the broken lives the "victim" leaves behind. While some suicides result from hopeless, zero-option scenarios like crippling depression, many adolescent suicides are self-centered acts of anger, a kind of terrible "screw-you" to the true victims, the loved ones who must survive the aftermath.

This harsh characterization is critical to understand for both potential suiciders and for their caretakers. Many adolescent suiciders exhibit anger, rather than the popularized withdrawal and depression, prior to taking their lives. It is impossible to predict whether or not someone will attempt suicide, but psychologists are able to provide good assessments as to the relative risk potential of an individual. Therefore, we must always act extremely conservatively whenever any possibility of suicide exists (more on this in Chapter 5).

Looking closely at this horrific trend gives clues about its nature. Teenage suicides often occur in chain reactions among circles of acquaintances or even locales. The "fame" that the media awards to victims can seem attractive to another troubled kid. We grownups also love to tell these stories, and thus romanticize them to our children.

Threatening to commit suicide (often on the Internet) has become a bizarre pastime among teenagers, along with a "rescuing" game on the part of the respondents, be they cyber or real. The problem is that the line between fantasy and reality becomes blurred with a few beers at 2 A.M., and frighteningly large numbers of these young people end up with a bullet in the brain. And most of the "successful" players pull a trigger on a weapon that belongs to their mom or dad.

I've had the terrible task of working with families seeking grief counseling and explanations about their teenage suiciders who spoke for months on the Internet about killing themselves. Tragically, in the cases I've seen, none of the scores of Internet respondents, some of whom were adults, thought to call these kids' parents or the police. When questioned after the fact, they typically respond, "Kids say this stuff all the time. I never thought he'd actually do it."

Again, before you become judgmental about how inferior today's youth are, let me harken you back to the days of your own youth, when the line between reality and fantasy got blurred a lot. We were fortunate in that suicide wasn't cool then. It kind of is cool now. We'll talk later in Chapter 5 about ways you can reduce the odds of having this particular nightmare, but for now allow me to jump ahead into quicksand while we're chatting about violence, adolescence, and suicide.

SPEAKING OF GUNS. . .

Get rid of your guns. I speak here not as a liberal, a conservative, Republican or Democrat. Just as a middle-aged shrink staring at a list of gut-wrenching names. These names are on files that tell the stories of families that were annihilated directly or indirectly by guns. This list is not offered here as objective data; it's very personal. But if you have guns, you'd better read this.

I won't venture into the more objective statistical quagmire that represents the current gun debate. For every study that links increased gun ownership with increased violence, another researcher claims that more guns equals less violence. I'll leave those numbers for you to sort out on your own, but there are two statistics that jump out at me as someone who works with teens.

The first is that as we Americans have armed ourselves in record numbers, the rates of violent adolescent crime have finally decreased dramatically after peaking mid-decade. This creates an illusion that having more guns around somehow should get the credit.

The second perplexing number is that the incidents of gun-related juvenile activity (shootings, gun threats, brandishings, and suicides) have continued to increase dramatically even in the face of these reductions in overall teen crime and violence rates. "Trickle-down" theories do work when it comes to the economics of weapons. Guns get to our kids with frightening ease.

You need to decide if you believe that the arming of America has reduced crime by teens. Most researchers shake their heads sadly at this theory, but even if you do think that guns reduce crime in general, you need to ask yourself what the potential cost is to *your child* of keeping those firearms in the house. You need to decide this quickly, because what we may be doing for your kid's generation is providing a deadly efficient means of expression for those dark and terrible thoughts that have been harbored at times by teenagers of all generations. I didn't have any guns in the house calling to me in my days of teen madness. Did you?

This is not about statistics or politics, it's just about TV, brain damage, and ballistics. I hope I've convinced the previously unconvinced that adolescents are nuts (due to wiring problems) and that the adolescent world is a dangerous place (just watch TV for an hour). So how can we justify providing these troubled human beings access to guns?

Simply put, guns work too well. Can homicidal kids bludgeon classmates out of this world with a baseball bat? Possibly. Can the suicidal ones overdose on drugs or cut a wrist and bleed to death? Sure. But the death literature clearly proves guns work best. Most homicidal bat swingers don't kill. Most suicidal pill takers and wrist cutters survive. As a tribute to technology, the body counts conclusively prove that the trigger pullers are all much better at their craft. The targets in gunfights survive much less frequently. The life-defining act of most successful teenage murderers and suiciders is pulling a trigger. Let me try this one last way.

If one night, God forbid, your kid or mine gets so far gone that she starts roaming around the house looking for a way out of this life for herself or her tormenter, what would you want her to find? And what would you hope she doesn't find?

Finally, please leash any fantasies about the childproof lock, the safe combination that only you know, or the secret hiding spot. Don't you remember when your child was eight he knew more about house locks, safes, or secret hiding places than you? If you think these things can protect your kid, in six seconds I'll name six children who aren't here anymore as a result of those very same fail-safe measures. And if you still want to argue, let me put you in touch with the parents of those kids. In the hope that it might save your child, they'll tell you about the lifelong agony, and I mean *agony*, they carry as the result of having once shared your "safe" gun fantasies. Mr. Murphy thought he kept his guns very safe.

Dad jumped in to take control of the conversation before his wife could finish her opening question about my political views on gun control.

"OK, Doctor, let's just get this straight from the beginning. You might be one of those liberals who hates guns and that might present a problem for us seeing you. Well, I like guns, and I know how to safely use them, and I've trained my kids how to safely use them to defend themselves. And when Bobbie was getting depressed, I locked my guns away in my safe that only I have the combination to. Even my wife doesn't have it. There's just no way anyone could have that combination. I take every precaution. I'm very responsible.

"And you know what else, if someone decides to kill themselves, they're gonna find a way, right? You shrinks are always saying how no one, even you guys, can prevent somebody from killing themselves. Am I right? So guns are not going to be the issue here."

First-session therapy notes of a couple whose adolescent daughter shot herself four weeks earlier with Dad's pistol from the impregnable safe. On her desk they found a copy of the safe combination, next to her last letter. She was well trained. She didn't miss.

Over 8,000 of our children died by gunfire last year. According to the Centers for Disease Control (CDC), folks who live with guns in their houses for "protection" have *five times* the risk of suiciding. Love guns? Fine. Love your teenager more. Get rid of your guns until he's out of the house. Keep your kid off my list.

Thank You for Flying Air Terror

This concludes the really frightening part of the tour. I do hope you're scared, because as the father of two kids, I constantly keep myself scared. We do better work when we're not complacent. It helps push us to do our parent jobs better, even when we're tired, sick, or just fed up. And once again, let me remind you that this parenting stuff is a job, and probably the toughest one you'll ever have. It certainly will be the most important, but, like any job, training is required to do it well.

Thus far, this training has taught you two vital things you'll need for the final exam: Kids are nuts and the world we've stuck them in is out of control. You suspected that, but now you can at least be comforted in knowing you have good instincts. You also have some bad information, but we're going to fix all that.

You can unfasten your seat belt for the time being, and feel free to walk around the cabin. Let's move on to Chapter 3 to look at the latest news on one eternal adolescent battle, known for its famous parental war chant:

"Oh yeah? Well, if all of your friends marched off a cliff, would you?"

Chapter 3
PEER INFLUENCE AND YOUR CHILD

O N THE FACE OF IT, it looks really scary. One evening, you have control over your child, and the next morning she's tuned to an underground radio station for mandates on how to lead her life. You had no idea that a cult existed right here on Elm Street. Her hair suddenly looks like the crayon box she used to carry, when was it, last week? At the clothing store she cruises past her old favorite Barbie aisle straight to the "flash & trash" section as if she's always dressed like that.

Parents of adolescents sooner or later feel desperately outmatched by the power that peers seem to gain overnight over their child. They anxiously fret, saddened and scared by the apparent loss of their teenager to the whims of this weird adolescent culture.

Contributing further to a tidal wave of parental hopelessness is the insistence of many experts that parents have much less influence on their adolescent's behavior than the teenager's peers. Others maintain that parents are more influential. But rather than giving in to the confusion and giving up, you must try even harder to maintain a connection with your kid, because as it turns out, in the long run, you have *much greater* impact on his ultimate character and value development than do his peers. Believing this while your kid is tantrumming for his third tongue piercing becomes an act of pure faith, and yet one you can't afford to neglect. In Part Three, you'll learn how to hold onto your kid as he negotiates these powerful currents of peer influence. For now, let's see what this peer pressure is all about. It looks overwhelming. It kept Laura's mom awake at night.

"My daughter Laura has become a starling. You know, one of those birds you only see in packs of 20, all moving precisely together. I can actually watch and see the latest 'papal peer mandate' rippling through her flock. It makes me laugh with the multicolored eyebrows. It terrifies me with sexual edicts, as in 'OK, girls, the Peer Supreme Court has just ruled that all cool 14-year-olds have sex with their boyfriends.' I used to try to talk with her about this peer pressure, but she makes me feel like I'm attacking someone's religion. So I just learned to shut up. On the radio they said that it's better to say nothing than entrench these behaviors, right?"

Well, yes and no. Before I answer, let's look at a similar problem Jeffrey's dad was facing. He had heard of a much different solution.

"Jeffrey and I used to be very close. We used to laugh a lot, and he seemed to share my own views about not caring what others think of you. I think I used to be important to him. Now he acts like I'm a circus freak and Gestapo agent rolled into one. The only things that matter to him are his friends and what they think of him. He wants to be on the phone constantly, and he refuses to wear the good clothes we buy him, choosing instead to look like a poster boy for the homeless. His hair looks like a car wreck, and he fights us on hygiene habits like brushing his teeth. He yells that he has to be his own person, but in a crowd he's indistinguishable from his friends.

"I saw a TV show that said you have to keep fighting with kids to force them to wear the right clothes and hairstyles. You have to draw the line with those smaller things, otherwise, you'll lose them to bigger things like drugs. Is that correct?"

Well, again, yes and no. Unfortunately, creatures as complex as adolescents can't be explained with simple rules. To better answer these questions, let's start by looking closely at the power that peers wield in competing for what you fear may be the soul of your child.

The Power of Peer Pressure: Ways You Can and Can't Win

The first measure of peer power is time. How many hours a week do you get to sit and talk intimately with your teenager? Don't answer that question out loud. It's usually an embarrassing number. I can tell you that your teen's peers get 21 hours, on average. Three hours *a day*, seven days a week. Do you get three a month?

OK, OK. So the opposition gets to control the ball for most of the clock. What are their strengths? When are they most powerful?

Peer power is potent for only a surprisingly short time. Middle school marks the zenith of peer influence. Younger kids are more immune, and older adolescents become less influenced by peers with time—but if your kid is in middle school, watch out! Someone else does have his ear.

OK, OK. My kid is in ninth grade. They've got him for now. In what ways do they get to impose their foreign values on my son?

In virtually every way that shows, such as clothes, clutter, language, leanings, sleep, sloughing, politics, piercings, religion, restlessness, foods, fads, fetishes, dating, dancing, diets, disgusts, and, of course, music (music?). *But the ways that show really don't mean diddly.* When you pull this peer research apart, you find some very hopeful insights among some scary myths.

With all of the chaos we see in our adolescents' world, we grownups often look for simple causes with simple solutions much as we have done for eons in explaining bewildering occurrences with mythology. These help us to have shorter "what's wrong with kids today" conversations and allow us to fall asleep faster at night.

Peer pressure has become a convenient mythological scapegoat for our fears. Kill the goat and our kids will all be OK, but trying to kill your kid's peer choices to keep him out of trouble works about as well as appeasing Zeus to avoid lightning. Let's look at these popular myths that not only don't help, but when acted upon, can contribute mightily to an already unstable adolescence for your child.

PEER GROUPS CAN'T RUIN KIDS

Myth Number 1 is that famous tale about how peer groups recruit and then convert good kids into bad ones. That's mostly Hollywood nonsense. It hardly ever happens in real life. Think of your own experience for a moment. Let's assume you're a reasonable, hard-working, caring parent. Tell me about your peer group. Aren't they mostly folks more or less like you? Did they come and recruit and persuade you to be like them, or did you just seek out people similar to yourself? Can you imagine a scenario where you suddenly join an outlaw motorcycle gang, dealing drugs and beating up foreigners for fun? I hope not.

In this respect, your kid is the same. She's much more likely to seek out a long-term peer group that *reflects who she already is, or what she already has the potential to become.* In other words, she *is* the peer group, for better or for worse. Parents of troubled adolescents often grasp at straws trying to explain why their child suddenly does terrible things. Blaming the kid's peers is one easy way out that can become a dangerous diversion from the real, more complex problems that underlie teenage craziness.

There is a cute variation to this rule of thumb, in which your honor-student, vegetarian, private-school, antidrug daughter pulls up one night on the back of a very large and very loud Harley driven by an even larger and louder assistant bouncer from Tiny's Tattoo Parlor. These jaw-dropping turnarounds usually reflect that brain damage-based impulsiveness we discussed in Chapters 1 and 2, and can become a test of parental values. As we will discuss at length in Part Three, you are in charge of the duration of these types of tests. If you manage to keep your cool and react minimally, you will probably have only a short quiz. Your child will be able to more objectively see (and smell?) the reality of this type of peer choice and will more quickly return to her own values, and get back to hanging with kids who shower. But if you lose it and go wild with protective but punitive groundings, Clarence (the assistant bouncer from Tiny's) will become a 300-pound Romeo to her, enshrined as the object of her lifelong, forbidden love. You don't want this to happen.

If you kept your cool in the Harley test and your daughter still maintains months of devotion to Clarence, something else is going on, and now's a good time to call for help (see Chapter 16).

PEER PRESSURE CAN BE YOUR ALLY

A second myth you've been told concerns what it is that peers pressure each other to do. Answer fast: When I say "peer pressure," you think (a) drug use, (b) having sex, (c) skipping school, (d) striving for academic goals. If you picked (a), (b), or (c), you've gotten some bad information. Researchers find that the most prevalent form of peer pressure teenagers "suffer" from is a demand from their friends that they finish school. And no, I'm not doing drugs. This is for real. Ask Lizzie.

Lizzie showed up with two friends in my office without an appointment. Since she was only 14 years old, she had always been driven by her mom until today. These kids had taken a half day of bus rides to get to me. When I explained I couldn't see them for two hours, Lizzie jumped up to say that she'd try again some other time but was cut off midsentence by her friends who said very firmly, "We'll wait."

Two hours later, they marched into my office, the friends shepherding Lizzie like sheriff's deputies. The oldest-looking girl of the group, Shana, had orange and green spiked hair, with three piercings that were visible on her lip and probably many more in places I preferred not to think about. In that unusual body sat the closest thing Lizzie had to a mother. Shana started speaking like she was 40. "Doctor, Lizzie has been bullshitting, uh, I'm sorry, I mean lying to you about everything. She does lots more drugs than she says and she's having sex with about every creep in the park, and she ain't using protection. This week she stopped going to school and her mother don't give a shi... uh, doesn't care. I'm, like, no angel but I'm not gonna end up some loser like my mom. Lizzie's, like, becoming a whore or something. She's gonna end up dead and she don't care. She was going to school be a hairdresser, but she's thrown out now 'cause she didn't show up."

Lizzie stared at the floor red-faced as her peers, or her "pimp and pusher friends" as her mom had described them, delineated their concerns. I was fascinated to see Lizzie sit so still to hear all of this terrible information. The last time I had seen her with her mother, Lizzie went nuts when her mom noted only a small part of this dangerous behavior. That was a month ago, after which Mom no-showed for appointments and finally told me on the phone that she was "washing her hands" of Lizzie because she was so disrespectful. The answer to my next question explained this difference in Lizzie's reactions.

"Shana, why are you guys here?" Shana looked puzzled that I had to ask. "Cause she's our friend and we love her. We're not gonna just sit by and watch her get AIDS or end up a drunk like her mom. She's got to go back to school or she ain't gonna have no life at all. You're a doctor, and a doctor's got to know the truth about a patient to help, right?" "That's right, Shana," I nodded, "And I'm going to need you all to help me help Lizzie if that's OK with her." Lizzie very seriously nodded her assent. "You know what, guys?" I asked. "I think you've already helped her more than you can imagine. What do you think,

Lizzie?" Lizzie began crying softly as a child greatly relieved, and nodded again.

Most peer pressure has the intention of what we grownups would call being a positive influence. These kids really do, to varying degrees, care about each other's welfare. They may express it in screwy ways (did I mention that they're brain-damaged?), but they pride themselves on being what they think are positive influences on each other. They maintain a moral-ethical code, one that you or I may not subscribe to, but one that is based on a core principle of helping one another.

A HA! GOTCHA! Dr. Bradley, in Chapter 2 you stated that the greatest motivation in female adolescent sex was to earn peer esteem. Now you're saying that kids see themselves as positive influences on their friends. How do you reconcile these two statements?

I'm glad you asked, because the answer to this question cuts to the core of this peer pressure concept in two ways. First, it shows how "pressure" from peers to do bad things is so dangerously misunderstood by adults, and second, it provides a great explanation of why some kids fall into bad peer groups and others do not. Peer pressure does not come from peers. It comes from within each child.

THEIR FRIENDS ARE NOT THE PROBLEM

With sex, drugs, and rock 'n roll (acting out), peer pressure can be very powerful, but only to those kids who are *predisposed* to doing sex, drugs, and rock 'n roll anyway. Remember that kids will seek out other kids who are similar to themselves, but initially the similarity might not be the doing of sex, drugs, and rock 'n roll. It might be the far stronger common sharing of feelings like anger, depression, self-loathing, or social isolation. And/or it could be the similarity of painful life experiences, like self-absorbed parents, busted homes, or an inability to do well in school. These are the complex and powerful factors that lead kids to self-destructive behaviors, and they exist long before the actual crazy behavior starts. The sex, drugs, and rock 'n roll are not the problem. These are the adolescent brain-damaged versions of solutions to the real problems. The acting out is only a symptom of the real problems.

In this way, an isolated, self-hating, well-behaved kid who finds a group of isolated, self-hating, acting-out kids may feel enormous *internal* pressure to do sex, drugs, and rock 'n roll to embrace and support that group custom, but that pressure doesn't come directly from peers. That erroneous assumption can be a dangerous diversion from the real crisis. As Damien explained to me, peer pressure is more complex.

"My folks are positive that my friends are why I do drugs. They're completely wrong. They don't get it. They don't get anything anymore." Damien got only part of it himself. "My father is, like, at the cops all the time, telling them how my druggie friends are pushing shit on me, like they hold me down and pour pills down my throat. He's so stupid. If he gave a damn to show up to see me once in awhile, maybe he'd know something about me [Damien's parents are divorced]. I do pills because I like to. That's all. This is who I am, and if you don't like that, well, that sucks for you. The people I know who do drugs are much better than the assholes I know who don't. I know I got too heavy into speed, so I'm stopping. And you want a laugh? It wasn't my father who got me to think about cutting back. My druggie friends are the ones who told me first that I was too heavy into the pills. My druggie friends are the only people in the world who give a crap about me. They are my family now. We're there for each other. My friends have never, ever let me down. Not once! You go ask my father and mother if they've ever let me down. I want to be there laughing when you do."

Damien's dad did not understand a big part of why his son was doing drugs. It wasn't peer pressure. It was emotional pain. Similarly, Damien did not really understand why he started doing drugs. He didn't just "like to." It was to embrace and honor the customs of his new family. He thrived on their love and acceptance. He wanted to be like these people who gave him these wonderful gifts. He thought doing drugs would help keep their love.

The peer pressure phenomenon is really a complex circle that starts with a child in pain and spirals out of control with the loss of respect for parents. When the respect is lost, the connections with parents that are so critical to stabilizing temporarily crazy adolescents are also destroyed. Without these connections, your kid is cast adrift in an insane world looking for replacement attachments. That peer group is just the safe harbor your kid might seek out if he's not attached at home.

In Chapter 7, we'll talk at length about the respect factor. For now, understand that your kid's friends are not the reason he's having problems. Peers typically don't hammer other kids to do sex, drugs, and rock 'n roll. Peers offer "solutions" to pain that they see as helpful, like sex, drugs, and rock 'n roll. Many adolescents have sadly come to believe that these "solutions" are positive. Where, you ask, do they get such crazy ideas? From us, of course. Watch TV for an hour and then reread Chapter 2. We've told them that this is how cool adults act.

Feeling overwhelmed again? I always do after an hour of TV and rereading Chapter 2—but there is a hidden silver lining in that scary peer research that dispels the most depressing myth of all: that you are unimportant to your kid.

Your Values Are Most Powerful to Your Child

There's a third myth you have to lose. Contrary to what you may think, you are more important to your teenager than a pair of wing-tipped shoes. You are more relevant than your Bob Dylan anthology. You're even more useful than that turntable (what is a record anyway?). *Even through the middle-school body piercings, you remain the most prominent force in your child's life.*

The research clearly shows that what I call the "real" stuff in your kid—values, ethics, and morals—comes much more from you than from that peer group, provided you've been able to earn your child's respect. I'm hoping this might begin to make some sense to you, as incredible as it may sound. Kids seek out peer groups to match their own values, and those values originated in you. In Part Two, we'll talk at length about how this occurs. For now, take it on faith that your kids are tremendously influenced by who you are. While I'm stunning you, also know that your kid typically reports having a "close" relationship with you as a parent, and get this, she holds you in *high regard.* I'm not making this up. It comes from the research, as well as from my typical experience with your kid.

But for a year now she's done the exact opposite of what I ask. She won't talk to me, she rolls her eyes at me, and I'm increasingly sure she's hoping a blood test will prove she's adopted. How can this closeness and high regard stuff be true?

Because she's pretty much learned most of the really important teachings she can get from you by the onset of her adolescence. For better and worse, she's incorporated your values, morals, and ethics (see Part Two). She may have put them in cold storage for a while, but I assure you, they're there, and they will reappear in time. You did your work. Now she's looking to other sources for alternative opinions about music (music?), hair, clothes, values, morals, and ethics. This is what she should be doing. This is how she becomes her own person. Did you really want her to have you as her advisor on how to act, talk, and dress cool? Do you really want to spend four hours a night talking to her about the latest teen singing group?

Of course, there's both good and bad news here. The bad news is that if your own house of values is not in order, you've got a rough time coming, and you need to make some quick and difficult changes. We'll talk more about that later on.

But what if your own house is in order, and you see your kid violate your morals? Is this the feared peer menace? Matthew's father instinctively saw what was really important when his test came.

Matthew's dad spoke softly, his quiet voice betraying a steely strength of knowing who he was, and of being at peace with that. "I got a call to come immediately to my son's school. The principal met me outside his office with a teacher, the security officer, and the disciplinarian. He told me that Matt was waiting in his office, having been charged with a drug violation. My son is an honor student who's never been in trouble." Dad's eyes began to mist. "They told me he was bragging to other kids about having been stoned on grass many times, and that he could get it for them if they wanted. I didn't know what to believe." His eyes were clear, direct, and open. He leaned forward to continue. "I asked how long Matt had been sitting alone in that office. They told me two hours. I brushed past them and walked into the room. Matt jumped up. He was terrified." Dad choked up here, but I couldn't wait. "What did you do?"

Dad spoke haltingly through his tears. "I hugged him as hard as I could for as long as I could. I told him that whatever this was, we'd deal with it, and that we loved him no matter what. We just hugged and cried."

Now two men sat in my office wiping tears. "God," I pleaded silently, "please let me remember what this wise man did when I get that phone call."

When I hear and feel things like this from parents, they're almost always the prelude to successful outcomes for adolescents. I know that the values and strengths of these parents reside in their children, somewhere. We just have to locate them. Your child will dabble at testing contrary values, but if you remember that what is really important is maintaining your loving, respect-based relationship *especially through the provocations*, the peer influence doesn't stand a chance. A kid's peers don't have the power to rewrite deep, respect-based values, but they can encourage a teenager to test prohibited behaviors. It's all part of the learning process. What Matt learned in his father's response could only convince him that this man who discourages drug use must know what he's talking about. From a teenager's eyes, any man tough enough to respond to that provocation with love is certainly a man to respect. Repeat the following phrase 10 times: *Respect is the key to teaching values to adolescents.*

Before we leave this chapter, there is a new-millennium twist on the peer issue that you must address as the parent of a new-millennium, brain-damaged adolescent: the Net effect.

Internet Insanity: Don't Laugh It Off

Any discussion of new-millennium peer influence is not complete without a reference to the Internet. Most kids pass through a phase of mildly excessive Net use, and the worst effect is usually a profound loss of sleep that they may recoup in algebra class. But for many kids, the Net can become a much more dangerous type of peer influence.

The Internet has been linked to teenage depression, isolation, and even suicide risk. Kids are creating "cyber relationships" to supplant "real-time relationships" in strange and sometimes frightening ways. On a late night, you might be able to convince me that the Internet was created by a hostile alien race intent on destroying our youth by providing them with an insane secret world in which their adolescent insanity becomes normal, and all things bizarre become possible. With certain kids, it scares me that much.

Many adolescents find "cyber" connections much easier to maintain than real ones because computers are great to hide frailties behind, at least for a while. The result is often a kid who gradually withdraws from taxing "real-time" involvements to the fantasy Internet world. If you've spent any time on the Internet, you know how dangerous this can be. Remember that adolescents are large children, and they still have problems distinguishing fantasy from reality at times. They are susceptible to seeing the insane parts of the Internet as some representation of normalcy.

We are now beginning to see kids who have actually established Internet "cyber families" and "cyber lovers" that carry unique risks. These are idealized and highly charged emotional involvements that can crash quickly and devastatingly, often at 3:00 A.M. for a girl alone in the basement, when exhaustion and depression-based impulses are more easily entertained. Make no mistake, these "cyber" relationships carry as much emotional power and potential pain as real ones, and must be taken very seriously.

David had one of the kindest, softest faces I've ever seen on a father of an adolescent boy. His lip trembled as he tried to retain his composure while telling his story. He was describing his 16-year-old son as a successful student in a prestigious prep school. "Tim's never caused us an ounce of worry. I mean never. We don't even have any hard rules in the house because he's never needed them. He's loving, devoted, and helpful.

"Last night when we came back from work we found a note he left. He had gone to join his 'wife' in San Diego (3,000 miles away) because her father was beating her, and he had to do something. Tim, of course, is not married. He told us not to worry, that he loved us and that he'd be in touch. His computer mail showed that he's had an intense four-month Internet relationship, if you can call it that, with this 27-year-old woman in California. We don't know where he is. He must be traveling by bus. What do we do when he finally calls? What should we say? What in the name of God is going on?"

In Tim's case, his Net "wife" was the antidote for a too-good adolescent who couldn't cope with the loss of his girlfriend a few months earlier. In Part Three we'll talk more about the "what to do" stuff. For now, believe that your kid's choice of Net peers is just as significant as his choice of real-time friends. Both are windows into the soul of your child. Learning about your teen's wanderings in this netherworld can help you get crucial information about his inner workings when he no longer speaks to you in sentences of more than two intelligible words. Place these Net peers right next to his real-life peers in terms of importance to and insight into your kid. They can hold equal power in your kid's life. And remember that a child's fantasy flight into those peer worlds, whether cyber or real, becomes dangerous only when the connections with you are lost.

In summarizing peer pressure, remember that tails don't wag dogs and peers don't make kids. You hold more power than you can imagine with your teenager. Peer groups and Internet bizarreness are really just windows into your child's soul, which ultimately is just a reflection of your own. Do not panic over one-shot values-testing provocations. They're just quizzes. Don't flunk. Keep cool for school.

Chapter 4

ADOLESCENT CHANGE

"We've been at this for four weeks, and Timmy stills rages at home. I don't think this is helping." Doctor: "How have you been doing with your own temper?" Dad: "Well, I'm trying, but it's really unfair of you and her [his wife] to think I can suddenly stop doing something I've done all my life." Dad, seeing wife about to zing him: "Don't say it. I got it. I was listening to myself. Man, this change stuff is hard. If it's this tough for me, it must be a killer for my son." Doctor: "That's a great thought. Share it with your kid."

YOU'RE READING THIS BOOK because you want things to change, right? You're sick to death of the problems and pain and will do anything to bring about a new way of coexisting with your teenager, right? Of course, right! Who would want to stay stuck in a lousy place? Welllllll, maybe many of us.

Human beings are definitely the most interesting creatures around. Those television nature shows that some find so intriguing are yawners in comparison with studies of human behavior. We are really quite fascinating. One of our most amazing characteristics is our tendency to sometimes keep banging ourselves in the head with hammers. Even when it hurts. A lot.

We seem to possess a great deal of emotional inertia, a tendency to continue that which is. Our need for consistency and predictability often outweighs our need to alleviate pain and dysfunction. We take great comfort in keeping things the same. We seem to fear change, even if the change may be for the better. Given a choice, we often will pick a painful but predictable future over a possibly pain-free but unknown one. Our usual instinct is to continue our present state, good or bad.

Even those adventurers among us suffer from the same malady. The woman backpacking through the Himalayas who flat out refuses to consider a more conventional lifestyle may actually be more afraid of the change than of the lifestyle. The very unpredictability of her adventurous life is her predictability. This fearless woman may become weak-kneed at the thought of an unfamiliar lifestyle. We all typically dislike change.

Adventurous adolescents and their boring parents are not immune to this tendency. I frequently find my cat sitting and staring at me much as I do at the nature show, both of us perhaps thinking, "Why do they do that? It makes no sense." We can all become trapped by our own behavior, driven to maintain the status quo. It's quite comfortable even when it hurts.

Quick Fixes Don't Work

Of all the changes humans hate the most, psychological change may be number one. Some psychologists believe we're designed to be change-resistant, that this is nature's way of keeping us sane. Truly insane folks can change a lot, sometimes constantly, and even lose a sense of who they are. Our love of consistency may be a defense against insanity. For whatever reason, real psychological change is tough. And slow. Forget the ads for the "quick-fix miracle therapy programs." The insurance companies love this stuff—and it just doesn't work. There is no fast therapy, weekend program, or book (mine included) that can achieve instantaneous, lasting psychological change.

Remember that, psychologically speaking, whatever exists now in a person has very powerful forces behind it, not the least of which is years of repetition (quitting nicotene is easy; breaking the *habit* of smoking is incredibly difficult). Behavior patterns and character traits are not written in erasable pencil. They're etched in indelible ink. You can try to rewrite them, but it gets messy and sometimes the paper gets torn up a bit in the process. Scars remain and defy our best efforts to completely delete the old writing.

In the movies, clients have these incredibly dramatic breakthroughs, achieving astounding insights that allow them to instantaneously and permanently reconstruct who they are. I love those movies. I also love those John Wayne war flicks. They're both equally (in)accurate in real-istically depicting human experience. They each take a mostly tedious and occasionally intense process and rewrite it into a fast-moving, highly entertaining facsimile. Very few people would pay money to watch the real thing in real time.

You Change First

Psychological change is more often trench warfare than it is a Hollywood cavalry charge. Progress is measured in yards, not miles. This is particularly true with adolescents. Beyond the universal human aversion to the unknown, adolescents have added reasons to dislike change. First, perhaps because their lives are in such a state of continuous flux, they hate changes in the things around them even more than the rest of us. She might have three hair colors in one week, but God help you if you shave off your moustache. He is never home in the evening, but goes bananas if you dare to start night school. And forget any silly ideas you had about moving. They're not going.

Second, adolescents demand that parents change first. We'll talk in Part Two about the effects of parental modeling, how your kid's behavior is intertwined with yours, and how child change requires parent change. For now, understand that from your kid's perspective, changing first connotes a loss of face that most teenagers can't accept. They want to be treated as adults, and in their heads this means not doing what parents tell them to do just because they said so.

Third, in keeping with the change-as-competition theme, many teenagers view any form of conformity as surrender to authority. Their need to rebel and define themselves as being separate from you is all-consuming. Asking him to "just hang up your coat, for God's sake" might actually represent a huge concession in his mind, equal to turning and running in the face of a schoolyard challenge. They'll cry "death before dishonor" (a.k.a. change) and be willing to pay outrageous penalties rather than "cave in." Remember, you're dealing with a foreign culture when you interact with your teenager. Your values and beliefs may temporarily be radically different from your kid's. Children with diabetes give us a good view of this "give me liberty or give me death" philosophy.

Adolescent diabetics often experience a period of apparent insanity when they suddenly stop taking care of their blood sugar levels. They rip off their medical alert bracelets and may deny being diabetic, even when hospitalized as a result of their negligence. They are willing to risk death rather than attend to the daily rigors of managing their disease. Known as diabetic burnout, this reaction seems completely crazy to adults, and completely understandable to teenagers.

Here's how kids explain it:

As teens, we become obsessed with establishing our autonomy. We jealously guard our spaces (rooms) and will fight passionately over privacy issues (e-mail). Any intrusion into our adolescent lives is resented, with special rage reserved for authoritarian, directive-type things, be they overbearing parents or overbearing diseases. Anything that inflicts unwanted daily control and demands is to be fought. Perhaps to the death.

For an adolescent, this loss of privacy and autonomy can feel so bad that death can look good by comparison. Thus, to the teenage diabetic, the disease seems to overwhelm her, to inflict an unwanted identity on her. Dying as her own person, refusing to give in to the controlling demands of diabetes, can seem preferable to living and caving in to the mandates of the disease.

As you shake your adult head in disbelief at this explanation, let me restate that adolescence is a culture foreign to you. If you judge a teen's experience based on your own view of the world, you'll do no good and possibly a lot of harm to your kid. If you can open your mind and listen without judgment, you've taken the first step to helping—but it can be very hard to listen to something that sounds nuts.

"Joe, you've gotten everything you wanted from your parents, everything you asked for in return for making more of an effort in school. Yet your mom tells me you still refuse to bring home the weekly reports you agreed to get. What's up with that?" Joe tried hard but couldn't hide his grin from me. It seemed to spread to a painful extreme, causing him to grimace. This must be some great joke. "You can't tell them this," he ordered, "but I'm actually doing great at school." I bit. "So why not let them see the good news?" Joe's grin broke into laughter.

"Because they would think that they won, that they forced me to change, that they broke me. Now they think I'm just screwing up again, and I'm just letting them think that. When my report card comes home, they'll be all set to ground me forever, and I'll be laughing my butt off as they read it. I'm getting SECOND HONORS, dude."

All this time Mom and Dad thought they were talking about helping Joe with his grades. Joe thought they were talking about imposing their power and control. The parents were seeing academics. The kid was seeing bullying. Did you know that a friendly pat on the head in one culture is an insult in another?

A final reason adolescents in crisis hate change is their built-in unwillingness to trust adults. The simple act of confiding in a grownup can be another form of disquieting change for kids. For crazy adolescents, we are the enemy. Before you talk to them, try to see the view from their side of the table.

Eddie sat back with half-closed eyes that burned mockingly into my soul. This 12-year-old had seen his whole world crash, first with the death of his father a year before, and now with the hospitalization of his mother for an apparent suicide attempt. As the oldest child of three, he had to watch as he and his younger siblings were separated to live among relatives until his mom recovered enough to get them all back together. "You're the third counselor the [social worker] ladies sent me to. What makes you think I'm gonna talk to you? Maybe some bitch judge can say I gotta come here, but no bitch judge can make me talk."

"You're right, Eddie," I nodded, " No bitch judge can make you talk. The question is, do you want to talk?" "To YOU?" Eddie sneered incredulously. "What could you know that could help me? You're just some white yuppie with your squeaky clean office, and your squeaky clean PISSSSSS-AT [his sarcastic name for the car he saw me get out of] and your squeaky clean children [my pictures] on the desk there. Man, you know jack-shit about a kid like me. Who do you think you are, anyway?" I paused and then asked, "What would you like to know about me, Eddie?" He went off. "Absolutely nothing! Man, I've been here before with those other counselors. This is where you counselors tell me what a rough life you had, how you grew up in a bad neighborhood, what a bad-ass you was and how you fought in the war, and all that bullshit. Man, I don't care about you. Get it?"

I let Eddie sit a bit. He sighed and wearily shifted his body to look away from me. He didn't move a muscle as I finally spoke. He didn't even blink. He was listening. I paused to painstakingly select each word to try to eliminate any sign of pretense on my part. "Look, Eddie, you're right about my squeaky clean life. Compared with your life, I'm like a lottery winner. But I'm not here to tell you war stories. My stories are useless to you anyhow, 'cause your whole world is so different than what I remember. I'm not here to tell you what to do. My job is to help you figure out what you need to do."

Eddie's voice softened, and he spoke words that sounded like he'd been rehearsing them. "I don't need nobody's help, don't want nobody's help, ain't gonna take nobody's help. My family ain't no charity case. We take care of our own." "OK, fair enough, Eddie. How about if we talk about how you're gonna do that taking care of your family. It sounds like as your mom's oldest child, this job has fallen to you?" Eddie nodded slowly. We had taken a very small step towards trust.

A psychologist attempting to engage a teenager must slowly interject himself into the adolescent's world at a pace set mostly by the kid. This relationship building is a painstaking process in which the adolescent makes a series of critical judgments about the shrink prior to deciding to confide. Kids look for things like trust, caring, acceptance, and respect. If the therapist passes these tests, only then does the kid look to see if the shrink can be of any help.

To communicate with your adolescent, you must pass all of these same tests while shackled by the chains of parenthood. The shrink's exam is much simpler in that he can remain objective and uninvolved in all of the nasty little battles that Mom and Dad have to fight. Emotional fallout from skirmishes about school, curfew, and so on can do a lot of damage to the parent/adolescent relationship. An uninvolved psychologist can raise behavior options to a kid without attaching the land mines of parental power and control. Being uninvolved makes it much easier. You don't have this tremendous advantage. This, incidentally, is why psychologists who seem so skilled at working with other people's children can become just as handicapped in dealing with their own.

So asking for a seemingly small change in an adolescent can have huge, unseen impact, and must be purchased with great patience and courage on your part. You must change first, without any indication that your child will reciprocate. It's kind of like turning an aircraft carrier or a '63 Buick. Crank the wheel and wait three miles.

Psychologists are usually suspicious of overnight transformations in adolescents. When parents begin telling us how talented we are since their teenager is now a model child after two sessions, we're unimpressed. Like painting your house, a lasting change requires lots of preparatory grunt work. The quick job washes off in the first good storm.

Two Steps Forward, Three Steps Back

Positive changes with adolescents don't occur along nice, straight, predictable lines. Usually, if you chart their behavior, you'll see a lot of wild variability, which looks whacky. One day seems great, the next better, and the third much worse than ever before. Two steps forward, three steps back, one diagonally, cha-cha-cha. When adolescents act out, the dramatic aspects of their performances can obscure data indicating that things may actually be improving. Experiencing a tornado can obscure the memory of what a beautiful week it had been up to that point. While you're cleaning up the wreckage from last night, the preceding four peaceful evenings provide little comfort. Only the recent storm feels real.

"How are things going? You want to know how things are going? I'll tell you how I'm going. I'M GOING OUT OF MY FREAKING MIND! THAT'S HOW I'M GOING! BUT I'M GOING TO MAKE DAMN SURE MY DAUGHTER GOES FIRST!" Mom exhaled, looking unnerved at the fact that she could get this upset. She explained that the night before her 16-year-old daughter Maria had swiped the family car to meet a friend for a snack at the diner. At the 24-hour diner. At 2:00 A.M. And, oh yeah, she had met this friend on the Internet. At 1:00 A.M. "Why in God's name would she do this? Up to last night we were having an OK week. But after last night, I feel really hopeless. This is never going to get better, is it?"

Actually, things *were* getting better. A lot better, by my records. But I wasn't the one up until 5:00 A.M. that morning picturing my kid lying in a gutter somewhere. Parents and baseball pitchers usually feel as competent as their last game. Even if we've won six in a row, getting blown out in the seventh makes us feel like all-time losers, like we've forever lost our edge. We can quickly feel hopeless and despondent, believing that we'll never pitch well again. Such are the pressures of major league ball, which are half as weighty as parenting a difficult adolescent.

These variable and dramatic factors can make it very hard to keep an accurate perspective on how your kid is really doing. If you track problem behaviors of your kid on a grid, you'd get lots of scattered points all over the chart. The trick is to find trends of change inside the mess. Looking at just a few days' worth of data might show chaos, but looking at an entire week might show a little movement. The month's view tells the real story—but that month's view is better done with a chart, not by a scared parent.

> "We've got to talk about sending Tina away. I can't have her in the house anymore. She's completely out of control. Much worse than ever before. Today I found a credit card she stole from her uncle. I've been doing all the things you recommend, but they clearly are not working."
> "What's your log have to say about her behavior?" I asked. Mom flipped through the record I'd asked her to keep, tracking the number of bad behaviors. Grudgingly she replied, "Well, this shows her to be doing better, but it just feels so much worse." Mom's anger at me rose from both her panic and her profound disappointment from having once again dared to hope that she'd get her daughter back. The recent peaceful days now stood as a painful contrast to the terrible, but now less frequent, behaviors.

So don't trust your memory. Trust a chart. Keep a detailed log of how your kid is doing on a daily or even hourly basis, depending on the severity and frequency of the acting out. This data serves two purposes. First, it provides the science needed to see if things are improving. More important, this log can become your motivational coach, helping you not to feel so despondent after a particular siege.

Successful changes with troubled adolescents are not sprints. They're marathons. The patient and tenacious parents are the ones most likely to survive well. Frequently, the game becomes one of simply putting one foot in front of the other, of maintaining a mindless discipline of repetitious responses to stay the course, even when you're sure you've got nothing left inside. The logbook can become your bible, your reassurance that what you're doing is working, even though it doesn't feel that way. As a coach once told me, "If you can't outrace 'em, outlast 'em."

The final trick with tracking changes in your kid is to focus heavily on the positives. The fewer these are, the more you must see them. Put golden mental frames around these times to remind yourself of what is possible, to know that the wonderful smile you once knew still exists underneath that unrecognizable scowl and will resurface one wonderful day—but this is sometimes hard to believe.

"Darby is gone." Mom spoke with funereal reverence of her daughter, who was slouching in the waiting room next door. "I have a picture here I want you to see. This was my daughter." Mom handed me a picture of a smiling, bright, and clowning girl, mugging it up with her mother. The picture looked like it had been pulled out a lot. "This was us just a year ago. I wanted to show it to you so you could see how far she's fallen. After our last session I felt like you didn't understand how bad off she is."

I recalled our last session, in which I cheerily explained to Mom how much better Darby was doing. After a long truancy she was now attending school regularly and seemed more in control of her acting-out behaviors. I recalled thinking in our last session that Mom didn't seem impressed, but I had neglected to ask her why. This picture was why.

"Do you look at this a lot?" I asked. Mom bit her lip and nodded yes. Fighting her tears, she tried to help me see what I could not ever fully know: the depth of her loss. "I know she's doing better in some ways, but I feel like her soul is still sick. She's so bitter and sarcastic. I don't think she's smiled in a year. How can she not smile and be well? Look at that face in the picture. Where has that smile gone?" Mom lost her fight with the tears.

Her pain felt terrible to me. Here I was promoting a happy view of Darby, all the while forgetting Mom's huge emotional loss and fear. She was right. How can a kid be better and not smile? I had to word the next part carefully. "Mrs. Wright," I said slowly, "Darby does smile. She smiles a lot in here and her teachers report that she seems happy most days at school now. She just doesn't smile with you yet. You see, you will be the last to get that award-winning smile again because you're her mom, and she's still trying to sort out all of that separation need she has. This is her way, for now, of trying to be independent of you." With glistening eyes Mom stared hard as if her stomach was hurting. "But please," I continued, "hear this next part clearly. That smile in the picture is still inside of your child. Others less important to your daughter are seeing it again and you will see it soon. For now, you must look at these charts that show how much better Darby is doing. She's on her way back to you. If you can give her some scowling space, and not take it personally, she'll smile all the sooner at you."

I thought to myself that I would not have accepted this explanation if Darby were my kid but it was the best I had to offer. It turned out that Mrs. Wright was stronger than I am. "It's OK, then," she said with quiet conviction. "I do miss her desperately, but if she's all right then I'm fine. I can wait. I realize I was silly to think that her smiling at me was the test of her being OK or not. Thank you for straightening me out." I shook my head in dissent. "No," I corrected, "Thank you for straightening *me* out. I hang out with adolescents too much. Sometimes I forget that parents are people too."

Speaking of this astounding insight that parents are also people, there is another area in which the humanity of parents becomes painfully evident. It involves that gut-wrenching fear that sets in when we find ourselves awake in the middle of the night thinking thoughts about our teenager that are too terrifying to share with our spouse: Is our child seriously mentally ill, or is she just suffering from the normal temporary insanity of adolescence? How do we tell the difference? And why can't we even give voice to these fears?

In Chapter 5, we'll examine these and other scary questions that disturb our sleep.

Refasten your seat belt. We're going back in.

Chapter 5

ADOLESCENT INSANITY:
WHAT'S NORMAL, WHAT'S NOT

Now that I've presented the case that, to some extent, all teenagers are nuts, we need to sort out the degrees of disturbances parents might witness, ranging from the normal to the unusual.

This chapter has two purposes. First, it will help worried parents of normal kids not to become too terrified of normal teen craziness by describing serious mental illness. Second, this chapter will help families of seriously ill adolescents see past denial mechanisms that can become life threatening when kids who need intensive help don't get it. The disorders discussed in this chapter represent only a few of the many serious mental illnesses that can hit a teen. These particular ones were chosen for their relative frequency and their similarity to normal teenage insanity, which can get confusing and frightening.

To help you sort out what's normal and what's not, this chapter looks at four areas of your child's life: acting-out behaviors, moodiness, struggles with food, and anxieties. In each of these categories, we'll look at the typical craziness that results from the disorder of adolescence (see Chapter 1) versus more serious problems that require a trip to the shrink.

If you feel your knuckles turning white as you grip the book at this chapter, the odds are that you share the common parental fear that your child suffers from a serious mental disturbance. Stop worrying. Calm down. Take a deep breath. Let me reassure you that, whatever the case with your kid, your fears are correct. He is disturbed, whether it's diagnosable or not.

Simply being an adolescent connotes substantial disturbance, so in a sense, most teenagers vacation at times in the world of mental dysfunction. Even the student council president-type adolescents will exhibit irrational thoughts and actions at times. However, when the occasional visit becomes a daily border crossing, it's time to consider the possibility of a mental disorder.

CALM DOWN. As scary as that sounds, the diagnosis of an adolescent mental disorder is rarely a catastrophe. Conversely, being judged "normal" is by no means a passport to a successful life. Sometimes, serious mental disorders are much easier to work with than many of the adjustment problems of normal teenagers. A child struggling with an obsessive-compulsive disorder may be more open and direct about himself than a normal, surly, and sarcastic teenager who brutally torments his siblings for entertainment. The quiet courage of the not-normal kid can make his prospects for recovery quite good, and his odds of having a happy, fulfilled life quite excellent. The self-centered, uncompassionate normal child can make me wish his parents had called another psychologist. That normal adolescent can be maddening to work with now, and unlikely to find happiness in the future. I've worked with many normal kids whose lack of character left me very depressed— and I've worked with many seriously ill teens whose character strengths of moral integrity and emotional maturity just awed me.

Rachel sat and stared at the floor with the saddest eyes I'd ever seen in a 14-year- old girl. She didn't know it, but I had been in touch with school and county social workers who told me off the record that her father was probably an abusive monster, a word they don't use lightly. They were almost certain that he had been neglecting and beating Rachel's three- and five-year-old brothers for years. Rachel had been denying this to investigators, presenting difficulties for legal intervention. They referred her to me for treatment of a possible dissociative identity disorder (also known as multiple personality disorder). Her psychiatrist felt she was in the early stage of this illness, hearing a voice and losing memory for some time periods in the day.

In earlier sessions, Rachel seemed to be constantly testing me on trust issues. Her school records suggested she was mentally gifted, perhaps extremely so, yet her grades were poor. Her poetry suggested that she saw the world through the eyes of a tormented, bitter war veteran, yet with stunning insight into the human character and condition.

This session she leaned forward in her seat and decided to take a risk. "I'm not dumb, but I act that way to get left alone. I really do have a dissociating disorder. I know since I looked it up before the school sent me to the doctor. I've got another Rachel inside of me." She paused. "Do you have any idea what it's like to wake up in the middle of your life, in the middle of your math class, in the middle of your conversation, in the middle of your sentence, in the middle of your word? When you can't remember what the first syllable of that word was?

"I know you're not dumb too," Rachel continued, "but I don't know if I can trust you." With a sad laugh, she sat back and added, "I haven't met many adults I can trust. Kids are more moral, you know. If they're gonna hurt you, they'll do it in your face, right away. Adults lie. All the time, and then they tell you why it was OK for them to lie.

"I need you to fix me fast. So I'll tell you what the book said you need to know. I was sexually molested from the time I can remember until I was eight or nine by my father's friend. He didn't know. Then I was raped twice by another of my father's friends when I was 12. That stopped when I put a knife to his throat. My dad never knew. Nobody touches me now. Even including my boyfriend. I told him I can't be sexual, or even hug him. I told him why. He understands." As I tried to clear my emotional head from this incredible picture she was painting, she knocked me over again.

"I'm officially telling you that my father never knew any of this. I want you to write that down on your paper there." I wondered what this thing in the fog was, what she was trying to tell me. I slowly entered the mist.

"Rachel, why would you not tell someone this stuff was going on?" She looked at me as if wondering what it must be like to have a life as protected as mine. "You really don't know, do you? It's because when you tell, they all just lie, and do nothing. When you tell, you just get hurt more, and watch your baby brothers get hurt more." I posed to get past her fences. "I can't believe that, Rachel. We have laws today that..." It worked. She jumped up and yelled. "Your laws SUCK. Before we moved east last year, I told. I told for the babies. And the babies got beat! On account of my telling! He don't beat me now, he's scared of me, but..." She froze. With an icy voice she said, "You tricked me."

I walked to my desk and handed her a picture of our newly adopted two-year-old daughter. "That's Sarah. She was born addicted to cocaine. She came from a hellhole like the ones you've known. She was almost starved to death when she was a year old. Rachel, I give you my word as Sarah's father that if you tell, no one will beat the babies. I don't know where you came from, but you're in my ballpark now. This just ain't gonna happen here."

Rachel had kept her silence for years to protect her brothers, for whom she was really a mother in every sense of the word. She was being held hostage by a "father" who threatened to harm the babies if Rachel ever left, told about the sexual or physical abuse, or even killed herself. Rachel's heart and will were so strong that her mind finally broke under the incredible load she was carrying. Her disease of dissociating was her last-resort survival attempt. Even now, at age 14 and mentally ill, her convictions held firm.

Rachel is a heroine of mine, my living reminder that mental illness is not a failure of character, nor is it a sign of weakness. She embodies a guiding thought that may be the most helpful idea you can take from this chapter and perhaps from this book. Whether your child is normally brain-disordered from adolescence or more seriously ill, *separate the disease from the child bearing it*. Remember that your child lives on inside that maddening and frightening bundle of symptoms. Her hopes, fears, courage, compassion, loves, memories—all those things that make her a person—don't disappear with the onset of illness. Far too often we allow a disorder to become our child in our eyes, focusing all of our time and attention on the symptoms instead of on the person we love. This allows the disease to rob our kids of so much more. It can further infect their souls and contaminate all parts of their lives if they see us repulsed and furious with them all the time.

Do we view our teenagers as pained people stuck with involuntary mental disorders or do we personalize their behaviors and write them off as arrogant bastards? Be honest now, because your answer can make all the difference in how much of your kid's life will be consumed by the disorder.

If you answered, "Yes, I see him as an arrogant bastard," I appreciate your honesty, but I must change your mind. It really is no fun being nuts, especially if you're a teenager. The invasiveness of normal adolescent insanity is a terrible experience for kids. What you see as Junior having a fun time raging at you is really a manifestation of his pain. It is no fun living like that, feeling yourself going crazy and hurting the people you love, and who love you. Even as she sneers at your deep sadness, she hears a voice inside asking incredulously, "What the hell are you doing this for? Are you insane?" She hasn't yet answered that very critical question, but you might answer it for her. If you take her behavior personally, you will lie to her and tell her that she is sane, but cruel and horrible. This will make her sadder, angrier, and crazier. If you can find the strength to use the training in this book to not take her insanity personally, you will give her the wonderful gift of looking past the repulsiveness of her disorder to find that struggling child within. You will sidestep the hurtful words and try to listen to the pain that fires them.

Sound impossible? Of course it is, just like the 10 other impossible tasks you will do because you love your child, and because you are a parent. But listening can be very hard to do.

Shane's father had been preparing this speech. "I've had enough of this coddling bullshit with him. If Shane really wanted to, he could stop washing his goddamn hands. What he needs is a good, swift kick in the ass. I'm not gonna listen anymore to this 'I wanna die' crap." Dad intoned a whiney, nasalized voice to mock his son, who sat next to him staring at the floor. "He doesn't want to die. He just wants all this attention. My father wouldn't have taken this for one second. No sir! He would'a cured my disorder in 10 minutes. With his belt. That's what this whiner needs. Did I have problems? Sure I did. But I didn't let them take over my life. That's what my father taught me, the hard way. And I turned out..."

Dad's eyes, wide with his own childhood rage, startled at the choking sound coming from his son. Shane's shoulders were heaving with staggered sobs, breaking through the boy's desperate wish to hold back. This kid who hadn't cried in years was tearing in half. He looked liked he wanted to die.

Dad sat shocked, staring in disbelief as the depth of his son's pain opened up before us as a great terrible chasm seeking to pull us all in. Dad's rage at his son's symptoms melted away in the heat of Shane's tears. As the truth about his son washed over him and his denial of Shane's problem vanished, Dad began crying too. "My God, son, I'm sorry. I, I didn't know. I just thought..." His voice trailed off as he heard himself about to say how he had abandoned his own son because of an involuntary disorder that Dad found repulsive. The disorder was pain enough for Shane. The rejection by his father was far worse.

An adolescent struggling with a mental disorder shares the same terrible burden as one with a physical disease such as diabetes, but with an even more excruciating twist. Adolescent insanity, whether the normal or unusual type, attacks your child's identity with a vengeance far beyond physical illness by forcibly altering him at his most personal and vulnerable point: his own mind. Feeling compelled to entertain irrational thoughts and actions shakes him at his most basic level of existence, of self, making him most envious of the diabetic. The diabetic can refuse to cooperate with her disease. She has the option of diabetic burnout (see Chapter 4), of being able to retreat to some private inner place where the disease can't own her. She has the option of dying from the disease, but dying with her own mind as she desires. If Shane died, he would die with these unwanted thoughts still in his head. His identity, his essence, his soul are now infected with his disorder. Think honestly for a moment. If that were you, would feeling like you wanted to die seem completely irrational? Is your kid feeling like he wants to die so completely irrational?

Our task as parents, then, is to help our disordered kids handle scary thoughts in two ways, which can be contradictory and must be balanced carefully. First, we must listen without making judgments or giving advice. Listening means saying as little as possible, trying to get your kid to vomit out all his terrible fears that you'll want to talk away. Listening means overriding that fatal parental urge to discount what your child says ("Oh, you don't really want to die..."). Listening means asking small, quiet questions to keep your kid talking. Think of those pent-up fears as poisoned food, and you'll see why you want your kid to keep throwing up for as long as possible. Listening means trying to feel their pain, to walk in their shoes. Listening means holding them for as long as they allow, and understanding if they push you away.

Second, we must simultaneously affirm who they are *apart* from their disorders, whether normal adolescent insanity or more serious mental illness. This means focusing on those aspects of our children that are special, wonderful, and most important, unique to them. We must help them find those things that the disease can't infect. Look to praise his compassion, his love of music (music?), or his green hair. Marvel at her reading, her dancing, or her love of animals. Remind them that they are not their diseases. Every day. As often as you can.

Why We Don't Get Help

Before we discuss specific disorders, let me save you from reading the same sentence repeatedly, throughout this chapter. It applies to all of the illnesses we'll discuss, and I'll say it just once: When in doubt, seek qualified professional help NOW. Be sure your expert is a credentialed psychologist, psychiatrist, psychiatric nurse practitioner, or clinical social worker (see Chapter 16). If I had a nickel for every nasty situation I've seen where earlier intervention could have saved a lot of pain, I'd have 20 or 30 bucks by now—a lot of nickels and a whole bunch of needless trauma.

Why should I have to state the obvious? Why do loving, attentive, and giving parents wait until the house is engulfed in flames before calling 911? Why don't we call when we first see smoke?

For lots of reasons. The first is denial. As Dizzy Gillespie said, "You sees what you want to sees." We just can't believe that *our* kid is in trouble. The child across the street, sure, but not our bundle of joy. The neighbor's kid is a thug. Our kid is a little difficult. It's just not possible that he's ill. It's only a phase. He'll be fine.

Yeah, well, if he ran a 103-degree fever for four days, would you guess that he'd be fine or would you get it checked out?

A second reason is embarrassment. Those fire engines in the driveway announce to the community that something's wrong. We really hate that. It makes us feel incompetent and somehow publicly stupid that we have to call a psychologist about our own kid. After all, we should know how to handle these things. We're parents, for God's sake—but exactly what expertise comes along with the title of parent? Should we feel ashamed if the neighbors find out that we hired a contractor because the air conditioner isn't working? Should we feel ashamed if they find out that we hired a psychologist?

Innocence might be a third defense for doing nothing. Naive belief coupled with a lack of knowledge about mental disorders can be a deadly combination.

Paul cleared his hoarse throat many times, like something was stuck in there that wouldn't come out. This father seemed stooped and bent far beyond his years. Mom sat motionless. "Jimmy was simply the best kid you could ask for. We never even had to spank him, not once. But gradually a darkness started to come over him. He became argumentative, surly, and isolated. He refused to do any schoolwork. We suspected he was also using drugs, but we figured this was all a phase. That's what all our friends told us, and they've raised teenagers. Mental illness always seemed to be something that could only happen to some other family, not ours." "How long did this phase last?" I asked. Dad, with hollow eyes, answered. "About a year. Looking back now, I can see all of the signs. Why couldn't I see them before?"

I knew what I was about to say would not help them, but I guess I had to say something to help me. "When were you trained to differentially diagnose depression from normal adolescent moodiness?" Dad shook his head to say never. "And how were you supposed to have predicted something that no expert can predict?" Dad started to agree, but Dawn, his wife, cut him off. "It was our responsibility and our obligation and we failed and now we have to live with that."

Notes from grief work with the parents. Jimmy committed suicide.

Most parents have no idea what unusual mental disorders look like because they hardly ever see them. Parents who would never consider doing their own house air conditioning or car brake jobs often feel as if they should not have to consult an expert on their child's problems. How does this make sense? Why should parents be expected to have such specialized knowledge, particularly when the risks might be so high? When did you go to school for this stuff? Should you know the normal anticipated temperature differential readings at your "A" coil in your house cooling system or do you just call the expert?

The fourth reason we let the house burn down is cost. In some communities, the fire companies charge money to put out fires, so many homeowners now have these impulses of trying to douse flames themselves rather than pay the $500 to the firefighters. This thought may seem logical when first viewing a small garage fire. It seems insane standing in front of the charred house ruins, hearing the late-arriving firefighter say that lots of people make the mistake of squirting gasoline fires with a hose. What seemed so expensive at one point can seem so cheap later. I don't mean to trivialize financial concerns. I do mean to make you carefully assess just what "expensive" means when compared to the risk.

The final reason we find for neglecting a kid's illness is neglect. A sad truth is that many parents really don't give a damn. Since you're reading this book, that is not you, but it may describe your neighbors, your in-laws, or parents of kids you teach or coach. I can't give you numbers here, but I can tell you that in my 27 years of working with kids, my impression is that emotional neglect of adolescents is epidemic these days. Part Two of this book talks more about this, but for now, understand that many parents really do not give a damn. This is hard to see at first glance in our wealthy society, but if you look closely, underneath the toys, cars, and sports camps, often you'll find a disordered child cast adrift by materially giving parents. These kids probably scare me the most.

Now we're ready to look at the four major categories of teenage problems: acting-out behaviors, moodiness, food problems, and anxieties. With each one, we'll distinguish the normal adolescent craziness from the unusual to help you decide whether to try a home remedy or go to a specialist. Remember, if you have any doubt at all, go to the specialist. Also remember that the normal craziness can be just as difficult as the unusual, and often is a lot worse, and a specialist can do a lot to help you deal with normal adolescent insanity, as well as more serious problems.

Acting-Out Behaviors

There are a number of serious mental disorders that get lumped under this one popular heading along with some illnesses that we create with words and inflict on kids with gossip. Words like "antisocial," "psychopathic," and "sociopathic" are often tattooed onto kids who act out. While a very small number of kids are seriously disturbed, widespread misuse of these labels can do much more damage than the adolescents themselves.

People are amazed to learn that we don't have an illness called Antisocial Personality Disorder for folks under age 18, and we don't have diseases called psychopathology or sociopathology. I quibble with the terms here because of the permanently damning implications of these labels. With thanks to Hollywood, these nonexistent diagnostic categories carry terrible gossip impact for children who are described as such. If a community (neighborhood, school, and/or family) begins talking about a child as being a Silence of the Lambs monster, the talk can create the reality. It's the ultimate in circular effects. As the talk pervades, people begin treating the troubled kid as a potential assassin. As the community withdraws, the kid is increasingly isolated and left with fewer opportunities for normal (and healing) interaction, and more chances for weirdness. This leads to more pain for the kid, which leads to more anger, which leads to more hurting behaviors, which leads to more talk. In this way, our cruel and irresponsible words can create mental illness in adolescents. Conversely, our kind and engaging words, particularly those used in the face of provocation, can cure it.

NORMAL ACTING-OUT BEHAVIOR

Are all teens antisocial? Only to parents, at times, and occasionally to the community. What appears to you to be antisocial behavior by your kid is usually just your child trying to grow up. The disorder of the adolescent brain (see Chapter 1) gets further scrambled by your kid's struggle for independence. Like that first birthing process, the rebirth of a child as a teen fighting for autonomy doesn't happen easily. It involves a lot of parental controlled breathing, contractions, exhaustion, and pain. Most kids will become obstinate, disrespectful, and "in your face" at times with their parents. Sometimes these outbursts may even escalate into a one-time push or shove from your child, and still be considered normal. As horrendous as this is when it happens, in the long run a properly handled push can be very healing for the crazed adolescent soul.

James entered my office quietly with his head down. I hardly recognized him. This 10-year-old had always made grand mocking entrances as his form of protest about being forced into counseling with his parents. This time his mom left us at my door saying, "Jimmy asked to speak to you without us tonight." When I looked at her quizzically, she shrugged her shoulders and lifted her hands towards James's back indicating that he wanted be the one to tell me something. Alone.

I was shocked by this sudden turn in James's behavior. Gone were his trademark arrogant slouch, his disdainful smile, and his Air Jordans upon my table. He sat up straight like a responsible young man. In a voice that I'd not heard before, he actually initiated the session, something unthinkable a week before. "I've got something to say, so I'd appreciate it if you would not ask questions until I'm done. I'm trying to keep a promise I made to myself that I would tell you everything, but it's real hard to do." He certainly had my attention. "You know how you kept telling me that I had to find better ways to argue with my mom than to scream and yell? You were right. I think I used to mess with her to see if I could get her crying and crazy. I don't know why and you've got to help me figure it out before I hurt somebody again.

" Last night," James paused here a second to muster his courage, "I had fiscoolcality with her." Fiscoolcality? My God, I thought, what is he talking about? I had promised not to interrupt, so I sat there like I knew what he was talking about. This happens a lot when you work with kids. "I was messing with her like I always do, but I noticed that I was really getting angrier than usual. I was screaming really loud at her when this strange feeling came over me. Then next thing I knew I like, woke up and found we had fiscoolcality. I'm really messed up, aren't I?"

I wasn't sure how to respond. Here for the first time this difficult kid was finally opening up to me and I didn't know what the heck he was talking about. I've found that the truth is often a good option in these situations, so I went with that. "James, I'm sorry, but I don't know what you mean when you say you had fiscoolcality. What exactly happened?"

James looked appalled and agitated that he was going to have to explain in detail. Very somberly he explained, "We had, you know, fiscoolcality. I got so mad that I pushed her away from me. That's the first time we ever had fiscoolcality, and believe me, it's going to be the last. That's what my teacher at school calls it when a word fight gets out of control and you shove someone: fiscoolcality. Haven't you heard of this?"

As a sense of relief swept over me I found myself working hard not to laugh at this critical moment in James's life. I decided to make the teacher out to be the fool. "I think, James, your teacher got the pronunciation of that word messed up. He maybe meant something like becoming physical, maybe physicality?" "Yes," James nodded wisely, "that must have been what he was trying to say."

"What did your mom do after you shoved her?" I asked, although by his reaction I was pretty sure of the answer. "Nothing," James said very sadly. "She didn't yell or scream or hit me back; she just got real quiet and just asked me if this was the way I really wanted to act. I didn't know what to say. I feel terrible. I couldn't even sleep last night." James's eyes were brimming with tears now.

He's probably right, I thought. That might be the last episode of fiscoolcality he ever has with his very wise and very strong mother.

These kinds of incidents are the normal, adolescent, brain dysfunction-based impulses that only become serious problems if they are consistently handled badly by parents who lose the respect of their child by responding in kind (see Chapter 7). In Parts Two and Three we'll train you on how to hit these curve balls well. For now, know that these insulting or confrontational trials are normally short-lived, meaning anything from a one-time shot to perhaps a month of snarling. These episodes may repeat periodically until the storm of adolescence passes, usually by 17 to 18 years of age. The worst usually occurs earlier in the 12- to 15-year range.

Most kids will also have an episode or two of what appears to be frighteningly antisocial behavior in the community. Most kids survive this. Some even become professionals.

"Michael has been a model child all his life. I've never heard him utter a disrespectful word in his 14 years of living. He's an honor student, was captain of the altar boys at church, and lieutenant of his school safety patrol. He's had newspaper articles written commending him for his community service. He's worked for his own money since he was eight." Mom paused here, and searched the wall with her eyes, unable to grasp the content of her next sentence.

"Last week, he and Walter, his best friend who's also never been in trouble, stole Walter's mother's car at 1:00 A.M., took a BB gun, and drove around town shooting out street lights. They threw Slurpees through the open window of an occupied car parked in a lovers' lane. Then they stopped at a construction site and dumped bags of cement off a bridge onto railroad tracks, risking a derailment. They were chased by the police and somehow got away, driving at speeds over 100 miles per hour. They celebrated their bravery by drinking beer they bought from some gangster they contacted." Mom was stunned hearing her own words. "I guess this is what they call a sociopath. He could have killed any number of people that night, and had absolutely no regard for anyone's welfare. Is he insane? What will become of him? What will he end up doing with his life?"

Notes of a conversation that never was, since I didn't get caught 35 years ago. I still feel really bad about the Slurpee.

I can't really explain what happened that night. Was it insane? Certainly. Did you do at least as much? Probably. Will your kid have such an evening? What do you think? But the occasional bizarre behavior or two doesn't rate as illness. The key in assessing possible acting-out disorders is to seek patterns of behavior. Look to the rule, not the exception, with your child.

We call those inexplicable, isolated (or two, maybe three) events of madness normal teenage insanity (see Chapters 1 and 2). In Part Three, we'll chat about how to respond to such normal adolescent craziness. But if Michael started making a habit out of those Friday nights, we'd have to consider the possibility of more serious problems that require the intervention of specialists.

UNUSUAL ACTING-OUT BEHAVIOR

While most teenagers act out to some extent in what we consider a normal way, there are some kids who act out in a way that indicates a serious problem. Here are the most common serious acting-out behaviors.

Oppositional Defiant Disorder (ODD): Adolescence Stuck In 5th Gear

These kids are hard to miss. While all adolescents will be oppositional at times, an ODD kid seems extreme when compared to his peers. He's in your face a lot of the time for at least six months. Like the label says, he's defiant, uncooperative, and plain old nasty towards authority figures to a point where his life is hurting. No request is too small to be complied with. Sports, grades, and home life all may begin to come apart. If the behavior seems aimed only at one authority person, however, it's likely not ODD that's the culprit. Something else is going on between the kid and his exclusive target (see Part Three). Usually he's not picky about who to "dis." Anyone in charge whom he knows well will do. Cops, teachers, and parents all can get anointed, although he seems to spare strangers: "Gee, Ms. Smith, Charles has been a model student for the week he's spent here...Gee, Ms. Smith, after teaching Charles for six months I'm retiring to something more relaxing, like kick boxing." The bulk of his act is verbal and obstinate in nature, and rarely involves physical aggression. Normally this behavior starts before age eight and not later than early adolescence. Like I said, these kids are hard to miss.

Connor roamed my office like a wild animal, stomping and screaming. He was demanding to go home, shrieking at his mother that they were to leave NOW! This 12- year-old seemed really scary at this first meeting. He ripped the file from Mom's hands and began tearing and throwing the pages into the trash can, while continuing to scream. On the outside, I looked calm, helping Mom to maintain both her composure and her conversation with me, trying to help her learn to ignore the tantrum behavior. Inside, I was scared. Where would he draw his limits? Will he stop at verbal aggression? Is Mom strong enough to ignore him? Will my new glass-topped coffee table survive? Why didn't I become a dentist?

Connor moved on to "demo-ing" his papers from his school bag. Pretending I wasn't noticing, I noticed that he was deftly selecting certain nonessential pages for ripping, and just throwing the more important ones in the trash can intact. Good! Good! He was also hoping to imply that he might hurt someone, but he didn't seem willing to get physical, at least so I hoped. We just ignored him, thereby calling his bluff and asking to see his cards. Whew! A pair of 10s. When we ignored his final frenzied warning that we'd better call 911, his gas gauge warning light popped on. He began running out of fuel. As he slowly calmed down, I untied the sailor's knot in my stomach and jotted in my notes, "Close, but no physical violence. Maybe ODD. Get rid of glass-topped table. Still glad I didn't go to dental school."

We don't really know what causes this disorder, but we do have one theory. Most of these kids were very tough as babies, often colicky and difficult to soothe or snuggle. They often eschewed physical comfort, causing parents to begin to withdraw, thus creating another one of those ever-worsening circles where both the child and the parent feel unloved and unwanted. That circle might slowly worsen over the years until the brain dysfunction-based impulsivity of adolescence connects with that deep pain of rejection like a match to dynamite.

If you suspect your kid has ODD, get help yesterday. Time is critical given the acting-out possibilities for new-millennium adolescents. Getting an ODD kid in treatment is very difficult. (See the section "How to Get Your Kid There: Controversial Kid Tricks" in Chapter 16 for some tips.) We do have treatments and medications that can be very helpful with ODD kids, but the longer this disturbance goes on, the tougher it is to treat.

ODD adolescents are impossible to live with, refuse to accept professional help (what a shock), and are in serious danger of getting admitted to the next and much more serious level of disruptive behavior: Conduct Disorder.

Conduct Disorder (CD): Graduate School for Rage

Having successfully completed all of the requirements for the ODD degree, some kids graduate and move on to the college of Conduct Disorder. CD kids are ODD children getting a master's degree in acting out. Their behavior progresses from being verbally rebellious and obstinate to becoming physically violent and aggressive. They assault, bully, steal, lie, cheat, rape, whatever they choose with no regard for the rights of others. They are definitely not nice, they're not subtle, and they are this way most of the time. If you have doubts that your child has Conduct Disorder, he probably doesn't. Parents of CD kids have no doubts.

As of this writing, we have no single definitive treatment for Conduct Disorder. It appears that this one disorder may actually represent a cluster of "mini-illnesses," each with its own causes and treatment needs. For therapists, these kids represent the toughest of cases, since gaining access to the inner thoughts of adolescents this hardened is like going one-on-one with Michael Jordan. The outlook for success is poor. This is why I run on about getting psychological help for kids earlier versus later. If you have any doubts about your kid, check them out. You may waste a few bucks having the psychologist say, "He's normal, go home," but isn't that peace of mind worth something? Besides, what do you pay for a pair of sneakers for him these days?

Trying Juveniles as Adults

Before we leave the subject of Conduct Disorder, I need to raise a very controversial issue that relates to this topic. Criminal prosecutors are now being widely applauded (and re-elected) for charging juveniles suspected of violent crimes as adults, incarcerating them with adult criminals, and seeking adult jail sentences. These are typically kids who suffer from Conduct Disorder. As someone who works with adolescents, it's hard for me to know where to begin to address this issue. I can start by saying that the insanity implicit in this line of thinking makes the thinking of someone with Conduct Disorder seem easy to understand by comparison. And if you think that seeking adult revenge against children is a rare occurrence in this nation, think again.

In 1998, we prosecuted over 200,000 children as adults. As of this writing, 10,000 kids are fighting for their lives while they serve sentences in adult prisons. Since 1973, we grownups have killed 17 people for killing, all of whom were still too young to drive or vote when they committed their murders. If you find this disquieting, you might take some comfort in the good company we keep in this enlightened approach to juvenile justice. Among all of the member countries of the United Nations, only two have refused to ratify a covenant outlawing these legally approved killings of children: the United States and Somalia. In fact, since 1990, only six countries have executed people who committed crimes as children: Iran, Nigeria, Pakistan, Saudi Arabia, Yemen, and the United States. Interesting grouping, don't you think?

The rationale offered by advocates of this bizarre policy is twofold. First, they note that certain juvenile crimes are so terrible that they supersede the intent of old legal codes developed for lesser child crimes. In other words, they say that the laws developed to handle kids who vandalized their high school cafeterias are insufficient to deal with the kids who now storm the cafeterias with assault weapons. Juvenile law does not allow for long-term punitive sentences. The second argument claims that sentencing kids under most juvenile laws ensures that they will be put back on the streets whether or not they represent a threat to society. We've been all through this debate before. Actually, your great-grandparents thought they had sorted this out, but what the heck did they know?

One hundred years ago we used to stick children convicted of crimes into adult prisons. Then, in Chicago, thanks to the efforts of three women who were appalled at what we did to kids back then, the first juvenile justice system was created. The basic concept was that kids are kids, whether they're good or bad, and thus, by definition, they cannot be held accountable to adult standards for their actions. These folks decided that what bad kids needed was help to become good adults, not to be thrown into snake pits with adult offenders. They intuitively knew then what we've just now proven with science: Your kid is crazy and you shouldn't take his behavior personally, and neither should society. The idea of juvenile court spread like wildfire across the nation and became the compassionate and enlightened arm of justice—until today's age of re-enlightenment.

Over the past 10 years, we've taken a vindictive and small-minded sledgehammer to this juvenile justice concept that once viewed helping troubled children as being the responsibility of a civilized society—but one that requires a lot of work, tolerance, and money. Our generation is much more efficient than our great-grandparents'. Today we portray sick children as vicious enemies and then we annihilate them. We're good at it, too.

In debates on the subject, proponents of adult prosecution of kids begin by referring to these children as perpetrators or offenders or sociopaths, only to often slip and call them what they are—kids. These hard-liners quickly retract the child references in their arguments, but too late for me.

These perpetrators *are children*. Dangerous? Often. Capable of doing terrible things? Most certainly. Big, imposing, coldly calculating, uncaring, and frightening? Yes, sometimes. Beyond rehabilitation? Maybe, but maybe not. Who is able to make that call? Shrinks? We'll be the first to tell you that we can't do that. Prosecutors feel that they have both the obligation and skills to make such calls, and now our laws give them the authority. They claim they're just protecting us all, but just how does someone decide which children we try to save and which ones we throw away? Who gives them this wisdom? And how can they justify prosecuting an 11-year-old as an adult knowing what you know about your kid: that adolescents are insane? Their brains don't work well (see Chapter 1), they are not competent, and they are too easily influenced by their environment (see Chapter 2).

Prosecutors are not dumb people; they're politicians. This means they must pander to us. In years past, they carried out kid justice based on what most of us seemed to believe about children. Under the law, human beings under the age of 18 were always presumed to be incompetent. Therefore, the law used to reason, acting-out children needed help, not punishment. This new view of juveniles likes to play both sides of the competency line. We still don't let kids drink, smoke, or even make promises (sign contracts) since they're presumed to be incompetent—except, of course, if they kill someone. Committing a heinous crime has now become the proof of child competency. "Sorry, kid, but you're too stupid at 13 to understand the consequences of smoking. We have to protect you from yourself. But blow away a few of your peers with Dad's guns and we'll immediately grant you adult status. Killing a few kids who you think were taunting you must mean that your brain is working well." So we seek out long sentences in adult nightmare prisons for these sick children under the guise of being tough on crime, which sells well come election time.

But don't blame the prosecutors. They're just like rap singers who advocate violence. If you hate their message, blame the society that keeps these folks in business. The prosecutors and rap singers are only playing what sells, and as a nation, we're buying.

Many people have gotten tired of coddling these nasty kids in juvenile treatment facilities. We got mad at them, got scared of them, and didn't know how to help them, so we did the only thing a sane, reasonable, and compassionate society could do: We reclassified them overnight as adults and began sticking them in hellholes called "adult correctional facilities." If you think "hellhole' is an overly dramatic description, visit a state penitentiary and then give me a call.

So why do we do this? First, it surely keeps the little creeps off our streets, right? Wrong! They just return as big creeps. And bad ones. Every piece of credible research done in places like Minnesota, New York, New Jersey, Pennsylvania, and Florida proves that the kids we throw into adult prisons come out and commit more and worse crimes than similar kids we send to juvenile treatment facilities—and they do this much faster. The rage-training schools (adult prisons) do a very good job.

Second, we think this approach must save money since it keeps us from having to spend the bucks to fund special juvenile treatment facilities. Wrong again. The number-crunchers keep quietly pointing out that treating children as juvenile offenders is actually much more cost-effective than incarcerating them with adults and then paying the price later when these horrendously victimized children return as vengeful and skilled adult criminals.

Third, we believe this policy avoids all the paperwork needed to revamp our penal codes and find ways of safely and humanely treating these kids, and at the same time, protect us from the dangerous kids who may require treatment beyond the age of 18, right? Correct! We would have to reformulate our laws to find ways of saving the lives of these kids while protecting our own—but it's just too much work. In some isolated cases, enlightened prosecutors and judges have found ways to skirt existing laws to do this, and we could easily standardize this approach if we wanted to.

Getting tough with juvenile crime has been effective in reducing crime rates, right? Wrong again. That mythology is based on bogus research that credits the recent drop in juvenile crime to the harsher treatment of these sacrificial lambs. You can use that same statistical method—called coincidence—to prove that rap music has cut kid crime in half. The truth is that child crime has dropped for a lot of reasons, not one of which is related to adult prosecution of children.

So what's the real, underlying reason our society does this to these children? *I believe it's because they make us uncomfortable.* Relabeling sick children as vicious adults makes things much simpler. It helps us feel better when we're eating our bagels, reading our newspapers, and feeling outraged, sickened, and helpless that one 13-year-old could blow away his teacher, another could stab a woman 60 times in front of her children, and an 11-year-old could randomly kill the first adult she saw on the street that day. When the news articles note that these children are really just small, vicious adults, we can more comfortably turn to the business section to see how the old mutual fund is doing. This magical transformation of very sick children into criminally responsible adults gives us the closure we need. It's hard to read stock prices when we can't get the picture of an 11-year-old's savagery out of our minds.

It is something so bizarre, so inhuman, and so repulsive that we need to avoid thinking about it. It is so complex, depressing, and confusing that it makes our heads hurt, so we do the adult thing: We pretend away the problem and cast sick young children into hell. This is the most criminal behavior of all.

If you ever have the terrifying experience of talking with these kids directly, you will leave the jail scared, but not of these kids. When you learn about their lives, you find yourself being drawn slowly into their childhood agonies until at last you are confronted by two true horrors. First, the horror of seeing yourself as capable of the same savagery as these kids, but for your own good luck, the love of your parents, or the grace of God in not having lived the lives of these children. Second, you'll know the horror of a society that condones the brutality of prosecutors *who know these things* about these twisted children, and yet vigorously prosecute and jail them in a way that eliminates any small chance these kids ever have of becoming decent human beings. It might be more merciful to strap them into the chair, but apparently none of us has the stomach to pull the switch on an 11-year-old. Not yet, anyway.

The new adolescent brain data clearly proves that rewiring of teenage minds is possible. If we continue to exterminate these sick, incompetent children in this fashion, I believe that one day, as this new data evolves into new ways of helping these kids, we will look back in disbelieving shame at our own inhumanity.

I don't have the antidote for a 13-year-old's savagery. Chapters 1 and 2 lay out some of the root causes. It's difficult to read because it makes us wrestle with terrible issues. Who is really responsible for that 13-year-old finger pulling the trigger? What is the depth of the insanity of our kids' world? What are the limits of our collective and individual obligations to help the very sick acting-out children with our taxes, and the not-yet-very-sick children with our time? Read it, and then you tell me what we should do.

Does this relate to your own child, who will never kill anyone? Very directly, because if you follow this insane trend and attempt to hold your own temporarily crazy kids accountable as responsible adults, if you take their outrageous behaviors personally and you seek to hurt them when they're hurtful, then you will lose your children as surely as we lose the ones in the jails. Please remember that your kid is a child. He's crazy, she's incompetent, and they're both insulting, infuriating, and maddening—but they need your love and your patient wisdom just when you feel that you have none left to give. It is our job as parents and as members of this society to shoulder this burden, not to push it away with simple and brutal thinking.

What have you done today to push back against the madness? What have I done?

Now as I climb down from my soapbox, allow me to regain my composure and talk about another acting-out behavior that is frequently found to be a root cause of the more serious behaviors we've just discussed: Attention-Deficit/Hyperactivity Disorder.

Attention-Deficit/Hyperactivity Disorder (ADHD): A Controversial Diagnosis

Sorry, but we can't leave the subject of disruptive behaviors without talking about ADHD. I know you're sick to death of this subject, with your level of boredom likely exceeded only by your degree of confusion. Unless, of course, you suspect your kid has it.

What constitutes, causes, and cures ADHD seems to vary by the particular expert you consult. This diagnosis takes on the fervor of a religious or political debate. I used to have potential clients interview me about my views on issues like birth control. Now monthly I get asked, "Do you believe in ADHD?" What's the upset all about?

The research nerds pretty much agree that up to 5 percent of the kids in this country truly have ADHD. Many studies, however, suggest that up to 20 percent of our kids get diagnosed with ADHD. Since the treatment for this disorder usually involves administering a powerful stimulant drug (called a psychostimulant), this means 15 out of every 100 of this nation's children may be getting a form of speed for no good reason, except that we don't like their behavior.

Everyone agrees that this should stop. Most folks also agree that government spending should be reduced. The tough questions are *which* spending should be reduced and *which* of those 20 kids don't need the drug?

Well, you reasonably suggest, let's give all of these kids the ADHD blood test, MRI, or whatever to diagnose them. "Can't," I respond, "since we don't have such a test. We diagnose this disease based on symptom observation only."

OK, you huff, slightly annoyed, tell me the symptoms and we'll pick out the right kids.

"Good idea," I answer. "In adolescence, ADHD kids can be inattentive, disorganized, overactive, and impulsive. Some are more this, others are more that, some are mostly inattentive, others are mostly hyperactive. And a bunch seem only impulsive."

Jeeeeze Louise, you whine, that describes *adolescence*.

"Yes," I nod, "but ADHD kids have those symptoms to a greater extent than most kids. They're this way for at least six months, and they show substantial dysfunction at school, home, and/or in their social lives (in two out of three environments). By the way, if they're doing something they really like doing, these symptoms can magically evaporate. An ADHD kid may sit for hours intensely concentrating on a video game. And here's another thing you're gonna love. Since we diagnose and medicate kids for this disorder based solely on symptom observation, checklists, and reports, the diagnosis can be very, very subjective."

You're making my head hurt now, Doc. Aren't you just talking about boredom? How is this different from my college roommate taking amphetamines during finals week to study for his dreaded biochemistry exam?

"Well, in one sense, it is similar. The difference is that we think the true ADHD kid can't focus no matter how hard he tries. Your roommate may have just been lazy, looking for an unfair chemical advantage, but distinguishing between the two can be impossible, so a lot of bored, anxious, depressed, and unmotivated kids get inappropriately dosed with speed in the name of ADHD. By the way, how did your roommate do in bio-chem? I only got a D, but I did it without drugs."

Doctor, why are you making dumb jokes when I'm trying to have a serious talk about ADHD?

Because, dear reader, this is a key to understanding what is and isn't ADHD. If I presented the above discussion to you in a boring, clinical fashion, your mind would likely have begun to switch off. In a brain process we don't fully understand, your ability to concentrate would deteriorate. Not having ADHD means you'd be able to exert a mental discipline to refocus, *if you chose to do so*. Having ADHD means it's *impossible* to refocus. You have no choice. But, again, distinguishing between the two in an adolescent can be more art than science, and more inaccurate than accurate.

So proceed very carefully up this diagnostic path. Never guess and say, "Let's try the medication and see what happens." Giving psychostimulants to a kid who's depressed or anxious can have disastrous consequences. Consult at least one expert who will help you gather observations from many sources before making a decision.

Most important, remember that kids' brains don't get rewired by medications. The pills can help give a child more of a choice in deciding whether or not to be disruptive, but she will need lots of other kinds of help to do the brain rewiring needed to truly be better. This can involve parent training, family counseling, and/or individual therapy. Don't just hand her the pills and go back to your TV show. The pills alone may help for a while, but I'll bet you dollars to donuts that within six months the behaviors will return. This is another complex, multifaceted problem that calls for the guidance of specialists.

Common Disorders of Mood

If there's one group of diseases that seems to typify adolescence, it would be what we call mood disorders. These diseases are just that: dysfunction of a kid's mood. Many parents describe adolescence itself as a mood disorder for their kids. As it turns out, there is now a scientific basis to support that intuition.

NORMAL MOODINESS

As we've discussed, the teen years are a time of tremendous psychological, physical, social, and neurological upheaval. No one, least of all a child, can go through these repeated earthquakes without becoming moody at times. It's normal for kids to cycle through up and down moods where they might seem as exuberant as a six-year-old in the morning, as intense and somber as an adult in the afternoon, and as peaceful as can be playing in a bubble bath at night. It's also normal for them to appear very dejected and depressed for a few days when they're not invited to Heather's party. It may be bewildering and worrisome for adults, but it's the norm for adolescents—and it's not a disease. But if the ups and/or downs become extreme, and they last a lot longer, get it checked out. You don't want to guess at this stuff.

UNUSUAL MOODINESS

The unusual moodiness that should encourage a parent to consult an adolescent expert is anything that seems extreme, longer lasting, or somehow very different from what appears to be the normal teenage experience. There are three forms of moodiness that can become extreme and potentially life-threatening if not treated quickly: depression, suicidal thoughts, and bipolar disorders.

Depression

If there is any good to be found in the madness of adolescent shootings and suicides, it would be that the world is finally realizing that kids can get clinically depressed—not just puppy-love distraught, but gut-sick, hollow-eyed, I-don't-care, ready-to-die sad. And it may not look like what you think.

A serious depression may last for months. It can also occur within only two weeks. For adolescents, it may take the form of the popularized symptom lists. You know the drill: emotional/physical/social/academic withdrawal, eating too much or too little, sleeping too much or too little, lack of energy, loss of interest in previously pleasurable activities, loss of concentration, feelings of hopelessness or worthlessness, sudden stress-related physical complaints, and thoughts of death and dying. Four of these things must be happening for at least two weeks to officially qualify for the title. Again, your normally moody kid might be like this for a couple of days, and convincingly so, but if she doesn't rebound soon, get it checked out quickly.

I have a question for you. How many of these depression indicators do you get to closely monitor in your kid? If your answer is, "I'd rather not answer," you've got a lot of company. By definition, adolescents will often avoid disclosing personal information to parents as a function of their normal struggle for independence.

To make this discussion even scarier, teenagers are often excellent at disguising depressive symptoms. My newspaper file on "out-of-the-blue" adolescent suicides grows every month. These are the kids everyone swears gave absolutely no indication of being depressed, only to leave behind a secret journal filled with tortured months of dark, depressed ramblings. Some very troubled kids try to be perfect children as a way of handling emotional pain, and in keeping with that goal, they won't share their emotional struggles with Mom or Dad. We preach at parents all the time to monitor kids for signs of depression, but in today's world, just how possible is that to do over a two-week window? Without a lot of skilled observation and interaction, it's very easy to miss subtle signs. Are you sure about your kid's sleeping patterns? When was the last time you were given access to her list of pleasurable activities? How do you judge his academic involvement when the total feedback you've ever gotten to this inquiry consists of four letters in four years: "How's school?" "F-I-N-E." How often do you get to monitor how much they're actually eating? And do you really want to see what they're actually eating?

Some seriously depressed adolescents can put a dangerous twist on this problem. What they often show parents is not a sadness, but an "in-your-faceness." This becomes very dangerous because unsuspecting adults may rage back and/or withdraw from this seemingly insolent, actually depressed child, inspiring very dramatic reactions.

The good news is that we usually have success in dealing with adolescent depression. When we see it, that is. The bad news is that we do a lousy job of seeing it, and thus often fail in getting depressed kids the help they need. Too often we just don't see the signs.

Suicide: Welcome to Your Nightmare

There's no easy way to talk about this terrible epidemic killing our children (see Chapter 2). In keeping with the urgency of this topic, let's take a short quiz on the common myths of adolescent suicide to help you sharpen your suicide alert skills.

Answer true or false:

1. Only depressed kids kill themselves.
Answer: FALSE. Many suicides do occur in conjunction with depression, but many do not. Many adolescent suicides occur out of anger, as a payback to "unfair" authority figures. Some occur impulsively following seemingly small rejections or losses. Some occur as a twisted romantic adventure. Many are "copycat suicides" that mimic the suicides of peers or others in the community.

2. Only adolescents with long-term histories of depression commit suicide.

Answer: FALSE. Some depressed kids who kill themselves do so after only two weeks of sadness. Remember that one day to an adolescent is a month to you. A bad day that you know will end becomes a forever experience to the adolescent. Your kid doesn't really believe that the sun will come up tomorrow.

3. Once a kid is given an antidepressant medication, she's no longer a suicide risk.

Answer: FALSE. Often the risk of suicide is greatest as the energizing effect of the drug starts to work before the depression is under control. It can give some kids just enough motivation to pull the trigger.

4. Kids who make weak attempts, or who just threaten suicide, never do.

Answer: FALSE, FALSE, and FALSE. A child who threatens suicide in any way has just gifted his parents. He has provided a wonderful opportunity to help. Any child threatening suicide needs help. Now!

5. Teens who talk a lot about dying never do.

Answer: FALSE. Statements 3 and 4 are a lot like saying small fires never grow into big ones. All fires, regardless of size, are life threatening. Call the fire department. Statements 4 and 5 hold great power as myths. We all use mythology or magical thinking to help defend against unimaginable horror, so when the question arises of a child threatening suicide, well-intentioned adults often cite these myths as a way of trying to provide comfort to distressed parents. At great risk, parents may use this kind of misinformation to avoid having to confront the issue with their child, often out of a belief in Myth Number 6.

6. Talking to your kid about suicide increases his risk by "putting the thought in his head."

Answer: FALSE, FALSER, and FALSEST. Do fear the reaper. Do it openly. Use the "S" word with your kid. Talking can only help. Remember, suicide, *regardless of the cause*, is a last resort. You want to stick other potential options in your child's head. Think a minute on this. If a causal factor is anger, your child might discover that calling you an overcontrolling bastard *is* an option to offing himself. In fact, it might feel good. If depression is leading her to the gun cabinet, the *simple act of your caring enough to talk* might light a small candle of hope in her world. If it's some "unbearable" loss that drives him, your own stories of catastrophic nights that break into new dawns can inspire him to try. As comedian Jackie Mason says, "It couldn't hoit." He's right. Talking directly never hoits.

Signs that a child might be thinking about or planning suicide include all of the symptoms of depression with a couple of additions. These include:
* Use of drugs (especially alcohol; see Chapter 2)
* Giving away prized possessions
* Sudden contacts with all friends, past and present (saying goodbye)
* Talking, writing, or listening to music with death themes

If you're seeing these behaviors, get help now. If you can't get to a qualified mental health professional immediately, take your child to the nearest hospital emergency room. They'll do an assessment to help you decide the next step.

Search the house and remove as many suicide devices as possible. Guns, drugs, and ropes head this list. And guns. And don't forget the guns. Myth Number 7 is *If they really want to die, they'll find a way.* I've got another list I maintain, just like the airlines—my "near-hit" list. This is a list of kids who are alive because they weren't able to use their first choice of suicide method, namely a gun, because it had been removed or locked up (see Chapter 2—removed is best). Throwing that monkey wrench into the suicide plans may give your kid the pause he needs to stop and consider another option.

Might all this be a lot of wasted time and energy? No. Not under any circumstances. Even if the doctor says she's not at risk, and your kid's real annoyed, you've let her know that you care and that you, as the adult, are recognizing that things are not going well for her. This is an important statement to make to distressed kids who can easily lose their perspective, and then maybe lose a whole lot more. Every day we lose 14 of our adolescent and young adult children to suicide. So go ahead. Be overprotective. It's your job.

CRITICAL DOs	CRITICAL DON'Ts
◆ Take any sign seriously	◆ Guess about or ignore risk sign
◆ Monitor your kid all the time	◆ Think this will never happen to you
◆ Talk directly about suicide concerns	◆ Think you'll put ideas in her head by talking about suicide
◆ Get help immediately	◆ Just hope that it will blow over
◆ Search for and remove weapons and drugs	◆ Assume "he'll find a way" if he really wants to kill himself. A 10-second delay can buy a lifetime.

Bipolar Disorders

If one mood dysfunction were selected by parents to appear on the flag of adolescence, it would be a popularized version of bipolar disorder called manic-depressive disorder. Parents often worry about the rapid succession of emotions that seem to roll over their kid in a day's time. It seems impossible that those ecstatic highs could be followed so closely by those crushing lows (*"If you don't let me pierce my tongue my life is over"*). Perhaps the best way to describe normal adolescent mood cycling is to contrast it against a true bipolar experience. The normal stuff is not what you're about to read.

"Kevin had been very depressed for at least two months. He got so bad he couldn't even get up to go to school. Then one day he called me at work. He sounded so upbeat. It seemed to be the miracle I had been praying for. 'Mom,' he said, 'I'm gonna be fine now. I feel so much better. I went to school today and got all my missed homework assignments. I've been working all afternoon. I know I can catch up. I'm also getting a job at the bank.' I couldn't imagine what job he'd get at a bank, but I didn't want to ruin his first good mood in months with questions. 'Thank you, Lord,' I whispered as I hung up the phone. But it wasn't the Lord at work with my son.

"By the time I got home, my son had completed a month's worth of homework in six hours. Or so he thought. When I looked at it, most of it was gibberish. It looked like it was written in Chinese. 'Don't you get it, Mom?' he implored as I puzzled over his scrawlings. 'This is that secret code teachers use. It was invented by NASA for communicating with extraterrestrials. Mr. Baldwin is one of the NASA operatives. He just pretends to be a social studies teacher to spy on kids like me who have special gifts. When he sees the code, his cover will be blown and I'll be free.' At this point Kevin laughed real loud and real weird—it's hard to describe just how—until he saw that I didn't get it. Then he spoke gibberish to me, and waited for a response. I was sure he was on speed, LSD, or both. His speech was like a machine gun. His eyes looked wild.

"I began crying and begging him to tell me what drugs he had taken. 'No drugs, Mom, and you've got to stop giving me those chemicals in that food you make. That's what got me sick. I realize I can't eat any food that's been heated. That's how...' and then he was speaking gibberish again."

Mom's face was ashen. I felt my jaw tighten as I began to feel the horror that she held inside. I pictured my own son entering that terrifying phase I knew was coming in Kevin's story. I shifted and swallowed hard to clear my mind.

"That was the beginning of hell week. He got worse and worse. He stopped eating and sleeping almost completely, and wouldn't take a bath. He looked like a shell of a boy. Roaming the house all night, talking nonstop with those wild, hollow eyes, matted hair..." Mom's face contorted into sobs. "I used to love to smell his beautiful hair. We were so close. Now he's this raging monster. He screams at people who aren't there, and he doesn't make any sense. The electric sockets are all stuffed with paper to keep the alien messages from getting in. Today he asked his four-year-old sister if she wanted to have sex with him, and began to describe his penis to her. He thinks he can fly. HE THINKS HE CAN FLY! My God, what is going on? I didn't know whether to see you or a priest. Is he possessed?" "Yes," I thought. "He is."

This was exactly the kind of behavior that inspired the old satanic possession theories. Looking into the eyes of an adolescent in a manic phase can be like staring at the Devil. It is often that scary.

About 10 to 15 percent of adolescents who suffer from repeated deep depressions can become possessed like Kevin with an evil called bipolar disorder. There are a few variants of this disease, but they have some common features. The first is a depressed phase, which typically looks like what we described earlier. Usually this lasts much longer than the second part, known as mania, which may last only weeks, but what occurs during those weeks can make parents wish for the depressed phase to return.

The manic post-pubescent adolescent is a fearful sight. He talks incessantly, and may stop bathing, eating, and sleeping. He develops wildly grandiose views of himself that make no sense. His speech is too rapid and he can't seem to stay focused on one subject. He may begin to hallucinate, to see and hear things that aren't there, and often he acts in ways that are sexually inappropriate. Some kids, like Kevin, truly believe they have "Superman" powers of flight, x-ray vision, and intelligence. Watching this is truly watching madness.

Watching this can also destroy a family. It is too much to bear, too dangerous to ignore, and too easily fixed to suffer through needlessly. So if your depressed kid suddenly becomes euphoric and grandiose, get to the psychiatrist now. Don't wait to see what happens. You don't want to see what happens.

Eating Disorders

Before we can talk about eating disorders, we need to understand their context, for the context itself is a disorder.

If we adult Americans were really honest about our national symbol, we'd replace that lean bald eagle with a pot-bellied pig. We eat too much, we eat all the wrong stuff, and we do this all the time. Just like developing nations, we devote huge amounts of our time and resources to the issues of food. But unlike them, our stomachs ache with surplus. We are tragicomically unique among the world's people, struggling mightily to avoid dying from monstro (versus mal) nutrition. We just can't seem to get a grip on this—but our strangeness doesn't end there. For our adolescents, we've cooked up something special. We've created this youth-weight paradox that only *The Twilight Zone's* Rod Serling could have dreamed up. We present them with a fat-saturated culture that wildly promotes excessive eating, while simultaneously idolizing unreasonable thinness. Twiggy promoting triple-cheese-quadruple-beef-Belcho-burgers. Is this a great country or what?

Today the simple act of teenage eating has become a complex adolescent behavior that very often goes terribly awry. Many psychologists are pretty much convinced that, similar to sex and violence saturation (see Chapter 2), we've bombarded our youth with pictures of how an attractive body is supposed to look.

On second thought, change that word "attractive" to "acceptable" since we've also told kids that their worthiness is based on their physical appearance. If you don't look the way we want, you get left out. Sorry, but you're not acceptable. And guess what? Not too many of us can look "acceptable" without sometimes using life-threatening measures.

Researchers ran a less popular set of body statistics (not the 36-24-36 type) on the Miss Americas over the past century and found that the recent contests have uniformly chosen medically definable undernourished women as the epitome of womanly beauty.

It's really gotten quite out of hand, particularly for girls. Every time we repeat these scary surveys, increasing numbers of increasingly younger girls report being upset about their weight (up to 80 percent, last time I looked). Jayne Mansfield and Marilyn Monroe? Fat pigs. I mean, like really, why didn't they do something about those thighs? Today we dig the way dying women look.

This absurdity has not escaped our children. Boys have had their brain definitions of "sexy" reset to mostly unachievable versions of female physiology. Don't believe me? Watch some music videos. Those professional dancers have now become the standard body expectation for females. Our daughters are dying to look like that—they're dying emotionally and sometimes they're dying physically.

"Theresa was always a model daughter. She always did everything we asked and seemed so eager to please. She seemed a little unsure of herself as she was growing up, but otherwise did very well. She didn't seem particularly obsessed with her appearance, or anything like that. She seemed happy just as she was.

"About the time she hit puberty, we noticed that she was getting very slender. Our physician told us she would get alternately thinner and heavier as she grew, and to just keep an eye on her weight. At 15, she started following a grapefruit diet to lose weight from what we thought was an already too-thin body. All her friends were doing it too. We got concerned with this and confronted her. I'll never forget how she broke down in tears telling us how fat and disgusting she was, and how we didn't understand that she couldn't live like this. This was with ribs showing! But when she saw how upset we were, she agreed to start to eat more. We felt a lot better. But she simply went underground.

"At first, she just used ploys to avoid food. She had always 'just eaten' at some friend's house, at school, etc. When a few of these stories fell through, we grounded her and demanded that she eat in front of us. Just like the magazine article promised, she did eat with us. She did this for almost a year, still losing weight. We wondered if she was throwing up or using laxatives, but all of our snooping turned up no evidence.

"Last week the dentist called. He asked if it was true that Theresa had a chronic nausea problem. When I said no and asked what he was talking about, his voice got real grim. 'You've got to get her to a psychiatrist and quickly. From the condition of her teeth, I'd guess she's been vomiting daily for months.' I heard the denial in my next question, asked in a hollow voice that sounded like it was not mine. 'Exactly what are you saying?'

"I knew damn well what he was saying. 'She may have bulimia. It's seems to be epidemic with my young female patients. Go to the psychiatrist immediately! Are you hearing me?'

"His last question exploded my denial. I was finally hearing, and seeing, and knowing that our daughter was dying and that we really didn't want to believe that.

"It humiliates me to have to say this, but our dentist saved Theresa's life. The psychiatrist put her in a hospital immediately. She had already developed heart problems. My shame is that I watched her slowly become this concentration-camp skeleton, and I lied to myself just like she does, that this was some type of harmless body fashion, like piercings. It just happens so slowly, so imperceptibly. I was allowing her to die."

What's Normal and What's Not

When your Monday diet-obsessed and Tuesday cheeseburger-eating girl drives you crazy by complaining openly and endlessly about her inability to ever look like a model, you've got normalcy on your hands. In other words, if her conflict is out in the open, and the battle between "I gotta look like a model" and "Who ate the last slice of double-pepperoni?" seems balanced, with neither side getting the upper hand, count your blessings. She may be miserable and whiny about her undefined abs, but she's most likely OK. It's when the food war gets quiet that things become deadly, with lonely, desperate, covert battles that you never hear.

The causes of these disorders are not known for sure, but all of the cultural food and body image struggles we stick adolescents with are certainly part of the explanation. Additionally, kids who have eating disorders often have family struggles over issues of power and control with rigid or authoritarian parents (*"Maybe they can control other parts of my life, but they can't control how much I eat!"*). Some are sports-obsessed and see starving as another cost of competition. Others have terrible self-esteem and either undereat to gain acceptance or overeat for comfort and self-punishment. As our knowledge of genetics and biology advances, we are beginning to see these as contributing factors for eating problems in adolescents.

There are three ways these disorders appear, and girls dominate the first two versions. All are nasty, life-threatening, complex, and very tough to treat, and just like with Theresa, they come on very slowly so that we can all pretend that the unthinkable is not happening to our kid. Some studies suggest that one-fourth of the kids who suffer from these illnesses live this way for over a year before they are diagnosed.

Anorexia Nervosa

This disease mostly strikes younger females, although we're now getting a wave of boys caught up in this body-image madness. In a sense, you could argue that anorexia is really a visual problem.

It works like those trick mirrors at the amusement parks. Your daughter stands with you in front of a mirror. You see the girl you love who is unattractively thin, looking emaciated and sickly. The rest of the world sees what you see. The trick mirror in your daughter's head literally distorts that visual data so that she sees a disgustingly fat person who desperately needs to lose weight. This distortion mirror only works when she's looking at herself. Her normal peers, some of whom might be a few pounds overweight, look fine to her.

Get this part real good because you won't believe it: *She's not lying to you when she says she's fat.* She truly is disgusting to herself. Her obese view of her body cannot be swayed by what others see, any more than if they tried to convince her that a truck rushing at her is not real. She sees both as terribly threatening and she can't accept what you say simply because you say so. In her head, she is not crazy, she is simply attempting to take appropriate care of her appearance. She honest-to-God believes her "dieting" is good for her, so she starts to continually reduce her daily caloric intake thinking to herself that she'll go back to normal eating once she looks OK. *But she never gets to look OK thanks to that trick mirror,* so her food consumption can gradually decline to virtually nothing of any nutritional value. Some kids eat nothing but lettuce.

While an anorexic girl can hide her problem for a while, the good news is that eventually the disease is hard to deny by virtue of its impact on weight. If you look closely, you'll have lots of evidence suggesting that something is wrong. In addition to the eating (non)behaviors and weight loss, you might also see menstrual interruption, digestive and sleep problems, as well as complaints of always being cold. And be wary of sudden, intense, and prolonged exercise jags that accompany the above signals.

Bulimia Nervosa

While anorexia tends to target mostly teenage girls, bulimia typically goes after older adolescents and young women. Estimates of this dangerous behavior in college women run as high as 20 *percent.* Although for most it's a temporary phase, this astounding statistic illustrates the power of the body-image demands we place on young women. A lot of these bulimic girls were anorexic in their earlier years. These kids will eat like they're "going to the chair" and then get the governor's pardon for dessert. That is, they feel compelled to rid themselves of the food by vomiting or abusing laxatives—and both options are quite dangerous. Like anorexics, bulimics are also great at covering their disease. Unlike anorexics, their disorder is much harder to spot since the binge/purge cycle may often nutritionally balance out to maintain normal body weight among sufferers. They can look really good until they collapse. The vomiting exacts a terrible unseen toll on that good-looking body.

Like the anorexic, that bulimic girl is not lying. To her, that food she ate *is* a poison, one she *morbidly* fears will make her fat. The terrible additional bind for the bulimic kid is that, unlike the anorexic, she *knows* that the binge eating part of her disorder is crazy, and she still can't stop it. The guilt and hopelessness involved in living like this makes a Russian novel seem upbeat.

Obesity

I'm still amazed that some of our kids are *not* obese, given the cultural bind we've created for them, but my amazement may be short-lived. As of this writing, 55 percent of our children are clinically overweight. Estimates of obesity among American children and adolescents run from 15 to 25 percent. *Twenty-five percent.* Say it slowly and let the impact sink in.

How do you know if your adolescent is obese? The book says 10 percent over the weight tables qualifies. My pediatrician friend says, "Just look, and you'll know." He also tells me that 8 out of 10 kids who are obese as teens will be obese for life. He gets quite passionate with parents on the subject, since he sees the emotional pain and physical health risks these kids experience.

An ironic cultural problem confounding this disorder of obesity is our view of fat adolescents. We bombard them with bad food options and then hate them. Everybody knows they're lazy and weak-willed, right? If they wanted to, all they gotta do is stop eating, for God's sake.

"You know," this 15-year-old girl offered sadly, "being obese means everybody sees your disease. I know lots of teenagers who steal, do drugs, and beat up on little kids. But they're thin, so nobody ever knows what they are when they walk through the mall. They can pass for nice kids if they want. Other kids like them more, the teachers like them more, and so do parents. When I think about this I feel mad and hopeless about my weight. It makes me feel like eating way too much. Sometimes even my own father says..." Susan couldn't finish her sentence.

I leave the topic of eating disorders with two critical points of research. The first is that the longer the disorder continues untreated, the longer the recovery process will take. The second is that the best chances for long-term recovery occur with the earliest age interventions. So if you have any doubt about your kid's eating behaviors, get help now.

Anxiety Disorders

Given the nature of adolescents and the world around them, attempting to pick out those kids suffering from illness-qualifying levels of anxiety is like picking the really nervous pigeon out of the flock. They all look the same, at first glance. Anxiety is perhaps the most common denominator of adolescent experience. They worry constantly, about everything. You only hear a tenth of it. The other worries they never tell anyone because they're too embarrassing to share.

This disease identification process is made only harder by the fact that adolescent anxiety takes on so many faces that it seems everyone could qualify. It may appear as shyness, nervousness, or restlessness. Anxiety may manifest as chronic aches and pains. Anxious kids may avoid their friends, or they may get upset whenever they're apart from their friends. Some compensate with bravado risk-taking behavior that includes drugs or sex. Some are incredibly good students. Some can't face walking into the school building. Some have panic attacks. Others never appear stressed since they methodically regiment every minute of their day to avoid feeling out of control. Have I left anyone out?

WHAT TO LOOK FOR

So how do you pick out the unusually anxious pigeon that needs to see a doctor? Look for indications that the anxiety is putting a hurt on your kid's life. If he seems unable to do the things he'd normally do, watch for extended patterns (months) of this behavior. If you see him struggling terribly to show up to practice for a beloved sport, or if she suddenly seems terrified to go to parties where she doesn't know all the kids, check it out. More than not, the anxiety will center on issues like physical appearance or acceptance by peers.

In addition to this generalized anxiety, you might see other manifestations of anxiety disorder. These include the following:

Panic Disorder

Feelings of terror without any real cause may result from a panic attack disorder. This is not the same as being normally scared. A kid caught in a panic episode will look and act as if her life is at stake. She might sweat gallons, seem to be choking, and even have trouble breathing. There might also be nausea, chest pain, and numbness. These symptoms can be so dramatic that some of these kids (and their parents) dial 911, fearing a heart attack. This experience is so frightening that your kid may begin to avoid situations that she thinks might bring on an attack.

Obsessive-Compulsive Disorder (OCD)

There are two parts to this nasty illness, which typically strikes boys in their teens and women in young adulthood. The obsessions are unwanted thoughts that take over a kid's mind and force him to excessively focus on things to a degree he knows is crazy, such as sanitation, neatness, or religious rules. If having your kid very clean, exceptionally neat, or incredibly religious still sounds good to you, then he ain't got OCD. That's because the second disease aspect, the compulsions, exact such a terrible price to maintain these qualities, that they wouldn't sound attractive to you anymore.

Compulsions are irresistible impulses to do certain things in an exacting pattern as an attempt to somehow live with the obsessions. If these rituals are not followed, the kid feels like the resultant anxiety will kill him. I'm not exaggerating.

> The banging and screaming in my waiting room sounded like a riot had broken out. My waiting room music is bad, certainly, but not that bad. I apologized to my in-session client, and went out to find my new client, Michael, sobbing on the floor, with Dad sitting on him. As I picked up a strewn chair, Dad explained while he gasped for breath. "He has this thing about having to wash his hands. He promised he wouldn't wash anymore today. Look at his hands! They're already red and bleeding. This is the only way I can stop him. I keep telling him to stop, but he doesn't want to listen. I know he could put it out of his mind if he really tried."

Dad was furious when I told him to let Michael go ahead and wash his hands for perhaps the twentieth time that day. Michael stopped sobbing. He knew I knew.

Compulsions can consist of excessive hand-washing, ordering objects by size, sorting clothes by levels of contamination, walking in certain ways, repetitious praying, and so on. They are usually terribly time-consuming and life-altering rituals that serve to maintain your kid's anxiety at some barely manageable level. These behaviors can develop so slowly that many parents become like Michael's father in that they don't see this as mental illness, but as an act of defiance or just another type of teenage weirdness staged to get attention. The resulting parental frustration and judgment feels like terrible rejection to your child, and it becomes another reason to feel anxious, which provides more fuel for the OCD behavior, which only makes Dad angrier, and so on.

Many teenagers can get significantly obsessive and/or compulsive at times, but not have the disease. This statement may seem absurd as you view (and smell?) your kid's room, but instead of picturing cleanliness rituals, think instead of how your child can relentlessly torture you for things like tongue piercings, scary chat rooms at midnight, or ultra-baggy pants. You'll begin to see the Felix Unger that hides out in that allegedly counter-culture adolescent body. Short bursts of absurd pre-occupation with seemingly weird things are the normal adolescent insanity. Month-long patterns of this stuff that seriously interfere with a kid's functioning warrant a trip to the shrink. OCD is another one of those disorders that is much more easily treated in its early stages. Left untreated it can become a way of life that can leave a child enslaved by demanding and crippling rituals.

For the last time, if you have any doubts about whether or not your kid has a problem, get it checked out by a professional. The potential risks of ignoring any of these serious, non-normal disorders are far too great.

And with that, dear parent, we come to the close of Part One. You can start to breathe normally now, for you've gotten about all the scary news I can think of concerning our kids today. You might want to take a break, get some tea, and do something crazy like go and hug your astonished teen. Tell her my son's line referencing my age and demeanor as I approach him, arms beckoning: "Oh no. Here comes another senior moment." She'll understand.

But as you pass the hall mirror, take a long look because we're moving on to talking about those former teenagers who were also once insane and are now roaming around the house, contributing their share of craziness to the chaos, all with the best of intentions and often with the worst of outcomes.

Hello, Mom and Dad.

Part Two

NEW-MILLENNIUM PARENTS:
UNDERSTANDING YOUR ROLE
AND ACCEPTING YOUR CHALLENGE

IN RECENT YEARS, many therapists have begun to change the way we work with kids, which often contradicts the way we were trained. In the old days, many of us were taught that teenagers were small adults and should be treated as such. We worked with kids mostly apart from their parents, providing extensive individual therapy with little feedback to or involvement with parents. I have very powerful memories from my internship of going out to waiting rooms to get teenage clients and being silently haunted by the frightened, pleading eyes of Mom and Dad, who were told little about their child's situation. I recall being criticized by a mentor who felt I was betraying the confidentiality of my adolescent clients by involving the parents too much. The implication seemed to be that the parents were somehow an enemy, or at best, nonessential people. It felt bad to me then. It looks even worse to me today. Today I have kids of my own. It was wrong.

Back then we also thought that your kid's peers held all the influence cards with him. Often, parents would throttle back their involvement with their teen after frequent and extreme rejections, thinking that it was pointless to try to interact with their child. They felt like they were imposing themselves on a fellow adult who just disliked them intensely (see Chapter 3). That thinking was also wrong.

This was all based on that bad science we had about brain development. We thought that after the initial explosion of early childhood brain growth, things slowed down. We reasoned that patterns of behavior, personality skills, and so on were all hard-wired in at an early age and not likely to change much. Boy, were we wrong (see Chapter 1).

Seeing all of this wrongness brings about a new view of adolescent treatment in which we now believe that your kid can rewire his expanding (although temporarily malfunctioning) teenage brain to incorporate new patterns of behavior. We also now see that adolescent insanity is a neurological condition that heals with time. All of which brings us back to you, dear parent. And in spades.

In this part of the book, you will learn that you are not only a key to your kid's behavior, but you are *the* key. Your child is much more influenced by you, for both better and worse, than by any other force in her life.

Many adolescent specialists now wisely refuse to see a teenager unless the parents are involved in the process as well. We now know that parents must be the real therapists with their kids. Shrinks are just consultants to that relationship, with comparatively little direct impact on adolescent development. The parents must become the primary change-agents, or little permanent good usually results. And just as therapists should undergo therapy to avoid doing damage to their patients, it is critical for parents to examine themselves to understand the role that their own personalities play in their kid's behavior.

Research shows that parental influence—both good and bad—is enormous on adolescents. In order to maximize the positives of this vital resource for kids, parents must undergo a self-assessment to understand and control their own good and bad behavior as it affects their children. The new science tells us that the ways we interact with our adolescent get burned into that mushrooming brain as permanent rules of how to be.

Through the brain-rewiring process, the sins of the parents do become the insanity of the adolescent. Likewise, the wisdom of the parents can become the salvation of the teenager. Part Two begins this journey. In Chapters 7 and 8 we'll see how incredibly important you are to that snarling, snapping teenager who is so repulsed by you wearing dark green ankle socks with black sandals that he refuses to be seen in the same county as you.

But first, in Chapter 6, I need to expose that terrible, sad secret you've been carrying. The one about the passing of your child.

Chapter 6

GRIEVING THE DEATH OF YOUR SWEET, COMPLIANT CHILD

Two parents sat in my office overcome with pain for their raging adolescent son, Dennis. Between sobs, Hal described the fistfight he had with his beloved son two days before. "Michael," he croaked to me in a voice still hoarse from the screaming, "in 13 years I never hit him once. Not even close. Last month I slapped his face twice. He warned me not to go for three. I had already sworn to myself it wouldn't happen.

"The other night I couldn't stop myself. That's how this fistfight happened. You know, I thought I was ready for every kind of provocation that I've ever seen from adolescents. Dennis must have read my thoughts, because he found the one I was not ready for: verbally assaulting Sue (his wife) with the worst possible language you can imagine. I was on him like an attack dog. . ." Dad took a minute to regain his composure.

"It was an out-of-body experience. For a second, I watched myself trying to hurt him as badly as I could. This was the same sickening, twisted rage I had when I came back from Vietnam. I can't feel those feelings again." "Hal," I asked softly, "what was your rage about back then?" Hal's eyes fixed on mine as the realization hit him. "Grief," he whispered, "I lost everything over there. My friends, my ideals, my country, my faith in God—my innocence." His eyes filled again as he realized the rest. "And now here I am 30 years later once again losing someone I love, losing the innocence of my relationship with my son. Christ, I'm grieving all over again."

Sue nodded. She knew Hal all those years ago. Looking at him now and remembering him then, she could see the truth of what he said. In a small voice she added, "My best times now are those grief-stricken moments of solitude when Dennis is not around. At least," she wept, "no one's screaming in my face that I'm a weak, f'ng whore bitch. When he's gone, it's quiet. Like a cemetery. It feels like he died, and yet he's still walking around." Both parents were psychologists.

If I had to name the one thing that parents of adolescents in crisis most commonly and powerfully but secretly share, it would be grief. Most have had close, loving relationships with a child who seems overnight to have turned into an unrecognizable monster intent on viciously hurting them by attacking their most painful vulnerabilities. The grief these parents feel for the loss of their child is profound and relentless in that the loss seems renewed daily. Each day dawns with renewed parental hope that the old Junior will reappear. Each evening seems to end with the echoes of the day's battles fading into night along with their dreams of getting their child back.

Few of us are aware of how close we are with our children until we lose them to adolescence. We really have no idea how much we have come to place our own need for nurturing and love in the hands of our kids until they shred it up and throw it in our faces. Sherree and Simon were both children who were lousy at taking care of the emotional needs of their mothers.

Sherree and Simon

Jill sat crying in the middle of the couch, facing her daughter. Sherree was plastered so hard against the opposite arm of the sofa, I thought she might break it. She looked like a cornered wild animal. She could barely stay in her seat. "Sherree won't let me touch her anymore," Mom wept. "She goes crazy when I get near her and ask for a hug." "Tell him why we fought coming here," Sherree challenged. "TELL HIM WHY!" Mom turned to me for help. "All her life we were physically affectionate," Mom explained, "and suddenly last year she starts going nuts whenever I try to hold her. So sometimes I just hold my hand as close to hers as I can without actually touching. That's what I did in the car that made her go nuts, cursing and screaming at me. She hates me."

Hearing Sherree's disgusted snicker at her story, Mom started yelling, "Is this a crime? That I ask for some crumb of affection, some something from you that says you care even a little bit? IS IT A CRIME TO BEG FOR YOUR LOVE?"

Sherree stared hard out the window and tried not to hear her mother's sobs. Like a bad lawyer, I softly asked Sherree a question I immediately regretted, but couldn't withdraw: "Do you love your mom?" Ten ticks of my suddenly loud clock echoed in the office silence. Ever so slowly, Sherree nodded yes. "Then how can you treat me like that?" Mom asked incredulously. Sherree's eyes filled as her voice rose. "BECAUSE I CAN'T TAKE CARE OF YOU. I CAN'T EVEN REALLY TAKE CARE OF ME. WHEN YOU KEEP COMING AT ME IT MAKES ME WANT TO SCREAM."

I suddenly had this flashback to a story that my wife, Cindy, told about having rescued a lab monkey she called Simon. After taking him back to her apartment, she found that the terrified animal would go crazy whenever she tried to approach to comfort him. After hours of watching this poor creature scream and threaten, she opened up the cage door and lay down on the floor, pretending to sleep. An hour later, Simon slowly inched closer and closer, and finally brought her to tears when he put his arm around her and lay his head down on her shoulder.

A woman like that you marry, if she'll have you.

When Cindy stopped trying to fulfill her need to comfort Simon, she was able to comfort Simon. When we stop trying to get our kids to meet our need for affection, sometimes they can become affectionate (OK, OK, maybe a teeny bit). But if we demand that they give us what we need, they recoil in disgust and often will savage that very need, setting off a chain of events that can destroy parent-child relationships and cause this grief reaction.

Adolescents often have snarling, scathing reactions to displays of emotional weakness by their parents. They're simply defending themselves because they cannot handle the responsibility of carrying their parents' emotions. Tearful pleadings by parents often precede eviscerating responses from the little darlings, and a vicious circle is born. The parents feel so crushed by this apparent cruelty from their child that they go back repeatedly to beg for acceptance. This causes the kid to move even further and more cruelly away until finally the parents begin to experience a profound grieving for the loss of their once-loving child.

This grief, in turn, does some nasty things. First, it is debilitating, sapping parents of the energy they need to calmly meet the adolescent challenges now in front of them. Second, if the grief is not acknowledged and dealt with, parents can unwittingly transfer anger onto the large, arrogant adolescent who "killed" and replaced their sweet, loving child. At that point, trying to feel close to your kid can be like trying to feel warmth for Charles Manson. Your kid has no idea why you're scowling at him all the time and you don't even realize you're doing it.

Finally, this whole process can isolate you from your friends and family, from your adult sources of emotional support. Even if you understand what has happened to you (and most of us don't), parents feel silly sharing this grief experience with others, just as they may feel foolish deeply mourning the loss of a pet. How do you explain your grief for the death of a living child? Don't try, except to your partner and to other parents of adolescents. They know.

Many kids seem to contribute to this death theme by becoming walking zombies at times, seemingly devoid of human emotion or even speech.

> Dad completed his verbal picture of Jarrad, saying that his "corpse-like" son now utters only one-word responses and stares blankly at any requests for shows of emotion. As I got up to say I was going to bring Jarrad into the room, Mom started humming a strange tune. I bit. "It's the theme song to that movie *Invasion of the Body Snatchers*," Mom explained. "Our little private jokes keep us sane."

So what do you do? First you grieve. You have experienced a deep loss, but you've been there before with this same child and you will survive. Remember when she started kindergarten and you cried watching her get on the bus for her first real school day? That was grief. You lost your toddler, and that was very sad. You cried, your stomach hurt, your throat closed, and you went home and rummaged through those old baby pictures with a box of tissues. I know I did. Maybe you didn't feel like laughing with your buddies for a few days and then you got over it, sort of. My wife and I still get teary-eyed talking about that first day of school. It's ridiculous, it makes no sense, and it makes us human. It's called grief. It's real, it hurts, and it's just a part of the plan.

It's OK, as long as we can cry, take out silly pictures, and talk about it with loved ones. If we do these things, we ultimately survive just fine. Sad, perhaps, but fine.

If you don't acknowledge and feel it, grief can become depression and/or anger, which can destroy your ability to start a new relationship with your "new" child, be he the kindergarten student or the adolescent. It's OK to terribly miss that sweet, compliant little boy you once knew. But do your grieving privately with your partner, not with your ex-little boy. Remember that the large teenager in front of you didn't kill your child. That large person in front of you is your child, reborn once again.

Lydia looked incredulously at me as I delineated how well I thought her 14-year-old was doing. I looked incredulously back at her, wondering why her face darkened with each piece of good news I shared about Mark. As I concluded the details of my assessment, I started to summarize with a good-news ending that I never finished. "So, in closing, Lydia, I think Mark is just fine. The behaviors you've seen are all quite normal, just part of the usual insanity of adolescence. He's a great kid. In fact, lots of parents would be envious. . .Lydia, what's wrong?"

"I don't know exactly why," she mused, "but I'm upset to hear you say that he's OK. He's not OK. He's mean and snappy and I don't know exactly what's wrong, but something terrible is happening with him." "Lydia, what's changed between you two?" I asked. "Everything," she snapped. "That's how I'm so sure he's depressed. He doesn't come into my room at night and lie on my bed and talk anymore. He won't let me make his lunch anymore with those silly notes on the napkins." Her voice rose here: "He won't wear the clothes I buy for him, he listens to horrid music, he's just. . ." her voice sank, "gone. He's a stranger to me, someone I don't know how to be with."

Watch out for this common parent trap with adolescents. Many of us refuse to accept our own grief, and instead make desperate attempts at maintaining that old huggy relationship with this new standoffish child. Some kids will be openly disgusted and angered, becoming loud and hostile. These are the healthy ones. Their anger is just nature's way of telling you something's wrong. Other teens may reciprocate this unnatural alliance and become arrested in their journey to adulthood.

Snuggles at age 13 are not worth having a homebound child at 33.

Another adolescent reaction to this parental clinging can be terrorism. Many kids hold their parents' need for love hostage, to be threatened if they don't get their way on things like cars and curfews. Don't ever go there. These are deals with the Devil. Love your child enough to risk losing his love and, ultimately, you never will.

One Door Closes, Another One Opens

In case you haven't noticed yet, you're not raising one kid. She is four or five children wrapped up in one evolving body. A small print item in your parent contract (you really should have read it carefully) says that you must grieve over old relationships and start new relationships with your one child time and time again. It's very hard work. The kid keeps changing the rules on you and you always seem to be playing catch-up, adjusting your game as parent to meet the new challenges presented by your child.

This process of change is never more intimidating than what is confronting you right now: Adolescence. These sudden and dramatic changes represent the most profound "dying and rebirth" cycle you'll ever have with your kid, but as you feel the sadness of grief for your lost child, keep an eye open for the excitement of getting to know your new young adult. Oh, I know she's nuts and all, but still, this growing-up stuff is quite amazing to watch. I understand that she won't snuggle with you anymore (that's just for now; read on), but see how adult she's become in taking care of her little nephew? She's suddenly talking about subjects like social justice, racism, or animal rights. I know her temporary brain dysfunction comes up with some screwy ideas on these topics, but still, isn't this pretty impressive?

I know there are serious, scary things going on with your kid, but stop a minute and think. There's also wondrous stuff happening. If you focus only on the bad, your kid will feel your need to have your old child back, and he'll hate you for it. He can't be that old kid any more than you can. Sort out the good changes from the bad.

Remember diapers? Adolescence is very similar. It's a rough time. It can be very messy and often smells bad, but it's temporary. It will end. Try to find the exciting, wonderful parts of this new child. Fall in love again with your daughter, but understand this must be a new, more mature kind of love.

Mom, know that she will no longer take care of your needs for affection (for a while, anyway) but she can give you a tremendous sense of pride as you watch her courageously head out into those frightening seas of young adulthood, confronting her fears and trying to make it through.

Dad, understand that he won't be impressed with your baseball skills anymore, but you can feel a tremendous, quiet satisfaction in accepting that you have taught him so well that you are no longer competition for him physically. It is this selfless, loving acceptance and understanding, Mom and Dad, that makes up the core of what you now have to teach your adolescents. And this lesson is probably the greatest gift you can give to them. You teach it by living it.

For you, this is a time for displays of strength, not weakness. Strength is showing your kid that you are in control of your own needs, and can stand alone quite well without his hugs. Sad, perhaps, but not devastated and not demanding. Strength is understanding her conflict, allowing for her need for some emotional distance from you, and all the while assuring her that you still love her very much and are there for her whenever she needs you, even if she turns away from you in anger.

A final thought on your grief: All of those wonderful qualities you saw in your ex-child are still alive inside that angry, snarling body. You just can't see them at the moment. We shrinks get to see all the good stuff you put in them that they won't show you right now.

"Jonathan is so cold," Grace lamented, " he doesn't give a damn about anyone but himself. He used to be the nicest kid we knew, always helping out elderly neighbors and always going out of his way to make little kids feel special. Now he's only focused on his own needs. He won't help around the house, he won't ever spend time with us, and he hardly talks to us. It's like he's lost all of his goodness. God only knows what's going on out of the house. He races to get the mail every day, probably to head off failure notices from school."

"Grace," I said, " I have spoken with his school counselor. She says he has commendation notes in his file from this year's teachers for things like community service and tutoring. One letter tells of how he pretty much rescued a ninth grader from a potential beating, risking a beating himself. Did you know any of this?" Stunned, Mom slowly shook her head. "We thought he always intercepted the mail to steal bad notices from school. What is it with him? Does he hate us so much that we're not even allowed to know what good things he does?"

What it was with Jonathan is what it was with Sherree and what it was with Simon (the monkey my wife rescued). Sometimes you have to stop grabbing at someone you love to let him work out whatever he needs to in order to move back towards you a bit. When you apply this to your kid, it means holding onto a very difficult act of faith with your child. It means trying to trust that all those good qualities you saw in your 8-year-old still exist somewhere in your 14-year-old. It also means finally accepting that the eight-year-old has passed away.

Miss her, and grieve her privately. If you can set aside your own needs to hold onto what used to be and stop clutching at her, the good things you remember in your child can begin to surface again, but this time in a more mature and stronger form that can enable those wonderful qualities to survive and even flourish in a tough adult world. Then you can celebrate the birth of this wonderful new child.

Jonathan Revisited

I recently received a letter from Grace, Jonathan's mother. As I opened the envelope, a newspaper clipping fell out. It described how Jonathan had organized a relief effort in his school to help earthquake victims in Turkey. In the margin, Grace had written, "If it weren't for the media, we would never know how special our son is. We also now know how he wishes to be special, which is quietly. Since we've begun to respect his wishes, he's back with us."

Sherree Revisited

In their final session, Jill and Sherree sat on that same couch that couldn't hold them together six months before. The ease of their relationship was wonderful to see. Jill began by reflecting on how their crisis had begun. "I'd been through too much loss, between losing my husband

and my father. Sherree was all I had left, and when she started to grow up, I was panicked. I clutched at her like I was drowning.

"I did discover a little trick you should pass on to other parents like me. I took out all of Jill's pictures and sorted them into piles, each showing a different stage of her life. I took the best from each pile, framed them, and placed them side by side. This collage became my reminder that each time Sherree left me, a new and more wonderful Sherree eventually appeared, although sometimes after some fireworks. Now I look at those pictures and can feel a sweet sadness for each closed chapter, and at the same time feel a joyous excitement for the new one yet to begin. I'm OK now. I understand."

Simon Revisited

My wife's monkey Simon grew up to be a loving creature with a great instinct for judging people. Cindy told me that he was warm and affectionate with almost everyone, except for her old boyfriend. Whenever my rival would visit, Simon would grab an armful of grapes, climb to the top of the refrigerator, screech as loud as he could, and hurl the fruit at her boyfriend's head with the accuracy of an all-star pitcher. That monkey survived adolescence to become a wonderful judge of character.

With the sounds of Simon's wise screeching fading into the background, it's time to move on to the most important chapter of this book. No, we're not at the "how-to" part yet. Before we're ready to "how-to," we need to take a close look at the "how-to-ers," at us: real people trying to be parents of adolescents. As real people, we have all kinds of weaknesses and shortcomings just like everyone else, even though we go to sedate parties and act like we're cool and in control. We don't have to look at our warts then. We can cover them over with a pair of Dockers and no one will ever know.

As parents of teenagers, we stand naked to the world. Every blemish, every imperfection, every embarrassing shortcoming gets shoved in our faces and displayed to the neighbors by our little darlings. Sometimes they'll do it directly with the good, old frontal assault: "You're a disgusting fat pig." These attacks are the easiest to defend. The worst are the more subtle firefights in which acting-out kids take us back to long-forgotten feelings of depression, rage, and insanity and we lose our cherished self-control. That self-control is our defense against whatever old pain we carry around inside. Seeing ourselves becoming nuts is much worse than watching our kids get nuts.

Probably the greatest benefit in aging is not to have to feel so crazy anymore. Most of us achieve a fair amount of peace of mind, serenity, or whatever you want to call it as we roll into middle age. But Mother Nature plays one of her great jokes by pulling the hand-grenade pins and then lobbing these brain-challenged adolescents into the center of our newfound serenity. BOOM! Maybe this is just her way of reminding us how very precious serenity and self-control really are. They are precious, but more to the point of this book, they're also crucial to getting your kid through these teen years alive. If you don't find a way to keep yourself controlled, your kid has no chance—and right about now, if you feel like you're in a foxhole wondering where the next adolescent shells are going to land, you may not be feeling very much serenity or control.

This is what Chapter 7 is about: Helping you do a thorough self-examination to find and remedy your own weaknesses as a parent, weaknesses that rob you of your serenity and control. I know it's hard work. Do it for your kid. Do it for yourself—because as you'll come to see, your kid *is* you.

Chapter 7

PARENTAL SELF-EXAMINATION:
HOW YOUR BEHAVIOR AND PERSONALITY AFFECT WHO YOUR ADOLESCENT IS

YOUR TEEN IS A VERSION OF YOU. In the future, she will be able to branch off and become more of her own person, but for now, that adolescent personality in front of you is mostly created from two sources: her genes and the time she spends with you. Which of these top two influences do you think is greater? To answer that, let's take a trip back to the world of brain neurology to play with the "nature versus nurture" puzzle a bit. It's worth the trip because here lie the keys to understanding how your teen came to be, and what you can do to make some changes.

Your child came down the chute on his birthday a lot like a brand new computer in a box: a little messy and full of a whole bunch of blank brain circuits along with a couple of preset programs. That baby did hold a genetic set of cards that would largely determine who she would become physically and mentally, but in two different categories of certainty. The first set controls physical traits like hair and eye color, which are not changeable at all, although my son tries constantly. A second group of genes offers predispositions or possibilities, like innate (not learned) musical talent, alcoholism, or shyness. It's this second group of genetic factors that we need to focus on—the predispositions. Here lies the art form of parenting, which is knowing which of your child's characteristics to leave alone and which ones to try to tweak. To learn artistic sculpting, you must first learn human anatomy. To do child-personality sculpting, you must first learn how your kid's brain works. Then you can learn the art of trying to shape that brain. It's very much like learning to play a violin: a lot of work, very boring, difficult to do, time-consuming, extremely frustrating, and easy to quit on—and there's a whole lot of bad noise along the way. But if you hang in there, after years of patient, tedious effort, the results of both violin study and parenting can be absolutely breathtaking.

Genetic Predispositions: Possibilities or Probabilities?

Genetic behavioral predispositions are prewired brain circuits that come as standard equipment with your bundle of joy—like being aggressive to get what he wants or having high control needs or reacting differently to alcohol. He didn't get these from the world around him. They were just written into his genetic code. Think of these as behavioral tendencies that may or may not become a permanent part of that growing child, depending on how many times his brain repeats the neurological sequences that direct those particular behaviors. The more those specific circuits fire off for particular behaviors, the stronger they become, and the more they become permanent parts of that child as his brain insulates and solidifies those neurological connections. This is called "hardwiring" a behavior. The less these connections for a particular behavior are used, the more they atrophy and eventually die off. The researchers call this "pruning." You could call this "use it or lose it."

The use or disuse of those circuits is dictated more by parents than by any other force in a child's life, but there are limits to what can be accomplished exclusively by parenting, both good and bad.

Good parenting alone cannot create a violin virtuoso, and bad parenting alone cannot create an alcoholic. If the predispositions *are* there, you only have the *possibilities* of hearing her solo at the Met or of watching her become an addict. The outcome of a child's life is based primarily on a blending of those two factors—parenting and predisposition—along with other environmental influences. The power of free will/free choice comes later as her identity and independent thinking evolve. The process of actually moving her toward or away from auditions or addictions takes us into the world of manipulating or shaping behavior, but we're still talking simple brain wiring here, not metaphysics or morality.

And, ladies and gentleman, you can do this at home. In fact, it is virtually *all* done at home and by you, whether you realize it or not. You shape your child with something called reinforcement. His soft genetic predispositions become hard personality realities as a function of how often they are repeated, which in turn, is a function of how they are reinforced, which in turn is a function of parenting. This is the first half of your enormous power with your child.

Reinforcement: The First Way You Shape Your Child

Most parents don't really understand what reinforcement is, thanks to a misuse of the terminology. Reinforcement means anything that promotes a specific behavior, causing it to become stronger and occur more often. If a pigeon pecks at a lever and a food pellet appears, the pigeon's brain associates that pecking movement with food. If you, as the behavior-shaper, associate that movement with food enough times, the pigeon's brain thinks that pecking at a lever is a cool thing to do, and hard-wires that behavior into the brain as a circuit, or a feature of personality. Once it gets hard-wired, it's written into that brain and you'll see that behavior over and over again. Getting rid of a hard-wired behavior can be tough.

I just dropped off a good example of this at day care. Our adopted daughter Sarah arrived at our door two years ago as a foster child after as bad a first year of life as you can imagine. Born to actively drug-using parents who abandoned her, she was in three homes before she ended up with us. She almost starved to death in one home, and the other two returned her as unmanageable. She screamed almost nonstop and was as physically aggressive as a one-year-old could be. She couldn't be comforted, couldn't be held, couldn't be put down, and couldn't be picked up. She could hit. When picked up, she would whack your nose hard enough to bring stars and tears to your eyes. She clung to my wife's leg and screamed for about three months, not allowing anyone else near her, including me.

Sarah most likely arrived in this world with aggressive genetic predispositions. As she utilized those innate tendencies, the people around her reinforced them either by being aggressive in return or being too comforting. Sarah's brain associated that stimulation with her aggressive and tantrumming behaviors, and suddenly, like the astronauts would say, "Uh, Houston, we have hard-wiring." *Note that being nice or mean can hard-wire or reinforce a behavior.*

Reinforcement is the primary tool of hard-wiring behaviors in your kid. Remember, that insane adolescent brain in front of you is very much like Sarah's one-year-old brain, bursting with brand-new blank circuitry just dying to get hard-wired.

There are a few other things you ought to know about this neurological wiring that largely determines who your child will become.

First, adolescents crave brain stimulation like they crave Big Macs. They constantly seek out stimulation. They can't stand no brain action (*"God, I'm sooooo bored!"*), so they're always stirring the pot to make things happen, to get that hit of brain activity, often acting on very crazy impulses with no apparent logic other than firing off new brain circuits (see Chapter 1).

A second point is that kids are like publicists who say there is no good or bad publicity, there's just publicity. Just like Sarah, many teens often don't seem to distinguish between good (nice) stimulation and bad (mean) stimulation; they just need the action. They'll go for the rewards if they can, but they'll often switch off to the punishments as long as that developing brain is getting its dose of activity. Have you had that punishment war of attrition yet with your kid, to the point where he's grounded until February 3, 2018? This neurology is part of why he keeps provoking you and getting extended punishments. He needs the brain action, and the punishment is more easily accessed at the moment. We'll explain more about the neurology of this in a moment.

Third, you need to know about critical behavior-shaping tools such as positive reinforcement, negative reinforcement, and your ace in the hole, extinction. These will be important weapons in your battle against adolescent insanity and will help you to understand why some of the tricks you'll learn in Part Three work. If you don't understand the science behind the strategies, then trying to do what I'll be training you to do in the face of problems like teen rage may become impossible for you. You'll have to understand how this works in order to have the faith you will need when situations with your child get hot. So please bear with me here as we get a teensy bit technical.

Both positive *and* negative reinforcement have to do with *strengthening* a specific behavior, not getting rid of it. When that pigeon pecked at a lever and got food, it decided to peck some more. That was an example of positive reinforcement—you *provide* something that causes the behavior to occur again. Negative reinforcement is when something is *withdrawn* that also causes the behavior to occur. You could blast that poor pigeon with a rap CD at full volume and scare the pigeon poop out of it, and then any time the pigeon pecked at a lever, you'd turn off the loud noise for a minute (and maybe offer it a soothing Charlie Parker ballad instead). Turning off that rap music (music?) would cause the pigeon to learn to peck at the lever a lot. Negative reinforcement often gets confused with punishment. Note that negative reinforcement is withdrawing a *pre-existing* undesirable element in the pigeon's environment in order to get the bird to do something.

Punishment is entirely different. Punishment does not promote or strengthen any behavior. It is intended only to stop a specific activity. It does not cause any other behavior to occur. In parenting words, you could say that punishment doesn't teach anything except to *not* do something. The biggest problem with punishment is that while it initially provides *the illusion* of working to shape behavior in a good way, it actually spins off all sorts of brain reactions that can come back to haunt you in other, and often worse, forms of bad behaviors that we'll talk about shortly. What you might consider to be punishments can actually be weird kinds of rewards to your kid, which is how you ended up grounding him until February 3, 2018. Here's how it works.

The incredible, critical, and rarely believed fact is that being hurtful to your kid can be a *positive* reinforcer, making the rotten behavior occur more frequently, not less. Screaming at a child is used by many parents as a punishment (a mean response intended to stop a behavior), but screaming at your kid for insulting you can actually stimulate that temporarily weird brain in all sorts of reinforcing ways, like getting your undivided attention and controlling your behavior (I call this running you around the room).

Thus you can actually link your kid's insulting behavior to brain stimulation, encouraging the disrespect to occur again. Putting your purple, raging, spitting face in his gets all kinds of adolescent brain circuits firing off. Your yelling can become very addicting to your child. Parental rage can become *positive* reinforcement, as can snide, demeaning comments. In the world of developing brains, what we think is very negative can be very positive to an adolescent brain. And very bad.

Daniel seemed stumped by my question. This father and his 14-year-old daughter seemed to fight bitterly and endlessly over next to nothing.

They would compete to see who could one-up whom in senseless verbal duels that were fought over things they had already agreed on. Daniel would work himself into frothy rages at her button pushing.

"What do you want?" I repeated to Daniel. "She does all of these tasks you request. So what is it that you want?" He thought for a minute and then with a note of triumph he found it: "I want her to goddamn respect me by accepting what I tell her without her constant comebacks." "Daniel," I said, "so far she does respect you. I know this because she does pretty much what you ask. I worry that she'll lose her respect for you because all I see from you here is you looking more like her brother than her father by raging at her. You compete in word games with her like a sibling."

Daniel was mad. "You mean SHE competes with ME, don't you? She insists on always having the last freaking word. I'm going to keep on getting in her face until she stops doing that. I've got to teach her to respect me." "Daniel, what you're teaching her is that with one last word she can get a 200-pound ex-Marine foaming at the mouth because he cannot stand to have his kid get the last word. Your screaming is very reinforcing for her and very costly in terms of her respect for you. Give her the goddamn last word and after a while this game won't be fun for her anymore. Think about what you really want. Do you want the last word, or a daughter who respects her father as someone tough enough not to get drawn into stupid word games?"

Daniel glared at me just like I do when someone nails me like that. He knew this to be true. He just had to sort out what he really wanted.

Changing these behavior patterns between you and your child can be the toughest task you'll ever attempt. Did I mention that this training stuff is as difficult to do as learning to play the violin? I was not kidding. Speaking of hard, let me tell you a bit more about my little angel, Sarah, because she is a smiling example of the concept of behavior *extinction* along with positive reinforcement. These are your trump cards to play with your own kid. Learn these very well.

My wife's strategy with our new one-year-old daughter was to give her *no* reinforcement for the aggressive behavior, and to reinforce Sarah's brains out when she was good. Whenever she was cooperative and pleasant, we rewarded her like crazy. When she did her Mike Tyson routine, we'd go into shutdown mode. Whenever Sarah knocked Dad senseless (this happened 10 or 12 times a day), she wouldn't get hit, screamed at, lectured to, or anything. She got nothing, literally. We isolated her in her room with the quiet words, "When you are calm, call us. Because we love and miss you. But you cannot hit."

The solitary screaming and tantrumming that went on in that room is hard to describe. Cindy said she kept waiting for the green vomit and the spinning head. We told jokes to try to keep our spirits up and had trust that one day we would win this battle for Sarah's soul. The depth of her rage reflected her withdrawal pain from her addiction to the previous reinforcement she received for those aggressive behaviors.

The healing formula for extinction of bad behaviors is simple. Isolate, and repeat 10,000 times. The doing is excruciating. My wife is the strongest and smartest person I know. She went through hell undoing the worst of the hard-wired behaviors. She won. It took 18 months and we still see occasional flashes of the old insanity, but the Devil lost this series.

Sarah is your troubled adolescent kid. Later on in this book, you'll get specific training on how to use these neurological principles of reinforcement and extinction to help your child, but for now, know that your battle is the same as ours was with Sarah in many ways, and much scarier in others. It's scarier because of all that sex, drugs, and rock 'n roll information I whacked you with in Chapter 2. Now that you know how stimulation and reinforcement work, what do you suppose happens when we bombard kids with endless sexual, violent, and acting-out messages, and reinforce these messages as being cool? Are we hard-wiring that stuff into an expanding, developing brain? Jeremy might provide a clue.

Jeremy smiled a warm, engaging grin as he chatted happily. He was one of those rare 13-year-olds who seemed so comfortable with adults that you just liked hanging out with him. I realized I was daydreaming about the nice parts of adolescents and forced myself to tune back into what he was saying. "...you know, it's one of those light punk-type tunes, you know, that you can't get out of your head. It just repeats over and over." "And what are the lyrics that repeat in this tune?" I inquired. "Kill your parents, kill your teachers, kill yourself," Jeremy responded airily. Then his face darkened. "I know that sounds really bad, but it's just, like, music, you know? Nobody really listens to the words."

Jeremy had been referred for a risk assessment after he wrote a note threatening to kill a teacher who gave him a hard time.

So what can poor, little old uncool you do to push back against the insanity besides reinforce and extinguish? Plenty!

You are the most influential force in your kid's life in yet another way, which may outweigh the power of both genetics and reinforcement: modeling. This is where parenting really gets personal. Who you are and how well you can control your own needs can write the script for your child's life through something he calls "walking the walk."

Modeling: The Second Way You Shape Your Child

The next huge point you need to understand about that exploding adolescent brain is the incredible impact of modeling. Those expanding frontal lobes in your kid's head are wide open to copying behaviors thrust before him repeatedly, particularly from role models. Since I've already established that you are the most powerful role model available to your teen (stop snickering), and I've shown you how you hard-wire behaviors in your kid, you should be very frightened to know that the source of most of these behaviors is you. Your child is constantly watching you, modeling who you are, and testing it all out. In other words, our kids confront us with ourselves, in all our wanton glory.

Jason plopped down on my couch, clearly angry and disgusted. This huge, athletic, and bright boy looked lost. "I took the S.A.T.s (College Board exams) like I promised, but I walked out halfway through. I was doing OK until I got to this bullshit story about this all-American family that has all these traditions and rituals they always do. The point was how close they all were. It was sickening. I felt like I was going to explode in the room. I really wanted to hit someone. I tore up my answer sheet and walked out. Why do they put that crap in there? I'm never taking that test again." Jason had spent the past two years watching his dad verbally assault his mom, trash the house, and stalk out. He learned a lot about how to handle conflict.

Feeling slightly pressured? Good. You should be—because as the parent of a difficult adolescent, you're facing two on, two out, one run down in the bottom of the ninth, and we're sending you out to the plate with the fans screaming. There's nowhere to hide. Who you are as a person may determine the outcome of this adolescent game.

Before you head out to the parenting batter's box, you need to learn a whole bunch of things about yourself before your opponent learns them, too. How do you respond to pressure? Can you hit a major league curve ball? Can you ignore the crowd noise and focus only on your job? What are your weak points (because you know that's just where he'll come after you)? How do you handle provocation? Does intimidation get you out of your game? Do you play for the team, or for your own needs? Are you willing to sacrifice?

We need to look at these issues of parenting as they relate to who we are as people. In the parenting game, our personal character determines success far more than any training can ever do. And among character issues, the first one we want to aspire to is being boring. Don't be too cool for school.

Good Parents of Adolescents: About as Hip as Plesiosaurs

If you had this need to begin with, give up your desire to be cool. It's a hopeless endeavor, anyway. Ever notice how dumb middle-aged people appear primping their hair and trying to look cool in those sports cars? Uh-oh, that's me in that store window reflection. Oh well, knowing that as parents we don't want to be cool anyhow can comfort us both. One thing that will make a psychologist sit up straight and start to worry is hearing a troubled 15-year-old describe his parents as "cool." Often, there's trouble there. An insider tip I have for you is that as much as teens may laugh at your lack of cool, they really don't value cool parents very much. You see, they're cool, their friends are cool, their idols are all cool, and your kids know that all of these cool folks are usually also quite screwed-up. They know that cool people are often those insecure ones seeking approval by talking, acting, or dressing in certain ways. What your kid is searching for is that next level beyond cool. He's searching for people he can respect. Joe's mother, Martha, was confused on this point.

Martha was looking in all the wrong places for the source of her dilemma with her son. "I go downstairs in the morning to survey the wreckage after my 15-year-old son's sleepover. SURPRIIIISE! There are two girls sleeping among the five boys. Dr. Bradley, how can I tell him this isn't right without him rolling his eyes, sighing that sigh, and saying I'm so out of it? He keeps saying how uncool I am. He tells me that the girls' parents know, and that they're cool with it, so why can't I be? I hate it when he makes me feel like that, so I avoid fighting with him on these types of things. Why does he have to roll his eyes? Why does he say I'm so out of it?" "He's supposed to roll his eyes," I answered. "That's his job. Why do you need him to think you're cool?"

If you need to have your kid see you as cool, hip, or trendy, you're in deep doodoo, and you've got lots of company. Many of today's parents made a fatal error of association on that cool issue as they were growing up. They remember their own parents (whom they may have disliked for many valid parenting reasons) as also being uncool. As teens, we often made promises to ourselves that we would never be like that with our own kids. We would be different. We'd be cool. We'd understand what it's like to be a teenager, so we give our kids cars, money, and lots of freedom. We won't make them bus tables like we did just to buy Valvoline for that 12-year-old Corvair that burned more oil than gas. And if we catch them with a beer or a joint, hey, we're cool about it. Our kids will love, cherish, and respect us because we'll be so nice to them. They'll know we're cool.

Wasn't that a wonderful fantasy? Did you also believe the one about how we would change the world by being nice? I really loved that one, too, but I don't think we changed the world. I think we found out that change is much more complex than just being nice. Many of us have also found out how dangerous it is to raise children today by trying to gain their approval. Cool parents become sort-of-friends or pseudosiblings to their kids, sitting and handwringing as they watch their struggling children slowly drown in a sea of irresponsibility and excessive freedom.

Good parents of adolescents are definitely not cool. They're usually annoying, corny, and about as contemporary as dinosaurs. They know that parenting means loving your kid enough to have her hate you at times, because your primary concern is for the long-term welfare of your child, and not for her approval. Good parents know that raising an adolescent is, by definition, a conflict-based relationship. They would like to be friends with their kid, but they choose to be a parent first.

Believe it or not, that's the way your adolescent secretly wants and needs you to be, even though she ridicules you endlessly. That's because dinosaur parents are usually also reliable and consistent. They fulfill promises and seem to take a heck of a lot of abuse without yelling back (*"How do they do that?"* your kid often asks me). They show up. They teach much more by example than with words. They stand as light-houses, as constant points of reference for their struggling teenagers. Their ever-shining, unchanging lights are beacons by which their children guide themselves as they try to navigate the terrible storms of adolescent seas. Sharon's mother knew this.

Sharon was yelling, begging, and threatening, desperately seeking some lever to manipulate her mother into allowing this 16-year-old to go unchaperoned to Mexico with all the kids from her circle, male and female. "All of their parents gave permission," she wailed, "They trust their kids. They're like friends to their kids—they're cool with them. They love their kids, not like you. If you don't let me go, you will never be my friend." Mom kept her composure, paused, and then quietly dropped a line I picked up and wrote down: "Sharon, I'm not your friend. I'm better than a friend. I'm your parent."

The Opposite of Cool:
Overly Controlling and Overly Critical

In parenting adolescents, extremes are dangerous. Just as the "too nice, too cool" parents can be deadly, so can the "Welcome to Parris Island, maggot" types. We've seen how our own needs for nurturing and acceptance can hurt our kids. What about our needs for power and control? How do these play out?

"Last night Ross was dawdling in the bath, once again. It was already 10:45 P.M. and I was exhausted. Somehow, it got in my head that he should be in bed by 11:00, goddamn it, because he should! After I asked him for the third time to please move it along, I started thinking that he does this every goddamn night, and I'm tired of it. He always finds other things to do. He doesn't respect me. I was thinking why can't he just once jump when I say jump. I could feel anger and frustration building inside of me as I started up the steps. The adrenaline was rushing as I got to the bathroom door. A set of suggested words flashed in front of my eyes: 'JESUS CHRIST,' I was supposed to scream very loud, 'GET THE HELL OUT OF THAT GODDAMN TUB RIGHT NOW!' I was also supposed to lean down into his face for effect, throw the towel at him hard, exit slamming the door, and wait to hear any faint remark of defiance. If Ross should dare say anything back, I was to go back in and jack him up against the wall by his neck to terrify him and reduce him to tears. If I made him afraid, then he'd love and respect me. This is crazy.

I love my son more than I can express. I also love and respect who he is as a person. Ross is kind, funny, honest, unfailingly loyal, and deeply moral. He is, without a doubt, the finest young man I've ever had the privilege to know. It terrifies, embarrasses, and sickens me to feel this insanity towards my wonderful son."

Notes from the personal journal of Dr. Michael Bradley.

We have needs for power and control that originate from two places. The first is today. How was your day? How is your life? Are things going smoothly and predictably or are things tough for you? You need to know this before you go to get your child out of that tub at 10:45 P.M.

The night that I was telling myself to assault my child over 15 minutes of compliance was the end of a bad day. Everything seemed to be unraveling in my life. Nothing was working out the way I wanted. I felt no power or control, so I expected my son to give these feelings to me. He just wanted to play. He's a kid. That's his job. But we get into deep trouble thinking that our kids owe us this emotional caretaking.

The second source of my insanity was my own father. This script was a replay from my memories of his patented "parenting through terror" techniques. Our memory tapes of our own parents come rushing back as "parenting directives," particularly when we're tired or stressed. Many of us survived this type of training that used fear-based motivation or *punishment* as its key.

The parents, teachers, and sergeants I knew all used fear-based systems as their primary method of instruction and development. Today's teachers and sergeants have largely changed their models. We parents are stuck with these old "how-to" tapes from the good old days of parenting when whacking your kid was considered legal and admirable. A controversy rages today about corporal punishment, with many advocates of spanking noting the correlation between the increase in troubling adolescent behavior and the decrease in physical punishment. So does hitting work? To answer, let me take you back a few years to look at a telling situation as handled by a world-renowned expert on the issue of corporal punishment.

Sister Helen Walter was a Sister of Saint Joseph and my Catholic grade school enforcer. This fierce nun would roam the halls searching out any small signs of dysfunction or rebellion to be addressed with the metal ruler she wielded with samurai precision. We used to joke, very quietly, that if you thought she "was Helen Walter, then wait until you see her on land." She had an interesting punishment system, wherein you had to hold out your hands perfectly still to get whacked across the knuckles. If you moved your hands to avoid a shot, the sentence was doubled. If you cried while getting whacked, the sentence was doubled. Touchy-feely she wasn't.

We used to play a game in school called "Sister Helen Walter," the object of which was to pretend she was looming up behind someone doing something wrong. If the person flinched and looked, you won. Unfortunately, this game cost someone his life—or so we thought at the time.

In second grade, Leo Iggy's father was legendary for his collection of *Playboy* magazines that Leo would occasionally smuggle into school. One rainy day as we sat eating our lunches at our desks in silence (as was the rule), Leo decided to hide a *Playboy* on his lap and surreptitiously thumb through the pages (for the articles, of course). Sure enough, Sister H.W.'s radar somehow zoned in on this evil incarnate in our classroom and she appeared at the rear door, slowly making her way up an aisle behind Leo. Our frantic warning whispers were ignored since Leo had often been the loser of previous games of "Sister Helen Walter." When she got to his desk, the big H.W. let out a war shriek we had never before heard. Her ruler was a blur as she beat Leo out of his desk, onto the floor, up the aisle, and down to the principal's office as a hail of mostly naked women in white fur garments (as I recall) rained down on us.

Leo was never heard from again. His distant echoing screams were his last communication with us. The eighth graders told us what happened to him, and we knew it to be the terrible truth as soon as we heard it: The nuns killed him and buried him that night on the golf course behind our school. It all fit.

Years later, I was astonished to run into a very-much-alive Leo. He explained that his parents had been outraged that he had been beaten so badly and had immediately withdrawn him from school. Since he lived so far away, none of us had seen him or had any further contact with him.

What so astonished me then—and now—is that I fully believed that the nuns were capable of killing Leo and burying him on the golf course. This is called fear-based motivation. In this system, I was never confronted with having to decide what I thought to be right or wrong. I was good simply because I was afraid. I did not do bad things at school because I did not want to share a plot on the 13th green with Leo.

The corporal punishment debate provides a great window into the issue of effective parenting, proving ultimately that it is based on respect. Both the hitters and the nonhitters raise their glasses to that point, but the hitters believe that fear of physical pain breeds respect, while the nonhitters say hitting erodes respect. My view is reflected in my grade school experience. I did not respect the brutal nuns. I feared them. I can remember wanting to respect them, but being unable to get past their anger. I never came to really know or want to incorporate their values. The only control they had over me was external. Their use of fear caused me to reject their values. Nothing really changed inside of me.

So does fear work as a method of discipline? Yes, to *temporarily* control behavior, as long as the enforcer is around. Does it teach? Yes, but not what you want it to. It teaches anger as a way of teaching. Remember me "instructing" my son to get to bed on time?

So why do teens in general seem so much crazier these days since many of us have decided that hitting is a lousy way to parent? In addition to the teenage cultural changes (see Chapter 2), there are two other factors. *One is that we've stopped hitting*. It is clear that slapping kids across the face for acting out in a restaurant will allow for quieter meals. It is a quick way to stop undesirable behaviors, and thus provide a façade of parental control, but only in the short term. In the long term, it creates deep, dark, and temporarily hidden rage that gets lots of reinforcement to eventually explode, particularly in today's adolescent culture.

The fact that many parents have stopped smacking their children as a way of controlling them means that many kids may *appear* to be more out of control than in the good old days of corporal punishment, but this is an illusion. While today's kids may look rowdier at McDonald's than we did at Howard Johnson's, they are typically not afraid of their parents. And without fear, there's the possibility for a relationship based on respect and trust—and the chance that you will truly be able to help shape your kids' values and attitudes.

Research into parenting styles confirms this. Parents who use corporal punishment get small, conforming children who become large, aggressive adolescents. Teens with serious acting-out problems usually come from parents with cold, demanding, inconsistent, and critical parenting styles. Kids can feel that these types of parents are really preoccupied with fulfilling their own needs for power and control, and are less concerned for their child's welfare. Just like those modeling and reinforcement theories predict, these children often become cold, heartless, self-serving adolescents. They become what they see. They see fear. They never know respect.

The second explanation for kids seeming worse since we stopped hitting them is that we have changed the rules of parenting—*but to what?* We took away a primary parenting tool (hitting) and then told parents to raise their kids in a crazy, out-of-control world. We did this with people who were mostly raised in a fear-based model, and never told them what to use instead. We went into Bosnia, took away our soldiers' weapons, and told them to keep on keeping the peace. "Uh, lieutenant, begging your pardon, sir, but if one of the locals, like, uh, shoots at us, uh, what would you suggest we do?" "That's all, sergeant. Get back to your post. I have every confidence in you."

Some jobs are hard enough when we have tools. Parenting adolescents without training is like peacekeeping without weapons. But your raised hand is a weapon, not a tool, and one you can't afford to use with your kid. Raising your teenager is much more complex than just keeping the peace. You must have other, newer tools.

Wait a minute, Dr. Bradley. I know of many situations in which corporal punishment was used and the recipients grew up just fine. My own father used to hit me occasionally, and I loved and respected him. And what about my football coach who smacked me around? I loved and respected him, too. So where do you get off saying I shouldn't hit my kid?

To answer, dear parent, I ask: Did you love and respect those people because they hit you, or did you love and respect them *in spite of their hitting?* Love and respect comes from knowing and admiring who people are as people, not as punchers. You saw that these people cared for you, and that they stood for something honorable to you. You wanted to emulate them, to copy their strengths, compassion, and loyalties. You're confused because they hit you sometimes and you still loved them. It wasn't the hitting that earned your respect. That bought your fear. Fear maintains order, but it does not teach true discipline, which is *self*-control and responsibility. True discipline emanates from within, not from a ruler or a hand. True discipline is born from *respect,* which is not fear. Fear is easy to earn. Respect is tough. Really tough. We need to look closely at this thing called respect, for in seeking it you are searching for the Holy Grail of adolescent parenting. It is well worth the quest, but it is an arduous journey.

Respect: The Critical Tool for Adolescent Parenting

Virtually every piece of research confirms that teenagers who respect their parents have a much greater chance of surviving adolescence with only a few scrapes. When kids are young, you can get by as a parent using their fear or their extreme dependence on you. In adolescence, you must have their respect. In describing competent parents of adolescents, we keep coming back to a maddeningly vague definition: *They maintain an elusive balance of firmness and nurturing. They have the respect of their kids.* But exactly what creates respect?

If I could bottle it, I'd be on *Oprah*. If I could define it, I'd be on the Supreme Court. Like pornography, it's much easier to spot than to define, let alone teach. I can see it when it walks into my office with some families. I can also see the black hole it leaves when it's missing, sucking up all of the warmth, love, and hope in a family. Let me tell you what your kid says about respect.

WHAT YOUR KID SAYS
INCREASES HIS RESPECT FOR YOU

Some of these comments you've heard yourself. Others may surprise you, but they are all typical thoughts kids share with me about this respect issue. Maybe you can figure out how you can use this for yourself. Be forewarned, though; it's a tough list.

- He says he respects your honesty, particularly the hard kind where you admit to your mistakes.
- She says she respects your consistency, like when you keep trying every night to help her with her homework, even though she coldly rejects you.
- He secretly loves that you keep showing up for his games even when he says he doesn't care.
- She admires how you always offer affection without begging for or demanding it in return.
- He says that not taking yourself too seriously makes him respect you. The fact that you laugh at your own goofs helps him listen to you about his.
- She says she gets really impressed when she sees you setting aside your own needs for her—like when she knows how important cleanliness and order are to you and yet you don't take her disorganization and messiness personally.
- He says he can't believe how you kept from going crazy on him when he dented up your car.
- Her eyes filled with tears of admiration when you apologized for yelling at her for denting up the car.
- He silently cried when you told him how sad and scared you were the night he came home drunk.
- She was stunned by your courage when you told her you got pregnant at 17.
- He gets awed by how hard you work to provide for him without ever complaining.
- She is mystified by how you handled that abusive racial slur without losing your dignity.
- He wants to know how you do that thing where you seem so strong, yet you never raise a hand in anger.

- She is so envious of the skills you have to keep your husband feeling special after all these years.
- He is curious to know about how you seem to treasure your wife after all these years.
- She wants to learn how to love a husband, raise children, have a career, and still be such a powerful and distinct individual, like her mom.
- He sees how you teach by living your life, and not by lecturing.
- She loves that you don't ever say, "I told you so."
- He is inspired by how you never take cheap verbal shots at him, even when he deserves it and it would be so easy.
- She says that you're, you know, like, really a grownup.
- He says that you're, you know, like, really a grownup.
- She says that she loves you for all those times you don't tell her what to do.
- He can't say enough about how you let him make lots of decisions that he knows you wanted to control, but you didn't because you wanted him to grow up.
- She says she listens to you about drugs and drinking because you do neither.
- They both respect you the most for staying calm when they go nuts. They shake their heads at your self-control, as if you were some Zen master. They sometimes ask me, "How do my parents do that?" I love hearing that question from your kid. I know it means I won't be seeing very much of him.

WHAT YOUR KID SAYS
DESTROYS HIS RESPECT FOR YOU

Be forewarned before you read this list, also. It's a tough one, too.
- She says finding your stash of marijuana caused her respect for you to go up in smoke.
- He says finding out about your sexual affair ripped his heart in half.
- She becomes disgusted seeing how small you look after your sixth beer.
- He hates it when you beg for or demand affection.
- She feels lost when she sees you getting cold with her because she's been acting like such a little snot.

- He gets frightened when you retaliate in kind for his hurtful words to you.
- She becomes panicked when you act as small-minded as she does.
- He cries hard tears when he finds out his father is so weak of character that he uses strength of muscle to punch his own son, even though the kid "deserved it."
- She sees you shrink in size each time you are sarcastic.
- He feels less hopeful each time you resort to anger to get him to do things.
- They both become terribly despondent when they see their parents become children. One boy said it frighteningly well:

Eric began speaking spontaneously, something this 16-year-old rarely did. "Now that my parents are splitting up I hardly ever chill with my old friends anymore. I'm always over at Susan's house. Her parents are the greatest. They treat me like another son. You wanna hear something really weird? You know how you've been on me for the grass I've been smoking on weekends? Well last Saturday night, you know what I did? I watched a stupid Disney movie with Susan and her parents. She actually likes doing stuff like that with her folks. Wanna hear something weirder? I liked it, too. My friends, like, are going nowhere. All they do these days is smoke up, every day, whenever they can. It's like they all just want to zone out, to not be around, you know what I'm saying? Another thing I realized—every one of my old friends has jerk parents, like me. Like you said, it's all about escaping. And the dumb Disney movie was fun. Can you believe that?"

Eric paused, leaned forward and put his head in his hands, with his gaze burning holes in my carpet. "When I was a kid, my dad and my mom were my heroes. Dude, my dad could do it all. Cars, sports, weightlifting, you name it. Now, after I found out about his sleeping around, he's like this asshole I'm ashamed to be seen with. And my mom, she used to always be there for me, no matter what. We'd talk every night when I came in, you know, just about stupid stuff. Now she says it's 'her time for fun,' and she's out every night. Every freaking night she's jetting around like one of my crazy friends." Eric's eyes lifted and locked on mine. "You know what's sad? I have no heroes now. Every adult in my life turned out to be a jerk. I don't know who to be like anymore."

I considered giving Eric the line about becoming your own hero, but it sounded so weak in my head that I just sat and nodded. He was right. It was sad. We adults were pretty much all jerks to him.

Not being a jerk to your kid means getting and holding her respect. So how do I summarize what earns the respect of adolescents? If you look at that list of their thoughts, you see it has to do with upward-looking admiration. They must see you as something better than they are. They prize people who "walk the walk," who selflessly honor their commitments 24 hours a day, seven days a week, especially when the going gets rough. Perhaps most important, teens respect adults who calmly understand and forgive shortcomings in others less competent than themselves—like their children.

How do I summarize the respect-destroying list? Anger, hypocrisy, and selfishness. Unleashing our rage, pretending to be something we're not, and placing our own needs first are toxins to parental respect.

When your kid respects you, you're home free in the parenting game, because if your child admires you, she'll want to copy (model) who you are and earn your approval. She will largely incorporate your values and morals as her own. This is what we call inoculating kids against insanity versus policing them. In parenting teenagers, earning their respect is the key to a calmer adolescence. Rigidly controlling their behavior sets up a jailbreak.

Simply imprisoning kids with anger and control doesn't work. In addition to the reasons I've given so far, add this one: As they reach these golden years of teenage insanity, *you can no longer physically make them do things they don't want to do.* The terrible fact is that you lose all your power with your child if the primary components of your relationship are fear and control. She will get faster, stronger, and be willing to be a lot crazier than you. There's a storm coming. You haven't shown her anything except how to behave as long as you're around, and as long as you still hold the title as the No. 1 controller in the house. Once she's away from you, or once you lose your jab, it's jailbreak time. Your kid will have no defense against all that craziness out there calling to her because you didn't help her develop a set of values and independent decision-making skills. You just ordered her around.

If fear and anger are what you've taught your kids so far, get yourself to a shrink now. The good news is that Mother Nature anticipated our parenting failures and gave us a second chance to reprogram our kids in adolescence (see Chapter 1)—but this is likely the last train. Don't miss it.

If you have built a respect-based relationship with your kid, congratulations! You have given him the best gifts he'll ever get from anyone: intrinsic values and decision-making skills that go with him wherever he goes in his insane world. You vaccinated him with loving respect for you so that when he comes up against the inevitable decisions about sex, drugs, and rock 'n roll, he will likely be immune to the lure of the insanity. This immunization only comes from respect. It never comes from control. And like love, respect can only be freely given. It can never be demanded.

It's That Simple, It's That Hard

Remember way back in the Introduction, when I promised that this book would demand changes of you before you could try to change your kid? Well, here we are, for respect is the silver bullet that slays the werewolf that has taken up temporary residence in your child. It is just that simple. *Earning* the respect is just that hard. It doesn't come with the job. It must be won with years of blood, sweat, tears, and mostly with patience. The title of parent doesn't innately mean respect to your kid. Respect is not a rank on your shoulder. It is an emotion held in the eyes of your child as she looks at you. It is fine glass, hard to create, and easily shattered.

When I get the nerve to confront parents about their own self-serving behaviors that destroy respect, I find I'm usually telling them things they already knew about themselves. They just never realized how profoundly this stuff would affect their kid. More times than not, the prolonged (versus normal short-term) insanity of an adolescent child reflects a problem within the family in general.

Kids are barometers of family function. They act out hidden stresses hurting the family that sometimes they don't even know about. It's very weird. My wife and I were always amazed at how our infants would start to fuss before we even realized we were having a snit.

So if you think that I'm asking you to inventory yourself before auditing your child, you're half right. When you realize just how critical your own character is to your kid's, it is time for serious self-assessment, but since your teen may also be acting out stresses of the household, we must next travel to the second critical part of that child-rearing environment: the family. Just as your kid is shaped by your character, he's also intensely affected by the character of the interparent relationship within the house. Let's journey now to Chapter 8 to look at that powerful adolescent-shaping group my father used to call "the God-famn-damily."

Chapter 8

THE FAMILY MATTERS:
PARENT TEAMWORK, DIVORCE, SINGLE PARENTING, AND BLENDED FAMILIES

L ET'S TAKE A MINUTE to review for the midterm exam. So far, we've seen that kids are nuts, their world is crazy, their brains are open to new programming, and who you are largely determines who this kid will become. That last lesson, who you are, is comprised of two parts: who you are individually and who you are as half of a couple. Everything we discussed in Chapter 7 about modeling and reinforcement applies in describing the enormous impact your relationship with your partner has on your child. That expanding adolescent brain is carefully watching, evaluating, memorizing, and reacting to how you interact with your other half.

The problem for your kid is that we parents don't do relationships very well. Even the catastrophic 50 percent divorce rate underestimates the degree of dysfunction in our marriages. My friends in the marriage therapy business say that what has changed in the marriage world is that the word "we" has become "me." Too often, we married adults see marriage as a place to get our own needs met, rather than as a place where we mostly set ourselves aside for the good of the family. Setting the needs of others above your own is also a good definition of maturity. If we adults are not doing this well, then we are largely a society of big children raising little children.

This calamity has a terrible hidden effect on our adolescents. Everyone yells about the impact of family dysfunction on young children in their formative years. The new brain research indicates that adolescents are once again in their formative years, and contrary to the popular view, teenagers are not isolated from the pain of family discord because they are more independent. I argue that adolescents are *more* vulnerable to this pain. Teenagers are insane enough under the best of circumstances. Adding dysfunctional parents to the mix guarantees trouble. Further, the new adolescent neurological research now raises the specter of family dysfunction getting hard-wired into that expanding teenage head as the model for your kid's own future relationships.

Once again, raising our kids brings us back to raising ourselves.

Feuding Parents: Adding Fuel to the Fire

If your marriage is in big trouble, your teenager is in bigger trouble. If the parents are not operating as a team, it's jailbreak time. Just like younger kids, adolescents are born experts at divide-and-conquer strategies. They instinctively use parental dissension to get what they want. If Mom and Dad are working at odds, a difficult kid will chew them up.

Most troubled adolescents are being raised by parents whose relationship is also troubled. But there are two very different groups of stressed parents, and it is critical to know which group describes your situation. One group has marriages that were bad before Junior got zits, and the other group saw their previously good marriages begin to burn only in the blaze of adolescent insanity. The question is, which caused which? Who is the chicken and who is the egg?

Adolescents often act as barometers of how their family functions, and teenage crises can frequently be the indicators of other hidden family stresses, like a bad marriage. But the crisis of struggling with a brain-damaged adolescent may itself be the stress that makes the marriage shaky. Trying to sort this out gets difficult, but it's very important in figuring out your next move.

Most parents of adolescents in crisis usually feel widening cracks in the cement of their marriages, be they good marriages or not. Minor relationship weaknesses that could be previously ignored can become glaring flaws under the stress of adolescent craziness. The onslaught that pounds a marriage from an adolescent in crisis is difficult to describe. The best relationships can sometimes be undermined by the relentless emotional stress and fear that your kid can cause. Often the parents feel like their partnership is dissolving under the weight of the crisis. It can be a terribly angry and lonely time even for two nice people who really love each other.

> After exchanging shouted criticisms for 50 minutes, Harry and Janet paused. These adolescent-in-crisis parents lapsed into a deadly silence, punctuated only by sharp, tearful breaths. "I guess that's it, then," Dad murmured. "I knew you were mad, but I didn't know how much you hated me." "I don't hate you," Mom sobbed, "you hate me. But sometimes I hate you for hating me." Dad felt like he had to say something. "You know what I hate? I really hate being hated. I hate that." They were both startled at this silliness, and began laughing through their tears. When the laughter stopped, Harry awkwardly took Janet's hand like she might refuse his touch. "When did we stop talking?" he asked. "When we hit 13," she answered, "or when 13 hit us."

If you feel that your marriage was in bad shape *before* Junior went nuts, get some professional help now. If the distance, anger, and coldness of the marriage have the familiarity of years, focus on repairing the marriage. Without marriage therapy, you are risking a lot more than your relationship. You are risking your child. If you don't care about yourself anymore, you must still care about your kid. It's your job. Raising a difficult adolescent in a dysfunctional relationship is impossible. If that kid does OK, it will be because she was one of those very rare ones who could raise herself well. If you are not convinced, reread Chapters 1 and 2, and then ask yourself how a kid can survive in this world with unavailable, self-absorbed, and angry parents.

On the other hand, if Harry and Janet's story sounds more like your marriage, take heart. The crisis you're enduring will probably only make your relationship stronger and closer. Remember diapers, four-hour feedings, and terrifying, unexplained raging fevers at 3:00 A.M.? Remember how those sleep-deprived snit sessions with your partner left you feeling cold and alone, like suddenly everything had been turned upside-down by the new baby? Remember grieving because you thought that your relationship was dying? This is the same experience.

That pre-baby marriage relationship *did* die. It was replaced by a much stronger, more mature, and wonderfully fulfilling partnership, secured by bands of steel forged by the pressures of those first-child challenges. Standing shoulder to shoulder through those trials gave your marriage something precious that can only be purchased with struggle.

Well, here you are once again. Sleep-deprived, angry, and feeling alone—and embarking on another life adventure that will only make you stronger and closer to your partner if you can find the courage to put one foot in front of the other when things look most bleak. I always hate hearing this from others when I'm in a crisis, but it happens to be true.

So the first job in helping an out-of-control teenager is rebuilding your parent team. And fast. Because if the parents are not a team, nothing else will work. Reconnecting with your partner always results in a calmer, safer kid.

Think of yourself and your spouse as two cops alone in a squad car at 2:00 A.M. in the worst neighborhood in town. If you guys are squabbling, the street will eat you alive. Some nights will be so rough, the only thing you can depend on is your partner. Keep in mind that your kid's insane brain will straighten out in a bit, and then he'll be gone. You and your partner have decades of life after that to share. Don't let go. You must maintain the thought that your child's insanity is temporary and manageable with the right skills.

At the same time, don't underestimate the emotional impact these teen years can have on a relationship. Parenting an adolescent today will likely be the hardest thing you'll ever do. The tremendous battering can exact a severe toll.

Marinda sat down wearily. This quiet, dignified woman looked like she hadn't slept in days. "No, I don't sleep very much now," she responded. "I have to keep half-awake to listen for Grant's footsteps sneaking down the hall to run out. Even when he's in his room, I can't seem to sleep until I know that he's asleep. And that's usually not until 3 or 4 in the morning. My husband, Charles, he sleeps very well. He's given up on our son."

Her head bowed. "I feel like I can't ever forgive Charles for doing that. I can understand wanting to do that, but I can't accept actually quitting on your own child. It feels like he's abandoned us, even though he's still there. I always saw him as so strong before Grant began having problems, and now my husband just looks so weak and cowardly to me. I don't think we have any relationship anymore." Her voice choked, "I don't think we ever will."

Marinda and Charles had survived and flourished in the face of 25 years of struggles and tragedies through raising three children, but their youngest had taken them to the brink of losing each other. What they had forgotten is what you must always remember: The health of the parent team must come first, for without that, the health of the child is at terrible risk.

The fact is that most of these marriages that go bad after the teen craziness hits can be rebuilt. When we scrape away all of the mud and debris that the adolescent hurricane can dump on a marriage, we usually find two scared, lonely, and bruised partners who still love each other. They just got buried under a landslide of teenage debris, and they forgot how to keep the team alive. Don't you forget.

Team-Building Techniques for Parents Enduring Adolescence

Good parent teams are like beautiful dance partners. What looks so easy and natural to do is actually the result of lots of hard work, discipline, and commitment, and once the partners achieve a level of excellence, they must continually work to maintain those high levels of functioning. Good teams are not built by accident, and parents don't just do team-building stuff whenever it's convenient. They schedule the necessary time and they demand of themselves the emotional energy needed for their partner. They know that losing the team is the first step to losing the family. Here are some tips for keeping your team intact.

1. *Date your partner.* Do you remember how? Once a week, you fix your hair, wash the car, put on deodorant, and go get a two-hour cup of coffee with your partner—out of the house, without any kids, and with no distractions (phones turned off). Going to the movies only counts if you have that two-hour cup of coffee. Be prepared to sit and stare at each other at first, because you may have forgotten how to talk together, you know, like people? You may talk a lot now, but you do that as parents, not as people. Parents are not people (just ask your kid). Parents are bureaucrats. Parents talk endlessly with other parents about the business of running families. They debate and argue about all

sorts of frustrating issues that usually have no clear answers. Parenting is a very tough business, as you may have noticed.

People, on the other hand, have *relationships* with other people. They like talking and sharing with each other and they don't talk business. They just like hanging out together. This is how your relationship started all those years ago. The marriage and the family all evolved from this small but very powerful seed. Yet too often, the initial relationship energy that created your family gets lost in the ensuing crush of responsibility. With it goes the love spark of the family. When that light goes out, the whole family feels the loss. Like a dying solar system, the warmth from that initial love relationship slowly dissipates, causing the surrounding beings to grow cold. Our children flourish in the warmth of our love as a couple, so give your kid a gift. Love your partner. Go get a cup of coffee together. Make it a large.

2. *Support your partner, almost unconditionally.* I like it when adolescents can't remember if it was Mom or Dad who said or did something. This shows that the kid sees her parents as people so similar to each other that she can expect identical responses from them. This view of parents as an inseparable team is very calming to troubled adolescents. When they are presented with a united parental front, most teens will eventually give up the attacking, probing behaviors. Remember our brain reinforcement discussion in Chapter 7? The more that adolescent gets no payoff from being outrageous, the faster the outrageousness disappears.

Short of serious risk behaviors on the part of a parent, partners should bend over backwards to support each other in front of their kid. If you disagree with your partner, take your fight out of earshot of your child. As far as your kid is concerned, he should feel that attacking one parent is the same as attacking both. Your child needs to believe that nothing can split the parent team. He should never hear one parent criticizing or degrading the other.

Support does not mean jumping in to take on your partner's fight. If Junior is verbally attacking Mom, Dad must overcome his overwhelming urge to leap to her defense. She must stand on her own to prove to Junior that the fact that he's twice her size has nothing to do with who's in charge. Dad jumping in will seem terribly unfair to Junior (two against one) and will only set up the next Mom ambush for when the old man isn't around.

More important, whatever form your support takes—whether it's quietly letting your partner handle a confrontation on her own, or holding your criticism until you're alone—backing up your partner shows her your concern for the primary and most important relationship within the family: the one between the two of you. Knowing that someone is covering our back helps us to stay calmer and do better parenting, particularly in crisis situations. Conversely, being criticized by our trusted partner in the middle of a battle only demoralizes and weakens us.

3. *Tag team*. As one parent's energy fades, the partner's reflex should be to seamlessly move in to cover the struggle, if invited. This does not mean that you should take over when you're not wanted, but you need to develop a set of secret signals where one partner lets the other know when he is emotionally spent and needs relief. At times, the skill level and discipline required to successfully parent a difficult adolescent today exceeds the limits of one parent. Learn how to pass the ball to your partner without ever missing a stride. Your kid should hardly notice that the relief pitcher is now in.

Peter's voice was rising. It was late at night, and this attorney/father was still reeling from a lousy day in court. As his 13-year-old son kept refusing to accept the curfew limit Peter had laid out, this exhausted father felt his rage buttons being pushed. Josh had a map showing each and every one. "Well, that's just stupid," Josh sniped, "And soooo predictable. And soooo you. You know, you're really lame as a father." Madeline saw the signal from Peter. His voice-clearing along with the bulging neck veins were Peter's red flares in the sky. He was about to lose it. Without moving, Madeline moved in. "You know that your father lost a case today that he's been working on for months," Madeline intoned in a quiet and steely voice, "yet he's patiently sitting here at 9:30 at night taking abuse from you because you want another half-hour of curfew time. Joshua, listen closely to me. I pray every night that someday you can be half as 'lame' with your own children as your father is with you. For then you would be a very good man. This discussion is over for now. We can talk more tomorrow if you want."

Joshua walked out feeling like a jerk, and much wiser for the experience. He never knew what hit him. It was something called teamwork.

4. *Chat-up your partner.* In baseball, there is a prime rule that gets drummed into every four-year-old's head even before the rule about grabbing your crotch. The rule is to verbally support your pitcher *especially* when it's hot and you're losing by 12 runs. You do this to let that poor pitcher know that she's not alone—that a team stands with her sharing the load, no matter what. That rule is there not only to try to keep spirits up for this game, but also to ensure that the team's morale survives to the next.

Keep talking to your partner, particularly when he's getting pounded and he's lost his fast ball. Remember that adolescents are psychosis-carriers. They can make you crazy just by having too much contact with you when they're nuts. Your partner's soothing, cheering voice is the antidote to the contamination. It helps us keep the perspective that the insane, brain-damaged thinking that your kid just hammered you with is indeed insane. This, in turn, helps us to keep our own cool. It also helps strengthen that vital love link between partners in affirming that they will stand together no matter what.

5. *Keep your sense of humor.* Much of life is absurd. If you take it too seriously, you'll break down. Your teenager is absurdity on wheels. If you take him too seriously, you'll all break down. The problems facing you may seem catastrophic, but you must find the time to find the humor to find the solutions, or to at least survive the pounding.

Humor is our last defense against fear. It can keep the terror from taking over our souls and causing us to do nothing but panic. As parents, we often feel irreligious or disloyal when we laugh about our kid's bizarreness, but go ahead. You've earned the right to tell offensive adolescent jokes to each other (not within earshot of your kid, of course).

The humor can also help you distance yourself from the emotional beating you may be taking from your kid. Being able to laugh gives us some sense of control in out-of-control situations.

Most important, laughing together at the scary absurdity facing you helps to strengthen your relationship. Laughter helps cement those critical bonds of shared fear known only to soldiers in foxholes, cops in squad cars, and parents of troubled adolescents.

So buck up! You probably do still love each other. You're just getting pounded and you've forgotten how to be a couple. You need to try to find that old spark, that thing that made your stomach hurt whenever you looked at each other all those years ago. Remember when it seemed to be the two of you against the world, but that was OK because you had each other? Parenting a tough adolescent is you and your partner against the world once again. Rebuild that team to be sure you don't visit the postapocalyptic family wasteland: divorce.

The Powerful Impact of Divorce on Adolescents

I'm sorry, I truly am. I've tried and tried to maintain some semblance of the view that teenagers who experience the divorce of their parents can survive that process without trauma. I've tried to believe that these kids can be made to feel as healthy, secure, and positive about their futures as children from intact families. I've read those books about how teens can transfer their unfinished parenting needs to a schedule of every other weekend and Wednesday evenings and be just fine.

It's not working. I may be burning out, but I've looked too often into confused and frightened adolescent eyes that stare blankly back at me when I try to sell them this view. Their eyes tell me what my stomach knows: It's just a lot of crap that we grownups use to rationalize our own failures to meet our commitments to our children. They know it. Susan knew it.

Susan's soft 12-year-old face looked as terrified as that of a deer caught in the headlights of an oncoming truck. She knew she was about to get clobbered, but she was frozen in place, unable to give voice to her real feelings. "I don't know why they're making me come here. No offense, but I'm fine. My mom and dad have talked to me a lot about how much they both love me, and how nothing really will change when Dad moves out. They've explained how things will actually be so much better for me 'cause they'll be happier when I'm with them. I know they're right about this. I think that they have a right to be happy in their own lives. That way I'll be happy too. Because if someone's not happy in a marriage, then there's no way they can be there for their kids. Isn't that right?" As I shifted uneasily in my chair, she probed again with a voice that got too tight. "What do you think?"

I threw away my book. "Susan, I think it sucks. I think that parents owe it to kids to stay together. I think that's their job. I think that we're always telling you guys how to solve your problems and we can't even solve our own. I think that..." With choking sobs, Susan cut me off, "IT'S NOT FAIR! IT'S NOT FAIR! I DON'T UNDERSTAND! I DON'T! WHY DO THEY KEEP TALKING AT ME UNTIL I HAVE TO TELL THEM IT'S OK?"

Her heartbreak filled the office. I just let her cry for a while. When she quieted I continued. "That pain and anger you feel are the truths about your parents splitting up. That other junk is just what we grownups say to try to make things seem better when they're not."

Susan nodded knowingly. "Like at Grammy's funeral. My parents kept telling me how Grammy was so much happier in heaven, and that I shouldn't be so sad. So I stopped crying in front of them. I didn't want them to think I was selfish, but..." She started weeping again, "I miss Grammy for me. I miss her more now than ever. And I'll miss my family so much it feels like I won't be able to live. My stomach is tearing in half. I know they're not happy, but why can't they work it out? I'm not happy a lot, but I'm not allowed to run away."

The wounds of divorce to an adolescent are deep, ugly, and largely unseen, often boiling over years later as acting-out behaviors. Adolescents react very differently from younger children to the splitting of parents in ways that can have terrible consequences.

First, many teens become darkly quiet. In keeping with their need to be cool (and not express emotion), they appear to shrug off the divorce, saying, "Whatever." They distance themselves from the family, retreating to their rooms or schoolwork or friends in what looks like a healthy adaptation to the change. What you're seeing isn't healthy.

What you're seeing is devastation. The parental bonds of an adolescent child are equally as strong as a young child's, just much less visible. Teens may try to convince you that they don't care about the family, but that's just a lie to cover their self-despised vulnerability. They act tough and cool, but they're often six years old inside. That distancing is a panic reaction from the overwhelming feeling of loss and fear of the future. They know they're not ready to solo yet. Surprisingly to parents, even problematic marriages maintain very powerful connections for children. As teens look out their bedroom window to see Dad packing up his car, they can feel the flesh-tearing pain of their family bonds snapping.

Second, adolescents of divorce become deeply cynical about life-sustaining values. Values we love to preach to them about become sardonic jokes, empty campaign promises littered about on an abandoned convention floor. Words like "commitment," "responsibility," and "selflessness" become just words, sounds devoid of meaning. Worse, the words can become cons, lies we use to throw away stuff after we tire of it—like spouses, kids, and families. And please spare yourself that other rationalization about how your wonderful new relationship with another person will teach those values to your child. From his perspective, you really only get one time at the plate. Kids see those values of commitment, responsibility, and selflessness as one-shot deals. Once you walk, they run a red line through those sacred parent vocabulary words and add qualifiers like "except when..." They can never mean quite the same thing to your kid.

Third, we rob kids of parenting just at the time when it is *most* critical. Between the neurological instability of the adolescent brain (see Chapter 1) and the moral instability of the adolescent world (see Chapter 2), teenage years are the last ones you want your kid to be navigating with newly divorced parents. As all of the research makes clear, a healthy, functional, and loving family is the best antidote for adolescent madness. Even difficult marriages usually provide more of these parenting elements than no marriage. The shared-custody fantasy can never provide the essential aspects of teaming, modeling, and reinforcing that are so critical to keeping that child safe.

The long-term scars of divorce are now becoming documented in very recent research that has studied children of divorce over decades. These studies are universally showing that these kids grow up to be much more prone to serious problems than children from intact families. These problems include crippling fears of loss and disaster, substantially greater use of drugs and alcohol, and marriages that fail much faster and more frequently. Divorce is clearly not a problem-free experience for children.

Allow me a minute to apologize to the divorced among us here. I know there are often compelling reasons for divorce, and I don't wish to inflict pointless guilt on those of us who have no choice but to leave marriages. I work daily with the fallout of problems like addiction and abuse that can rip a relationship to unmendable tatters. There are many times when staying in a sick relationship might cause much more damage to an adolescent child than sticking it out. The hard reality is that some marriages are so toxic that they must be ended to minimize the damage to the family members, but remember, ending even abusive marriages can cause adolescents to grieve for the loss of the family.

Unfortunately, I see too many marriages with children ultimately shatter simply out of the unwillingness of the adults to tolerate the tremendous frustration and hard work of rebuilding a failing marriage. Too often, I've watched pride and self-centeredness whisper into parents' ears that "you deserve to be happy, too. Your kid will be fine. It's not like he's six. He'll adjust. They all do." For those folks, I need to puncture the fantasy balloons we carry around to comfort ourselves about the impact of divorce on adolescents. When we try to sell these myths to our kids, we wound them even more.

The point of my loading on the guilt here is twofold. First, if you've already divorced, stop kidding your kid that this is better for her. Maybe it actually is in the long run, but I guarantee she doesn't see it that way. Be open to her anger and grief over the split. Let her know she is right, that this just sucks, and you did let her down—that it was your job to somehow find a way to make things work out since you owed her a two-parent family. Tell her that you tried and failed. *Even if you had no choice but to end the marriage.* Be the grownup and let her know that the buck stops with you. Remember that kids can accept your failures with your straight-up admission. They'll still be wounded, but much less so. What can take them over the edge is your promoting some self-serving notion about how your divorce is healthy for them. Give it up. For when you do, your child will be able to move past his anger and slowly begin to see that maybe you really did try the best you could, and that maybe the marriage did need to be ended. And he will love and respect the fact that you were big enough to accept full blame for a tragedy that was not your fault.

Second, if you're on the brink of divorce, read this chapter over and over and get heavy into the guilt. Timely guilt can be a very smart thing. It often lets us know when we're about to be dumb. If you're about to pack your bag, about to have an affair, about to retain your lawyer, STOP NOW! First, call a one-year time-out with the luggage, lovers, and lawyers. Second, call a shrink. If your marriage is unsalvageable, you can always go ahead and divorce after the pointless marriage therapy. But if there's even the slightest chance you can work it out, is a year so much to ask?

Before you yell, "YES, IT IS TOO MUCH," go and look at your sleeping teen. Isn't it strange how in sleep that arrogant 13-year-old face melts away to that sweet 6-year-old one you miss? There's some truth to that illusion, because that 13-year-old is as soft inside as that 6-year-old. Stand there and gaze a while and then answer my question again. If you still can't find the courage to take a shot at retrieving the marriage, think ahead to how you will feel explaining to that soft face why you needed to destroy the family to find happiness. If that conversation ultimately occurs, you will need to know that you left no stone unturned in trying to preserve your kid's world. You will need this in order to survive the gut-wrenching look you will see on your child's sleeping, peaceful face.

The final excuse that I offer for guilting you on divorce is the aftermath I witness in my work with these adolescents. Their description of life after Mom or Dad's car screeched out of the driveway is like walking a battlefield the day after. The bodies may be gone, but an eerie stillness sets into the devastated landscape. In your kid's world, the stillness becomes a hundred painful little things that symbolize the one huge loss. Things like no Friday pizza because the money is so tight. Things that nobody fixes anymore, like dripping faucets and broken screen doors. Things like the circles under the eyes of an exhausted mother who tries so hard to keep life and limb together that the child learns not to ask if Mom can come to watch his game. Things like the hollow, too-loud words from a very sad Dad promising what a great time they're going to have even without Mom there. Things like strange noises never before noticed in a house that's suddenly too large, empty now of the smell and comfort of the missing parent.

These adolescents of divorce develop a subtle weary sadness around the eyes that doesn't fit with their young faces, and it seems to never leave them. I've come to believe that, at best, these kids limp along with lifelong scars in their values of intimacy, responsibility, and commitment.

This teenage wounding may be a key factor in the recent startling statistics on young adults from the National Marriage Project at Rutgers University, which shows these kids staying unmarried and unintimate well into their adult lives. Oh, they have sex, and lots of it. What they don't have are true partnerships—marriages. They idealize the concept of marriage, say they want it, and yet never seem to find a suitable mate. The women are the most pessimistic about ever finding a good partner, and unhappily report having to gear their interests and sexual habits to those of men. Real intimacy seems to be seen as something dangerous and threatening, something to be avoided through a shallow and self-serving lifestyle. Something perhaps they've had wired into their adolescent brains by watching divorcing parents? Doesn't it make you stop and think? It worries the heck out of me.

If the divorce has to happen, so be it, but be fully aware of the costs to your teenager before you pack that bag. Please, stop and think. The fact that your kid is an adolescent only increases the devastation for her, in both the short term and the long term. You may be handing down an heirloom of family dysfunction that can run for generations to come. This is serious game time.

As I finish trying to dissuade you from divorce, let me close with my most powerful weapon—to describe to you that very thing you are contemplating, that impossible activity that we're now somehow doing in record numbers: single-parenting adolescents.

Single Parenting: The Toughest Job You'll Ever Hate

Single parenting is one of those bizarre aspects of new-millennium life that has become so common that we forget how strange and difficult it is to do. Parenting an adolescent alone reminds me of that Ginger Rogers line about having to dance with the great Fred Astaire—and doing it backwards and in high heels. With more than half of the children in this nation being single-parented, we now have unprecedented numbers of homes with one parent trying to do the jobs of two. These are the Iron Men and Iron Women of the adolescent parenting world. They have to be the toughest of individuals just to survive.

The experience is much like having to suddenly live life with your leg in a cast—everything becomes four times as difficult, in a thousand ways you can't imagine until it happens to you. Like having no one to go look for her when she is three hours late because you've got little guys in bed at home. Like not being able to make sure he's not talking to the Internet crazies again because you literally cannot lift your head up at 2:00 A.M. to go look. Like stealing your teen's birthday money to buy diapers until that support check arrives, hopefully. Like weeping uncontrollably in the bathroom because the kids are pounding at the door as you try to sit on the toilet. Like getting that "late again?" look from your boss because you stayed home too long to hold your crying daughter's feverish head as she was throwing up. Like waking up to the immobilizing agony of a migraine headache, knowing you've got no back-up to help get the kids ready for school. Like being surrounded by a thousand different half-finished tasks, not one of which you can do to anyone's satisfaction. Like having life become an endless set of reminders of your inadequacies.

Remember that critical couple's skill of knowing your limits and tag-teaming, handing off the interaction to a fresh partner? Single parents go it alone, 24/7, rain or shine, rested or exhausted—and almost always, exhausted. I really can't imagine a tougher scenario for parenting teenagers, and yet these folks often measure themselves against the effectiveness of parent *couples,* and then consider themselves failures by comparison. If I played golf daily with Tiger Woods, I'd feel as incompetent as Linda.

> Linda was making my stomach tighten. This single mother of two small kids and one crazy adolescent had just finished outlining her daily schedule that starts at 5:30 A.M. and ends at midnight. Every single day. And within those 19 hours is no unfilled time. "And I get this dream a lot. I'm in my car, driving through this desert, with no landmarks. I just drive, and drive, and drive. I never seem to get anywhere. It just continues on forever, the same bleak, gray landscape..." As her words trailed off into silence, I realized I was unconsciously shaking my head, and she had noticed. "I know," she sniffled, "you must be thinking that I'm a real screw up. I can't seem to do anything right." "What I'm thinking," I responded, "is how incredibly strong you must be, and how I know I could never be tough enough to do what you do." I was not kidding. And she would not believe me.

People like Linda must first get a perspective on the enormity of their challenge and then adjust their expectations of themselves to more reasonable levels. If you find yourself embarking on this road, there are a few things you need to do before Day One.

Task One is to redefine success, both in your head and in a conversation with your adolescent. Success does not mean preserving your teenager's lifestyle to the predivorce standards. Success means you and your adolescent surviving with the important things intact. You will get carried out the door in a white coat if you try to do it all, and you will do your adolescent no favor in the attempt. Teenagers need to learn that life is full of bumps, and that they must adjust. Involving them in calm and realistic discussions about the changes can help them greatly in their maturation. Let them know specifically about the new money, time, and privilege constraints, and how you will need their help and cooperation. Delineate specific chores that need to be done, and ask your kids to pick from the pile. This gives them some control and freedom, while enlisting their help.

Before you have this talk, be sure your own understandable panic is in your hand and out of your kid's sight. No tears and no "Oh my God, we're all gonna die!" talk. Perhaps unfairly, you're the sole captain now, and quite impossibly, you've got to project an air of calm and quiet but realistic confidence. I know it can't be done. Just do it. It's another one of those parent Medal of Honor acts that will give you peace of mind in your old age. DO NOT DUMP OR LEAN ON YOUR TEEN! He may look grown up, but he's just a big, crazy kid. He's not there to support you. You are there to support him. This is your job. Remember that the impact of what you say and do right now is enormous for your child.

Be prepared for an initially angry kid, furious that she has to pay for her parents' failure at marriage. She has every right to be mad, but also look for a possible pleasant longer-term surprise. Adolescents relish any opportunity to appear grown up, and many will see this as a chance to advance their status a bit, particularly if there are younger siblings around. Changes like getting a job to pay for extras can be very therapeutic for teenagers, even though they'll act like they got drafted. Many give up a lot of craziness when confronted calmly with serious family demands.

Task Two is to preserve as many of the old rituals as possible. If you used to eat out with your teen every Friday night, keep some version of the event going. Try finding cheaper but special alternatives, like making pizza together. These symbolic rituals are enormously reassuring to an adolescent reeling from a recent divorce. Trust me on this one, because he'll act like he doesn't care. He does.

Task Three is to hold fast to the rules. Expect some testing to see if you can still enforce the laws around the house now that you're alone. It's nothing personal; it's just what teenagers do. Stay calm and keep reminding her that many things did not get lost in the divorce, one being your memory of her curfew. The testing may be aggravating, but you'll see that this is how your adolescent will eventually calm herself and settle back down to the rules.

Task Four is to enlist help. And lots of it. Line up friends, neighbors, and relatives as back-ups for adolescent crisis situations. If you are of the opposite sex from your kid, find some same-sex role models for your teen, particularly if your ex runs off to Mexico and doesn't come back. Many issues of adolescence can only be easily shared with someone who uses the same rest room.

Task Five is to reset your priorities. You cannot do it all, so be sure what you do counts the most. If you plough into this tough time on automatic pilot, you will burn out doing things no one will really miss anyhow. Then your kid will really miss you. Take time to write down your list of tasks, customs, and rituals, and start to prioritize items. The comforting and protecting parent-child activities all stay. The silly status and neurotic cleanliness items get red-lined. For example, no, the laundry does *not have to* be folded. Yes, you *have to* check out the parents hosting that sleepover. No, you do *not have to* buy him Abercrombie & Fitch for his birthday. Yes, you *have to* make a cheap, but big, embarrassing fuss over his birthday. No, you do *not have to* buy her those CDs. Yes, you *have to* show interest in her music (music?). No, the rugs do *not have to* be vacuumed daily. Yes, you *have to* check on his homework daily. No, you don't *have to* scrub the sink every night. Yes, you do *have to* lie on a bed together every night for at least 15 minutes staring at the ceiling fan and yacking about her day.

Task Six is to go back to Task Five and strike the least important *have to* and add one last nonnegotiable item: Keep yourself healthy. If you don't survive with some sanity, no one else will. You must find the time for a weekly restorative activity to keep yourself OK, or no one in your family will be. Do one activity that brings you some peace. For some, this is coffee and browsing at the bookstore. For others, this is a bruising game of over-40 basketball. For many, it is a single-parent support group. These support groups can be wonderful places to hear survival tips from veterans who have faced those same fears confronting you and lived to tell about it. You may think you have no free time for this, but you'll lose your sanity if you don't make the time.

Will your kid get mad as you head out to the bookstore when she wanted you to stay so she could have friends over? Do bears poop in the woods? When she protests, what you say is, "Gee, I'm sorry, honey, you have a right to be mad, but I'll be back in two hours." What you think is, Gee, I'm sorry, honey, you have a right to be mad, which is what I'll become if I don't get two hours away from you.

Task Seven should be in red letters since it is so important and so frequently overlooked: Hold on to your child. Find something that brings you together—an organized activity, a weekly movie night. It's far too easy to let him spiral away from you given the extreme demands of parenting solo, his size, and his incessant mantra that he's old enough to be on his own. He's not. Don't start believing the mythology of brain-damaged adolescents.

While we're exploding myths, let's talk about that fantasy that often arrives on the heels of divorce while under the boot of single parenting. It's that magical merging of two existing partial families with adolescents into one happy, smiling group. Welcome to the alchemy of the new millennium: the blended family. Somehow we've convinced ourselves that we can take two sets of wounded people, mix them together, and like the alchemists of old, turn lead into gold. By the way, did you hear that some of the Brady Bunch have rap sheets?

Blending Families with Adolescent Children: Welcome to the Playoffs

The peak of the single parent's dream is the valley of the divorced adolescent's nightmare: the blending of families with adolescent children. It's a recipe for disaster.

Take all of the tumult of standard adolescence and put it in a large bowl. Mix in a few years of parental feuding to include late-night screaming sessions, icy-cold silences, spouses not coming home, emotionally unavailable parents, and extramarital affairs. Now add the spices of divorce, like shredded parental bonds, fear, vulnerability, hopelessness, and loss of respect. Age this mixture a bit, then place it over the heat of children watching parents dating other people. When the sauce is truly volatile, toss in a flaming match of remarriage and bringing strange kids into the family as instant siblings. Stand back and be sure to act shocked and appalled at the amazing explosion in your child. Is this kid insane, or what?

Blended families are an aspect of new-millennium life that is so common and so bizarre that we've become blind to how impossible a concept this is for adolescents to deal with. They go along with it for a time and act like it's normal because we act like it's normal. But it's not normal. Like divorce, this is a limp-along process, not a restorative one. Doing this exacts a cost on your teenager. It doesn't build them up.

Divorced parents contemplating remarriage usually feel like they've found the oasis of salvation after trudging alone for years in a horrid desert. The exhaustion of single parenting can cause a selective blindness to the impact that dating and remarrying can have on an adolescent child. Let me remove the blinders by describing a typical blending process from the eyes of an adolescent.

Initially the divorce trauma rips up much of the old parent attachments for the kid, and redistributes them along new parental loyalty lines. These new alignments are shaped by things like which parent the child sees as the victim, which he blames for the divorce, which he thinks needs him the most, and so on. Adolescents more than younger children are forced to make these terrible loyalty choices since courts usually let teenagers pick their custodial parent. This sets up a scenario where the child (known as "loyal child") usually goes with the victim (known as "victim parent"). Humming "You and Me Against the World," victim parent and loyal child set off to try to cope with this new hostile universe.

Things often calm down here, as basic survival becomes the all-absorbing and unifying goal for parent and child. Suddenly Mr. or Ms. Right appears and seduces victim parent away. Loyal child acts happy for the parent. He won't express his feelings of betrayal out of his duty to protect victim parent from further pain. Loyal child sees victim parent becoming more and more distant, and loyal child becomes more and more scared while smiling his approval.

Just when loyal child is barely hanging on, victim parent announces remarriage and introduces strange-looking, weird-smelling, instantly disliked instant siblings who are also straining to maintain that same hollow smile as loyal child. Victim parent takes to the pulpit daily to preach about how wonderful it will be for loyal child to have a family once again. Loyal child begins to secretly cry at night, thinking that he already has a family that's been scattered to the wind, and feeling that this new family is mostly just to help victim parent pay for Friday-night pizza, fix the drippy faucets, and repair the broken screen door. The truly crushing realization is that, once again, a parent chooses to act on his or her own need rather than worry about the hidden needs of loyal child. Before it was the "bad" parent doing this. This time it's victim parent. Now loyal child truly knows the meaning of alone.

Loyal child attends the wedding, moves in with instant siblings and smiles a lot for a while. Then all hell breaks loose when stepparent orders loyal child to stop leaving soda cans in the family room. Victim parent brings loyal child to shrink's office to have him fixed since he's obviously crazy.

This script is an oversimplification, but one that basically describes too many kids I've worked with who tell me these things. In the shrink world we have lots of sanitizing words to make us feel better about this particular scrapple recipe we mix with our kids. We describe the process of blending families as going through neat little stages that lend an air of normalcy to this abnormal process. Younger kids can make these transitions better than teens. For teens, the blending process can be of the Waring variety.

The psychology-scrubbed version of this seven-step process for families goes like this. First is the "fantasy" part where we think our new family will be The Waltons. Second is the "fake assimilation" where we all pretend we're doing fine. Third comes the sinking feeling that we label "awareness." All hell breaking loose is a good way to describe the fourth and fifth steps, called "mobilization" and "action." "Contact" and "resolution" are the happy ending terms to describe the coming together and bonding of this new family. Sounds comforting, doesn't it? It's like neatly packaging red meat in plastic so that we don't have to think about the reality of the slaughterhouse.

In much the same way as visiting the slaughterhouse, working with adolescents has changed my views of the impact of family blendings. It's that last part of the seven stages, the adolescent happy endings, that I quibble with. Where divorce and remarriage are concerned, teenagers are different from younger kids and have a much tougher time fitting in. They have longer histories and stronger loyalties with the lost families. They have higher cognitive abilities and much less tolerance for hypocrisy. They also have enough cynicism to power a Russian novel. Even after achieving "resolution" with the new family, adolescents often maintain a scornful and sardonic view of those values that are so critical for their maturation: respect, commitment, responsibility, and selflessness. They see the value of these words degraded, first by divorce, and then by the "re-using" of the marriage vow by their parents.

It shows in their language. Years after the fact, adolescents talk of Dad's "new wife," not of their stepmother. They refer to Mom's "new kids," not their step- or half-siblings. They call the replacement group their "new family," not their family. The unspoken, perhaps unrealized, inference is that these are like new and better appliances. An adolescent is smart enough to know that all appliances get worn and need repairs, and that we grownups love to get shiny new replacements rather than work to fix the old dented ones. Knowing this makes them sad.

Randy paused to reflect, and then opened up "My new family's OK, I guess. At least for now. Dad sure acts happy. He's, like, bouncing all over the place yelling 'Happy, Happy, Joy, Joy.' He's speeding. I've never seen him like this. Now that I think about it, I guess he's scared. He should be. He doesn't know it yet, but I can see that his new wife is gonna be a lot worse for him than my mom was. What made him think this one was gonna work out better than my mom? How can he act so happy when he just crumpled up our old family and threw us in the trash can?" Randy's pain was quiet now. It would likely get louder later. "The worst part is how he keeps telling me how his new wife is like a freakin' Mother Theresa. This is while she's looking at me like she wishes I'd get abducted by aliens. He gets so stupid saying this crap, I can't even talk to him anymore."

So how do you shield your adolescent child from pain in a family blending? First, you stop thinking that you can. Recognize the fact that this is another one of those things that just sucks for your child. When we try to tell kids how great something is that isn't, we lose them. Allow your adolescent her pain. Respect it as real. Don't try to happy-talk it away by rationalizing your remarriage decision or discounting her feelings. She hates it when you say things like "I'm sure you'll feel better later on." Just sit and listen to what she has to say, particularly if it is critical of your decision to remarry and start a new family. You want her spewing the poison out of her, not holding it in. The simple act of quietly listening to your kid knock you for remarrying is helpful. Your nonjudgmental support helps her remember who you are, or at least who you were to her. It helps rebuild that parent-child bond that seems to be breaking up. Sometimes the simple listening can be the start of some healing.

Michael sat with that 16-year-old gunfighter slouch next to his father on the couch, staring away from Dad as if he could not possibly muster any more disinterest in the old man's words. The first five of the eight years since Dad left had been marginally OK, but the last three summers saw father and son grow completely apart, with Michael becoming more and more dysfunctional and Dad becoming more and more angry. After Dad tried the usual "why can't you be" lecture and got the usual "screw you" response, I asked Dad why he was here. After all, I noted, they had virtually no contact now with Michael living at his mother's full time, so perhaps they didn't want a relationship?

The big, imposing, and controlling man disappeared. A much smaller, softer, and loving father took his place. Looking confused and hurt at my question, Dad quietly answered, "Because I love and miss him, of course. He's my son. Why do you think I fight with him?" A glistening, watery light in Michael's diverted eyes showed me something I'd never seen in him in six months of work: real emotion. "That's a lie!" Michael stammered with a quivering chin. "You love your new wife and your new kids more than me. You do whatever she says and take her side even when you know she's wrong. Your new kids, they're just perfect! They make their beds, never argue—they do all that junk I can't do. I'm sorry! I'M GODDAMN SORRY BUT I'M NOT THEM! I'M JUST ME, DAD, REMEMBER ME?"

Michael paused to take a breath. His words came now between sobs. "You used to joke about my messy room and then help me clean it up. Now you tell me how upset I make your new wife, and what a bad example I am to your new kids. You made it real clear, Dad. I'm not good enough for your new life. None of us were ever good enough for you. That's why you left to get another family. Why don't you just say it like a man?"

Dad's chin now quivered exactly like his boy's. Tears began streaming down his strong face, tears that Michael had never before seen. With a voice that broke under the weight of years of repressed guilt and pain, Dad brought all of us to wiping our eyes. "Michael," he choked, "I do remember you. You are my son. My first-born child. You are the greatest miracle of my life. I remember that I held you in my arms the minute you were born and I promised you I would always be there for you. You opened your eyes and looked right into mine like you had heard me." Dad waited for his throat to clear and then finding no voice left, whispered the rest. "I didn't keep my promise. I'm sorry. I know I let you down."

Dad's head dropped in weary sobs. Michael instantly shed his 16-year-old punk veneer and tearfully turned towards his father. "I'm sorry, too, Dad. I know I've been a prick. But you never talked to me like this before. It seemed like you really didn't give a damn anymore." Michael began to open up and explain, "Look, Dad, I just can't be part of your new family. I don't fit, and you're always caught in the middle. I don't like them and they really don't like me. I'm rap music and street hockey. Your new family likes going to a country club. I want to be with you, but I think my being there just makes us all crazy. Maybe I just can't live there with you."

Michael eloquently stated the real dilemma of the adolescent in family blending. Sometimes it is impossible to create new family bonds with the replacements for the old family members. The very assumption that this should be possible is dangerous. If you're attempting this family-blending maneuver, lower your expectations and get help. It's very hard work. Don't lose whatever connection you can maintain with your teenager by compulsively chasing your fantasies about unifying the new family. As the Rolling Stones would say, you can't always get what you want, but if you try, sometimes, you just might find you get what you need.

What you might need now to get some of what you want are additional tips to minimize the tumult when blending families with an adolescent. Remember that these are ways to reduce, not eliminate, these feared problems.

Tip Number 1 is to not fear the problems so much. Think of these as flags that let you know which inevitable problems need to be worked out. The faster the flaws in the new family are recognized, the better the odds that they can be minimized. Keep those initial fantasy expectations low.

Tip Number 2 is to find some megadose patience vitamins for the new adolescent stepparent. That person needs to reread Chapter 7 a few dozen times, particularly the discussions on respect. You see, that new teenage stepchild who is smiling at you is being so nice now because she doesn't see you as a parent. She's got two parents already and has no intention of breaking in a third. You're just some semipeer who seems to make her bio-parent happy. She thinks it's cool that you love her parent, but in her mind this has nothing to do with her. That's why when you criticized her for coming home late she looked at you like you were crazy, just before she went crazy. Remember, having respect is critical to having any control over an adolescent, and that respect is something that can only be earned, never demanded. Earning that respect is tough enough for bio-parents over a lifetime of interaction. Stepparents get to try to do this over eight weeks at Parris Island.

The key is incredible patience. The stepparent must start out very slowly in the discipline role, leaving the bulk of that to the bio-parent. The new parent must meticulously build up a parenting bank account of respect currency, and only withdraw what has been earned. There's no credit in the respect game. So at the pace you think you're earning this kid's respect, you can also ease into setting some limits. Start small and slowly build your involvement. If you overdraw your account, the adolescent explosion will be your insufficient funds notice. Don't sweat the first few notices. Everybody bounces checks until they get this straight. It is very, very hard. Err on the side of conservatism, meaning when in doubt, keep your mouth shut and let the bio-parent wade into the mess with the kid. The two of them likely have an established set of rules by which they sort out these conflicts, and you need to sit back to learn these while you build up your respect fund. If you go in like General George Patton, your sweet stepchild will redefine "blood 'n guts" for you.

Tip Number 3 is for the stepparent to give the adolescent stepchild lots of control in setting the rules of engagement. Let the child take the lead in establishing how intimate she wants the new relationship to be. All kids are different, and they themselves won't even know how they want things to be until they get into the new family and muck around a bit. The stepparent should always display a gentle invitation to closer ties, but let the kid set the pace. Remember Cindy's monkey Simon in Chapter 6? That's the idea here as well. Even if the stepchild never shows that she wants a close relationship, she will nonetheless respect the wise stepparent who doesn't force herself into the kid's life. That may be sad for the newly married bio-parent and stepparent, but it also may be as good as it gets in these tough scenarios.

Tip Number 4 is a message directed at that sad other bio-parent who is sitting on the sidelines watching some new rookie take his place with his ex and his kid: Watch out for your own capability to be small. One of the few guarantees I can give you is that your adolescent child will be bursting with terrible stories to tell you about your replacement. He'll do this out of loyalty to you, out of anger at having a third parent, and out of a "never say die" desire for his bio-parents to reunite. DON'T GO THERE WITH HIM. If you do, you will be throwing firebombs into that new family that is barely surviving now.

If you relish that thought of hurting your ex, then think about your kid. Sitting and gossiping with her about that new low-life stepparent is one sure way to guarantee extensive and needless pain for your teenager. If you contribute to a war within that stepfamily, the casualties will include your own child. Your impossible goal now must be to help your teen adapt to the new family. Listen supportively without judgment to the stories, but keep suggesting that she take her complaints back to the new family for discussion. If you have serious concerns about what you are hearing, secretly talk these over with your ex. Never, never get down into the mud. If it helps you to do the right thing, be comforted by the fact that over time your kid will come to respect you for having taken the high road here. And you will teach her wonderful lessons about selflessness that she will carry forever, and pass on like diamonds to her own children.

You can take your helmet off now because Part Two, alternately titled "Let's Beat on the Parents," is finished. Get your next cup of tea and find that yellow highlighter (it's in his backpack under that half-eaten Moon Pie). You're going to want it handy as we venture into Part Three for those down-and-dirty, straight-up, and field-tested strategies for surviving your child's adolescence.

Yes, you're finally ready.

Part Three

PUTTING IT ALL TOGETHER:
FIELD-TESTED STRATEGIES FOR EFFECTIVELY
PARENTING YOUR ADOLESCENT

THERE WAS ONE GOOD THING about those good old days of parenting. It used to be easier to keep the insanity away from children.

Maureen began to breathe more easily now. As she finished her story about finding out that her 11-year-old son was part of a neighborhood ring that had weekly afternoon booze parties, she began to speak more slowly. "Dylan kept it all hidden so well. If he drank too much, he'd wait it out before coming home, saying that he was having dinner at someone else's house, or sleeping over. It's so embarrassing to say this, but none of us parents had any inkling that this was happening. The kids hid it amazingly well. If it weren't for the one girl who got drunk so often, we still might not know.

"It was like that movie, *The Great Escape*. The kids had systems worked out to do this without getting caught. They knew which parents had liquor around that was never used, which parents were not home at certain times, which parents might be more suspicious, which breath mints worked best—it was incredible. They had cover stories to explain away all of the potential problems." Maureen paused and shook her head. "I grew up in the projects. I don't remember anything like this happening there. We had our share of craziness, for sure, but most of us just never did this sort of thing. Why was that?"

She began to answer her own question. "First, no one had any booze that the parents wouldn't miss. Second, I don't think we had that much spare time. Most of us were working by the time we were 11 and 12. And drinking hard liquor never appealed to us and most of us would have gotten beaten even more than we were already if we got caught.

"But there's another thing here that's very different. The craziness comes to you. We now live in a beautiful neighborhood, with very successful families. I remember thinking when we first bought this house that my children will never know the insanity and despair that comes with living in a project. I thought these pretty houses would protect my children." Maureen laughed sadly here. "I asked Dylan how this whole drinking idea came about. He told me that the kids were all home alone one afternoon in a neighbor's basement watching music videos. One came on showing kids just a little older than them drinking brandy and cruising around in fancy cars. It looked really cool, so they started the weekly drinking club."

Maureen leaned forward to emphasize her point. "I asked Dylan if he thought this was a cool thing to do. He told me that he actually hated the taste of the liquor, and he didn't like getting buzzed, but that he knew he had to 'acquire a taste' for booze, since this is what high school kids and adults drink all the time. He didn't want to be seen as a geek when he started high school in the fall. Dr. Bradley, he's 11 and he's trying to acquire a taste for brandy?"

She shook her head once more. "There is no shielding of children anymore. There's no innocence. You can't move away from the insanity. It comes to your door. It's in your basement. It's in your CD player. It feels hopeless to me."

Maureen touched on what may be the biggest change in raising adolescents today. The insanity is indeed in your basement. It rains down on your brain-damaged adolescent's head 24 hours a day, 7 days a week. The old days of removing children from bad influences are gone, just as the old days of beating children are gone. It used to be easier to physically move children away from sources of insanity, or terrify them so they would avoid the insanity. Today, we must *vaccinate* our youth to resist the exposure to this plague that we know is constantly attempting to infect them.

This concept of *inoculating* adolescents against the craziness versus *isolating* them from the insanity is a complex challenge for contemporary parents. It is five times the job that confronted parents in the past. Parenting teenagers is no longer a game for well-intentioned, naive amateurs. Today, it is a game for well-trained, savvy professionals. Welcome to Part Three of your training.

After all of that preparation in Parts One and Two, you are now ready for the "how-to" of parenting adolescents. Before we proceed, let me emphasize two points that apply to all of the chapters that follow. First, remember that this model of parenting teenagers is based on all of the information and training provided in the previous chapters. Using the suggestions in Part Three without the grounding provided by Parts One and Two would be useless. As you understand now, it's more *who you are* than *what you say* that leads to success in raising teenagers.

Second, try to become comfortable with a new and uncomfortable parenting concept: Your goal is not to create perfect adolescent behavior. This is not possible, anyway. Your goal is to build unprecedented parenting skills so you can respond with discipline, strength, and love to your kid's imperfect behaviors in order to inoculate her against the greater insanities awaiting her in the world.

In this part of the book, you'll learn to not be so terrified of the screw-ups that are bound to happen, and to see them not as horrible failures, but as wonderful learning opportunities for your children that will strengthen them so much more than if they are perfect for you— that is, if you learn to use the screw-ups wisely.

A core concept of this inoculating model works just like vaccines do. When your kid got vaccinated, the nurse injected her with the very disease you were hoping to avoid. The vaccine was a weakened version of the virus that allowed your kid to develop an internal defense system to the bug. You had to give her a little of the disease to save her from the disease. She had to be able to defend herself when the unavoidable exposure ultimately occurred. She couldn't live a normal, healthy life if you tried to just isolate her from the virus. Isolating her actually increases the risk of terrible damage when the inevitable exposure occurs.

With the inoculating model of parenting, you want your child to get small doses of the insanity in a safe, controlled environment (his house, his family, his loving supports) where you can supervise the resistance-building exercises.

If your son abuses alcohol while he's still at home, you can teach him about the dangers while he's still in a safe, controlled environment. You don't want your kid's first exposure to alcohol to be 500 miles away at a frat party at 2:00 A.M. If your daughter lies to you about her friend stealing her parents' car, you can teach her about what trust and friendship really mean in a place where the stakes are much lower. You don't want her deciding these issues when her roommate asks her to lie to the police about the heroin the roommate is using.

The reality of the world today is that you are not powerful enough to keep the madness out of your child's life, but you can become strong enough to make your child strong. How you do this is what Part Three is all about. Chapter 9 begins this process by teaching you the basics of how to successfully interact with today's teenagers.

Chapter 9

THE 10 COMMANDMENTS
OF PARENTING YOUR TEEN

Ever take tennis, music, or karate lessons? Remember how the instructor started out by teaching you a bunch of small, unconnected movements that you eventually linked together into one complex, smooth-flowing response? Well, here you are again.

The basic movements I'll describe in this chapter are the small pieces that make up the more complex responses you'll learn about in upcoming chapters and that you'll be using to handle the countless teenage crises I don't include in this book. Think of it as a puzzle. I'm giving you the pieces in this chapter, which you'll use to put together different puzzles of your own.

Just as with those other training lessons, these techniques are easy to talk about and hard to do. The skill development occurs with practice, not with reading.

Myron was an airline pilot and a father to an adolescent. During one session, he was reflecting on how much better things were with his son since he began responding differently to his son's provocations. "You know, there's a lot of similarity between the training for parenting and the training for piloting. It's often not the problems that cause crashes. Frequently it's our bad reactions to the problems that create the disasters. Until recently, I didn't know how to react to my son in a crisis. No one showed me. My training was bad.

"All my life," he mused, "I thought I had been trained on how to parent. Not from watching my father, but from watching TV. I thought *Leave It To Beaver* showed me all I needed to know to calmly raise my son without screaming and hitting like my father did with me, but I must have missed the episode where Wally gets in June's face and screams that she's an evil bitch. I used to wonder what Ward would do then.

"At least now I know what I'm supposed to do, but it's not easy overcoming my earlier training. I think I'm doing well about 80 percent of the time. I know the more I do this, the better I get at it. Just like flying."

There are three things that have completely changed the rules of parenting adolescents. We now know that kids are crazy (see Chapter 1), the world we've created around them is crazier (see Chapter 2), and we can't beat them up anymore (see Chapter 7). These realities of the new millennium reshape the way you must approach the entire exercise of parenting teenagers in its most basic form. This encompasses everything from how to touch your child to how to talk with her.

The rules that follow are presented as commandments for reasons other than humor. Just as with the biblical commandments, these general rules are subject to interpretation as dictated by the individual differences of your child and yourself. Feel free to improvise and build on these concepts to fit your particular situation. The best version is the one that most closely applies to you and your child.

The first commandment offers a model for parenting adolescents that applies to every other rule. Where did I get the inspiration for this model? From getting traffic tickets, of course.

I: Thou Shalt Be as the Dispassionate Cop Unto Thine Own Child: Be Cool, Not the Fool

When interacting with your teenager on any issue that might get her upset (which could be anything at all), remember your experiences with the heat. All those moving violations you accumulated in your crazy days are about to pay off now that you are confronted with someone else's crazy days.

There are two kinds of cops who give you tickets for blowing through stop signs. The first type is angry, sarcastic, and bullying. She has her spotlight in your face, her hand on her gun, throws the ticket in the window, gives you a nasty lecture, pretty much dares you to say something back, and then storms off into the night. What's in your head as this goes on? Calmly reviewing your bad driving habits and thinking of ways you can improve your behavior? Not likely. You're completely focused on the *cop's* behavior, not your own. You're writing down her badge number, demanding her commanding officer's name, and so on.

What you're doing is raging back, although quietly if you're a sane adult versus an insane adolescent. You're completely engaged in plotting ways of getting even, of responding only to her rage, and not to the real issue: the missed stop sign. Your own driving behavior is the last thing on your mind. You might even feel justified that you jetted past that sign, since it's such a stupid place to have a stupid stop sign, anyway. And if you pulled up to that same intersection tomorrow and saw that cop sitting there staring at you from her squad car, wouldn't you feel a strange, suicidal urge to maybe not come to a complete stop just to show her you're not afraid?

There's a second cop who tickets you for the same offense. He's the nicest guy in the world. He's respectful and calm, and in a monotone voice he quietly points out that you missed that stop sign. He seems almost sympathetic *even in the face of your distress.* You get the same ticket. He says, "Sorry about this. I can see you're in a big hurry, but please be more careful. I'm sure your family would prefer you arrive home a little later, but safely. And, by the way, watch out ahead. There's a traffic jam on the expressway; you might want to take a right on Elm so you'll miss it." He wishes you a nice day and drives away. As this cop disappears, what are you thinking about? Are you mad at the cop, or at your own driving behavior? Which cop would have the greater chance of influencing you to drive better?

That second dispassionate cop is the smart one in two ways. First, he keeps the focus of the whole disciplinary exercise on *your* behavior *in your own head* by not triangulating this scenario as that first angry cop did. She took the two critical elements of you and your behavior and then interjected herself into the middle by being angry. Her anger became a diversion for you so you didn't have to think about your own behavior and responsibilities. In a sense, she let you off the hook by pushing you around.

The second dispassionate cop was much tougher. He got in and got out of your situation quickly and smoothly without distracting you with his behavior. He made you confront your own.

That dispassionate cop's approach was smarter in a second way: He has far fewer physical confrontations. His calm demeanor deflates any ideas you might have had of becoming furious or disputing his control. That first angry cop had you thinking about nothing *but* rage and control. The second cop never lets these rebellious thoughts become options since he's so calm and confident. He lets you know you're not in his league in terms of power and control by *never referring* to his power or control. He never even allows them to become issues. It's just implied and immediately understood without any words being spoken. He's completely unthreatening, completely unintimidating, and completely in charge. You're a minor leaguer talking to the Cy Young Award winner. You can't make him nuts. He keeps his cool. Even if you begin losing your own control, his calmness seems contagious, helping you to regain your composure. If you snap and yell at him, he just stays calm and says, "Sir, no one's yelling at you."

How does he do that? Training, training, and more training. The fact is that the entire approach to law enforcement has undergone the same transformation that is now required of parents of adolescents—and for many of the same reasons. In the old days of parenting and policing, both sets of professionals were able to use brute force a lot more to get the job done (see Chapter 7). But times have changed, and we aren't allowed to rough up offensive drivers or offensive adolescents anymore. The cops had to learn a whole new set of people skills to replace the old billy club skills. Just like you, they had a terrible time in the initial transition as physical force was outlawed as a routine enforcement technique. Many officers couldn't believe that this dispassionate approach could work. They saw it as being weak and becoming vulnerable to abuse and assault. This model was completely contrary to both their initial training and their own experiences.

When the cops overcame their skepticism, they found that this dispassionate approach actually *lessened* the chances of physical attack and reduced the frequency and ferocity of verbal abuse, as well as increased the chances for voluntary compliance. It works well for cops. It works even better for parents. Using this approach helps your kid not get diverted by your own angry behavior, increases the rates of voluntary compliance, and greatly reduces the odds of having a physical confrontation with Junior.

The sobering fact is that we have to rigorously train police officers in this technique even after preselecting candidates who possess these skills to begin with, since dispassion goes against our innate reflex of lashing back at displays of anger or control. We must even more rigorously train parents in these techniques for two additional reasons. The first is that we don't select parents based on their psychological skills. In the business of shaping human beings, it's pretty much potluck who ends up doing the shaping. Many people who parent need lots of training. The second reason that parents need more training than cops is that having your own child provoke you is more difficult to handle than the provocation of a stranger.

As hard as these techniques might be, the obvious payoff is well worth the effort in both parenting and policing. Of those two styles, the angry one or the dispassionate one, which do you see as the stronger? You might be more afraid of the angry authority, but which would influence you more? Which one would you see as being more powerful and more likely to earn your respect? Most important, which of those people would you want to emulate, and whose opinions would you value more?

Which one of those cops would you want to be? Which one of those parents do you want to be?

Take a minute and be sure you understand this dispassionate approach to exercising parental power. As we proceed through the remainder of this book, we will often be referring to this dispassionate cop model as a prerequisite for all the skill training that follows. If you find you cannot interact with your kid calmly, get some coaching now (see Chapters 7 and 16). Nothing else will work until you master this first skill of the dispassionate cop: keeping your cool.

Having learned that, you're now ready to learn the next two skills in the program, ones that you thought you learned when you were two years old: how to talk and how to listen. But talking well with a teenager is like learning to play the blues. Before you can play, you've got to do a whole lot of listening.

II: Thou Shalt Listen Even as Thine Own Child Shouts

The first part of learning how to talk has nothing to do with talking. It has everything to do with listening, which typically we're really lousy at. Not that you don't have a good excuse to be that way. As parents we are bombarded with nonsensical noise, much of which emanates from our offspring when they are small. We get used to not listening since we have so many other things we need to focus our attention on. As our small children talk, we frequently nod and grunt "Uh-huh, uh-huh" assuming that there's no intelligent life in there (*"Mommy, mommy, watch this. Mom, are you watching? Watch this. Mommy? Mom?"*). This is an understandable, but bad, habit.

As these mush-mouthed creatures get older, they get a lot smarter and start to say a lot less. We chase them to get precious adolescent sentences out of their mouths, but we are crippled by our bad habit of discounting what they finally say as stupid, arrogant, or that worst of worsts for teens, childish. These unthinking parental responses are the death knell for communicating with your kid. What they said may have seemed stupid, arrogant, or childish to you, but these are precious, important thoughts shared by very vulnerable people. Their initial presentation may be poor, but don't judge the book by its cover. The more they talk, the more sense they will make to you as they sort out their thoughts. They may not speak or think so well yet, but they are just learning the difficult art of adult discourse and thought. Criticizing their initial efforts is a sure-fire way to get them to become entirely mute. Let's look at a few examples of good and bad listening.

Bad Listening:
   Teen: "I hate school. I'm going to drop out."
   Parent: "That's stupid. You don't hate school. And I forbid you to drop out."
   Teen, thinking: *"OK. Screw you. If I can't drop out, I'll just flunk out."*

Bad listening means criticizing his words and telling him what he has to do, thus ending both the conversation and any chance you had at influencing his thoughts. You might win this one battle and force him to go to school on Monday, but you'll never help him work out his thinking, which might win 100 Monday battles at once. Now that he's an adolescent, the days of safely disregarding what he says as unimportant are over. You would not allow him to drop out of school anyway, but what is the payoff in immediately jumping on his head with your bottom-line position? Why not let him talk it out? There can be great advantages in listening well.

Good Listening:
    Teen: "I hate school. I'm going to drop out."
    Parent: "I'm sorry school feels so terrible. Can you tell me what it's like for you?"
    Teen, thinking: *"I feel better just having brought this up. It's nice Mom's not flipping out on me. Maybe I'll keep talking. I really don't want to drop out, but I'm having this problem..."*

Bad Listening:
    Teen: "Not one person in this world loves me, especially you."
    Parent: "That's crazy, honey. I love you, your dad loves you, your goldfish..."
    Teen, thinking: *"I'll just shut up since apparently I don't even know what I feel."*

Good Listening:
    Teen: "Not one person in this world loves me, especially you."
    Parent: "It must be awful to feel like that. I'm really sorry. What tells you that no one loves you?"
    Teen, thinking: *"Maybe Mom does care a little bit. She's actually listening to me without telling me what to think."*

Good listening means saying as little as possible to get your kid to say much as possible. It means showing respect for your kid's thoughts and feelings by allowing him to express what he feels, particularly if you vehemently disagree with his view. You can always go in later with your evidence showing how people love him, but keep this as a separate discussion from the one in which your kid actually shares his feelings with you.

That kid *knows* that people love him. Yet he *feels* like no one does. What we know *cognitively* and what we feel *emotionally* can be very different. Of the two, you want to focus on your child's emotions. This helps your kid to *talk* crazy more often and *act* crazy less often.

Acting crazy can actually be a direct consequence of bad listening.

Bad Listening:

> Teen: "There is no God. Your religion is lame. I'm not going to church anymore and you can't make me, and another thing you might want to know is that I think religion is only for weak-minded people."
>
> Parent (interrupting): "Oh yeah? Well, nobody's asking you! You're going, and that's that!"
>
> Teen, thinking: *"I wonder if he's still fast enough catch me if I just jet out the door."*

Bad listening is interrupting, asserting your power, and inviting a confrontation. It's letting your anxious urge to protect your child run ahead of your parenting training. It's taking your child's words too seriously, forgetting that being a brain-challenged adolescent means having lots of impulsive, illogical, and provocative thoughts that don't necessarily represent what the kid was trying to say. Bad listening doesn't allow adolescents to see their more important thoughts, which are hidden beneath their opening words. Listening well can help your kid get there.

Good Listening:

> Teen: "There is no God. Your religion is lame. I'm not going to church anymore and you can't make me, and another thing you might want to know is that I think religion is only for weak-minded people."
>
> Parent: "I'm sorry if it feels like I've been forcing something stupid on you. Tell me more about your thoughts on God and religion."
>
> Teen, thinking: *"I never thought she'd make me think about this stuff. I thought she'd just snap out. What do I really believe about God?"*

Good listening means modeling the critical first step of communication: *good listening.* If you want your kid to learn this, you've got to show her how. Over and over and over again. Listening means trying to set your own thoughts and feelings aside to let your kid talk without judgment. It means putting yourself in her position, seeing the world from her vantage point—not to see *if* it makes sense, but to see *how* it makes sense, at least to her. It means doing this particularly when you are tired, scared, or mad.

Michael's eyes filled with tears as he recalled the story of how he had listened to his son about as badly as anyone can. "I was in a rush that night. I had a couple of last-minute cancellations that allowed me a rare opportunity to have dinner with my family. I was particularly on edge because we had adopted a very difficult one-year-old just a month before, and we were all stressed and exhausted. I had this fantasy picture in my head of taking my ragged family out for a rejuvenating and relaxing dinner. I rushed into the house yelling for everyone to get ready since I only had a little time. My son, Ross, who had patiently suffered the most from all these adoption changes, began dragging his feet to get ready. As I pushed and prodded him to hurry, he began to talk. I began to not listen. 'ALL RIGHT, ALL RIGHT,' he yelled, 'I'm just getting my CD player. GIVE ME A MINUTE, WILL YOU?' I saw tears of frustration in his eyes, but I still wasn't listening. 'GET IN THAT CAR NOW,' I barked in my best army voice. 'DAD...' he appealed one last time without finishing his thought. I cut him off and repeated, 'NOW!'

"Ross became very upset. He jumped into the car and began punching the seat in frustration, causing the baby to cry. She had definitely been neglected in a previous foster home and possibly abused, so seeing my son go nuts in front of this scared baby made me do the adult thing in response: I went nuts, too. 'HOW DARE YOU!' I bellowed over and over. 'HOW DARE YOU! GET UP TO YOUR ROOM! NOW!' I chased him up the stairs, yelling and releasing all of my frustration and anger. As his door slammed and I heard him crying inside, I turned to my wife to share my outrage over his behavior. As I began to tell the story, I finally began to listen to Ross—except it was my wise wife talking for him.

'He's had it very rough this past month,' she said softly, 'Tonight he was looking forward to just having some quiet time to himself, something he's had very little of recently. He didn't want to go out with the baby. He's had enough and needs a break.' My wife quietly blew gaping holes in my rage justification. I hate it when she's that smart.

"If you looked up the word 'jerk' in the dictionary that day, you'd have seen my picture. Now I had finally heard what my son was trying to say, but only after I had demolished him. I hung my head, went upstairs to his room, and explained how I screwed up, that all the rage he felt from me was not about his behavior, it was about my own shortcomings. I apologized for not listening to him.

"Ross made me feel even worse. He didn't have the decency to scream and yell at me. He just forgave me, apologized for yelling, and hugged me with tears still in his eyes. I carry those tears in my own eyes now. They help me remember to listen."

Entry from the personal journal of Dr. Michael Bradley.

If you don't want to find your picture next to Webster's definition of "jerk," you must engage your kid on her adolescent brain-dysfunctioned level to get her perspective, and to do that you must often sidestep a provoking, arrogant, and apparently crazy initial exchange of words. *The fact that her words or actions are crazy does not mean that the underlying thoughts and feelings have any less value to her than yours do to you.* Listening means valuing your kid's thoughts and feelings as being important to her, and thus more important to you. If you don't learn the art of listening you will never learn the art of helping her to think, because helping her to think requires that you master this next commandment of interacting with adolescents, which you can only do after you've got Commandment II down.

III: Thou Shalt Not Shout: Speak Thou Wisely

One of the worst things you could do to yourself is to tape-record your critical conversations with your adolescent—those little talks you have when he's not doing so well that seem to blow up all the time. Listening to your own words will sound like dragging your fingernails across a chalkboard. About 90 percent of what we say to our teens in these situations is useless, loud, and often inflammatory. Our discourse is mostly comprised of messages that are maddeningly repetitious, hopelessly predictable, painfully obvious, or childishly patronizing. When we're giving adolescents negative messages, we use too many words, we talk too loudly, we issue challenging ultimatums, and we get in their faces to be sure they've heard us. Sometimes when we're really mad, we stand too close and raise our hands and maybe even jab them with a finger. In short, we break about every rule the teen culture prizes about effective peaceful communication. We talk about as well as we listen.

Here are the rules for speaking when visiting the adolescent world and conveying difficult messages. These basic guidelines will be expanded in the chapters that follow. *Before you skip over this list thinking that these are silly suggestions that cannot make that much of a difference in communicating with your kid,* harken back to your classroom days. Remember that English teacher you loved who used to jump all around the classroom, act crazy, and make you do most of the talking? Remember that history teacher who used to stand in one spot and read his yellowed notes for 50 minutes in a monotone voice while he twirled his nose hairs? The presentation of the message *is* the message. If you take the time to respect your child's needs in communicating difficult messages, he will know that you care about him. He might even listen.

Here's your list:

- Use fewer words in shorter sentences. The more you talk, the less they listen.
- Don't repeat yourself. Don't repeat yourself. Don't repeat yourself. (It's very annoying.)
- Lower your voice. The louder you are, the less they hear.
- Keep your hands down, especially when your kid is upset. Hands in faces are very provocative to teens. Never crowd them physically or verbally.
- Use "I" statements. Speak more about your feelings than their behaviors. Talk about how sad you were when he was mean to his sister, rather than what's wrong with him.
- Organize your thoughts before you start to talk. This art of adolescent communication is hard work. Edit the first draft of what you want to say before you speak. Like my Chinese fortune cookie once read, "Open brain first, then mouth. Foot hard to put in brain."
- Gauge your kid's mood before starting tough discussions. Monday mornings at 7 A.M. are bad times to bring up school issues. Timing is everything in the world of adolescent discourse.
- Don't cram too much into one conversation. Take frequent breaks if you see frustration building on either side. Once it gets hot, you won't get anything good done anyway. Don't hesitate to say, "Let's continue this tomorrow."
- Allow your kid to use the pressure-relief valve of walking out at times. Although it might appear as simple defiance, it might also

be her way of avoiding snap-outs. Let her know that her walking away is OK if you pick up the conversation again later.

◆ Don't go to ultimatums unless absolutely necessary. Kids see ultimatums as challenges to be risen to no matter what the cost. If you feel an ultimatum coming, it's time for a time-out.

I saved the most critical rule for last: Don't ever talk down to your adolescent. If you can't get your head into a position of respect for his feelings, don't start the conversation. Take the time to look past the parts of him that are making you mad and find those good things about him to build on. If his schoolwork is sliding since he made the track team, go in leading with your pride about his athleticism and his ability to devote so much time to that discipline. DON'T FAKE THIS. Find something that you genuinely like about him, then ease into the "but I worry that this takes too much of a toll on you" part. Express concern for him, not marching orders.

Finally, some contradictory advice. Talk a lot to your kid about non-difficult issues. Sports, weather, news, whatever. With these, be chatty. And go on endlessly about what your kid does well. He may think you're a little silly and too talkative, but that's OK if this happens in *noncritical* conversations. Communication works better the more it's used. If you guys get into the habit of shooting the breeze, it not only draws you closer, but it makes conversation seem normal. Many adolescent parents get into the bad habit of approaching their kid to talk only when there's a problem. The very sound of your voice can then become a signal to your kid that another grilling is coming. It's tough enough talking to a teen. You don't need them hearing your first words as an air raid siren.

Bug them for time together to allow for these silly and critical conversations. Negotiate, whine, and bribe to get a few mealtimes a week with them. Don't get put off by the eyes rolling and the "Oh Mmmm-mmoooooommmmm!" sighs. Admit to being hopelessly corny and sentimental. Don't stop selling just because you get a few doors slammed in your face. Your kids really do want you to want to hang out with them, even when they turn you down. It protects them when they are reminded of your unconditional caring, of the bond you share that goes with them wherever they go. It helps them remember that the beacon of your love is always there to guide them home when the storms hit hard.

IV: *Thou Shalt Add 15 Minutes to Every Interaction Involving Thy Teen*

Successfully raising a brain-dysfunctioned adolescent is a job for professionals, not amateurs. No matter what the specialty, the pros are set apart by their habit of meticulously planning their moves, while amateurs just react. Pros know that they can't have an immediate answer to every situation, so they build in contingency plans to cover the inevitable problem solving they must do. They are confident enough to freely admit when they don't know something, and they allow themselves the time to figure out a good response. Amateurs tend to panic and respond quickly and poorly because they think they should know all the answers all the time.

Nowhere is this distinction more critical than in the profession of adolescent parenting. By now you have learned that, if nothing else, your kid is unpredictable and has a talent for presenting you with complex situations when you have no time to think.

As an attorney, Debra was trained to think on her feet. "It's what I do for a living," she explained, "so why am I so lousy at this with my 14-year-old? There I was rushing out the door late for court when my son Stephen asks if he can sleep over at Ron's tonight. Ron's father is the rabbi at our synagogue. 'Of course,' I laughed, 'as long as there won't be any booze or girls there.' Luckily, I glanced back to see him look away. That always means trouble. I froze in midstep. My eyes got big. 'Ron is going to have beer there?' I asked incredulously. He shook his head no. My eyes got bigger. 'Girls?' I nearly screeched. 'GIRLS?'

"Stephen went on the offensive. 'It's no big deal, Mom. Everybody has coed sleepovers these days. We're not all uptight like you guys were when you were kids. There's not like any real sex going on or anything. Everybody's going to be there. I have to go! I really, really have to!'

"My head felt like it was going to explode. My mental list of court tasks evaporated as a maze of bizarre thoughts and questions flooded my head: The rabbi approves of this? Am I uptight? How hurt will he be if I say no? What was I just doing? Oh, yeah. Preparing to help decide the fate of someone's life. WHAT THE HELL DOES HE MEAN 'NO REAL SEX IS GOING ON?'

"As I picked up my dropped briefcase I was astounded to hear my own voice saying, 'Well, I guess it's OK if the rabbi's going to be there, I guess?' I half-mumbled something else that even I didn't understand and rushed off to court. Two hours later as I'm listening to an important witness drone on, I saw a message flash across my eyes that said, 'ARE YOU CRAZY?' At the break, I raced to the phone. When I told Stephen I had changed my mind he went berserko. I'll spare you all of his screaming words by summarizing his theme. It focused on how stupid and weak I was for always changing my mind. His reaction would have not have been one-tenth as bad if I could have taken the time to sort out that decision on the spot. It wasn't my job to find out if the rabbi was actually allowing this. It was my job to let my son know clearly and calmly where I stood on the issue of coed sleepovers. I'm not going to allow myself to get ambushed again."

As a professional parent you must develop the habit of tacking on 15-minute bumpers to every schedule and every interaction you have with your teen. The potential consequences of your reactions to your kid are so high that you must never get backed into schedule commitment corners when making tough decisions. I know you have no time. I also know you don't have the luxury of having no time. You must build in these 15-minute contingency slots for these emergencies. If there is no time, refuse to make the decision and tell your child that you need to have the opportunity to talk this over with him later. He won't like it, but he'll learn that ambushing you will not assure that the dice will roll his way.

The primary reason you need to develop this habit is not just to make safer decisions. The real goal here is to provide yourself with a controlled system of decision making that allows you to incorporate all the positive parenting principles we've discussed so far, and some you've yet to learn. This includes elements such as consistency, teamwork, discussion, planning, teaching, modeling, and that perennial favorite, respect.

The second goal of controlled decision making is to reduce the frequency of nasty experiences such as tantrums, threats, inconsistencies, and holes in walls. These will cost you dearly in your parenting efforts.

V: *Thou Shalt Vanquish Thy Foolish Pride*

Go find that trash can where you threw out your need to be cool. You'll want to toss your pride in there as well.

As the parent of a young child, you got used to winning control skirmishes. You usually could out-talk, out-think, and out-run your child whenever you wanted to. This was very bad. It gave you a feeling of control that created a false pride, particularly as you saw the abuse that other parents were taking from their adolescents. Outwardly, you were sympathetic. Inwardly, you were smug: "My kid will never act like that when she's a teen."

Mother Nature, God, or fate hates smugness, and the payback is called adolescence. Suddenly, you can't out-talk, out-think, or out-run your child. She's louder, smarter, and faster than you are. She's also willing to be a lot crazier. These are fatal factors for your old style of parenting where you thought you could raise an adolescent with decorum, style, and foolish pride. Give these delusions up for now. They will only handicap you in the long run.

As we talk about more complex response strategies in the upcoming chapters, I will be assuming that you have left your old, foolish pride on these pages. What does it look like?

Foolish pride means having to get in the last word. The last word to your teen is an astronomical concept called infinity. It will go on forever.

Foolish pride means thinking that because you said "jump" your kid will jump. To your teen, the shouted command "jump" means sit still and sneer coldly at your parent even if it costs you your life.

Foolish pride means being terrified of looking like those weak parents you used to be smug about, those silly ones who "let" their kids act that way.

You need to change that foolish pride to a more mature pride. What's that look like?

Mature pride means giving your kid the last word because he's crazy and in pain, and because it teaches him things he doesn't yet understand, like patience, tolerance, and giving someone else the last word.

Mature pride means giving your kid lots of space to rebel when you've asked for compliance on something. It means giving up your own childish need for control—to see your kid jump just because you said so. It means understanding that your kid's eventual compliance with your request is a huge victory.

Mature pride means giving up your need to look cool in public. It means that you never change your behavior or your rules with your kid just to avoid a public scene. It means taking your public verbal lumps without raging back at your teen and then seeing those parents of pre-adolescent children look at you with their outward sympathy and their inward smugness. Feel sorry for them. You know what's coming in their lives. Paybacks *are* tough.

Mature pride means surviving rage without raging back because the lessons you can model for your child are more important than your own feelings.

Mature pride means setting aside your own needs and focusing exclusively on your child, on the long-term struggle to create a decent human being out of this creature who specializes in short-term devastation.

You can hold onto your foolish pride and lose your child to the insanity of adolescence—or you can embrace a mature pride and forge a loving connection with the heart of your child that no adolescent storm can break. It's your choice.

VI: *Thou Shalt Not Kill* *(Thou May Entertaineth Thoughts of Killing, But...)*

Congratulations! You are now officially discharged from the army of hitters of children (if you were ever in that group). As the parent of an adolescent, you must assume the status of conscientious objector. You don't do violence anymore. You don't hit, smack, butt, throttle, jab, or even look like you might ever do any of these things. You draw an invisible circle around your kid and you never cross over that line uninvited.

You will do this for two reasons. The first is that hitting doesn't work, anyway (see Chapter 7). The second is that smacking an adolescent is an experience very much like whacking at an old stick of dynamite. Often, it doesn't explode right away, but when it does, it will demolish everything around it. The question is why would anyone whack at a stick of dynamite or at an adolescent?

"Because he dared me to," Jack answered when I asked him how he ended up smacking his 14-year-old son Damon the first time. "He told me that he was bigger and tougher than me, and he asked what I was gonna do about that. He said that I was no longer in charge of him and that I'd better not mess with him because I'd go down. He got up in my face. He called me a pathetic old man. You have to answer challenges like that from your son, don't you?"

"How did that work out?" I asked, avoiding his question for now. "Great," Jack answered, "at first, anyway. Damon calmed right down. He apologized and everything. Then a month later we did the same thing. Now we do this almost weekly and the fights are getting worse. I broke his tooth last week. That's what brought me here. I don't know what to do when he gets in my face. I think we both hate this, but why does he keep provoking me? And why is it getting worse, not better? It seems like Damon is getting worse."

Damon was not getting worse, he was learning. Jack was teaching Damon that their weekly boxing matches were how he should sort out issues like who's in charge and why. Slapping an aggressive adolescent is the same as slapping a mentally ill adult. Your kid is just nuts right now, and he'll get better unless you start to hard-wire in this aggression by rising to its physical challenges. It's normal for all kids to have the realization that you are no longer their physical equal. A few kids will test this out to see what the new rules are, *particularly if you made a habit out of spanking them when they were smaller, which told them that physical strength was the source of your parental power.* If you are or were a believer in corporal punishment, start training for that teenager test now. Even if you have never touched your kid, you might get provoked into reacting physically.

What do you do if challenged to a fight? Nadine had a good response.

"Derek got right up in my face. He's only 13, but he's huge and very strong." Nadine swallowed hard, as if recounting a terrible trauma. "He was screaming that he didn't have to come home until he felt like it. He was trying to back me down. He shouted, 'I COULD PICK YOU UP AND PUT YOU THROUGH THAT WINDOW IF I WANTED TO, AND THERE'S NOTHING YOU COULD DO TO STOP ME.'

Then he waited to see what I would do.

"I knew that what I said next would be very important. It felt like I was on trial. I stayed real still, lowered my voice, and looked him straight in the eyes. I said, 'Derek, I know I'm no match for you physically. I am very proud that you have grown into such a strong young man. When you were so sick when you were a baby I always prayed that you would be bigger and stronger than me, but I've never thought of that as being part of our relationship. I'm afraid I don't understand your point. What does your physical strength have to do with my being your parent?'

"Derek stared for 10 seconds with those furious eyes, and then he blinked. When he blinked again I knew I could breathe again. The rage just drained out of him as he unclenched his fists. He walked away without a word and I let him. Later he came back to apologize. He felt terrible. With tears filling his eyes, he told me he thought he was going crazy that he could do such a thing to me. I told him he wasn't crazy, he was just young, and it was all right. He let me hug him for the first time in weeks.

"Maybe I shouldn't jinx myself but, you know, in my heart I believe he'll never do that again. I think he learned something important that day. It was just the way that he had to learn that was scary. I guess some teenagers have to learn like that."

Derek was one of those. His now-estranged father had smacked him around a lot.

If you got as white-knuckled at Nadine's story as I did, then you were wisely remembering all that scary stuff you read about teens in Chapters 1 and 2. These poor kids are brain-challenged, hormone-saturated, and living in a world that loves and honors rage. In Chapter 12, we'll talk at length about how to respond to adolescent rage, but until we get there, please don't take a swat at that unstable mass of adolescence in front of you.

On a related issue, be careful about all forms of physical contact with your kid—even the ones you think are nice. Tousling his hair might be a favorite of yours that drives him up a wall. Maybe you can't pat her rear end anymore. Even though you still see her as a little girl, she might be operating on woman rules now. Check out these forms of physical endearment with your kids and get their permission. Don't take their silence as their approval. They might just be acting nice. They sometimes do that, you know.

One of the ways they become nice is by learning the most critical skill we imperfect beings must master in order to survive in relationships: the art of apology. For here lies our salvation and redemption as human beings.

VII: *Thou Shalt Apologize at Every Opportunity*

The most powerful weapon in your arsenal of adolescent parenting is the one I see used the least: the apology. We've been talking a lot about how talking a lot at your kid is a poor way of communicating. Lecturing, admonishing, threatening, and commanding are useless methods. His anger just shuts you down after a very small exchange. His defenses and rebelliousness don't allow you to finish a sentence. So as you stare at his fortress walls and wonder how to get inside, remember that tale from Greek mythology about the Trojan horse. A parental apology is that Trojan horse you so desperately need.

Teenagers are expert at deflecting adult discourse. At peak periods of rebelliousness, they can repel any advance you might make at starting any conversation in which you might (gulp!) actually try to teach them something. (My son has a sign that reads "Attention teenagers: Move out of the house fast while you still know everything."). But they have one glaring weakness that makes them vulnerable to emotional growth: They don't know quite what to do when a parent apologizes, except to sit and listen. It neatly sidesteps all of those obstructions of anger, rebelliousness, and denial, and provides a rare, direct line to their souls. It's great!

Apology provides you with a vehicle for sneaking in all sorts of important lessons for your kid—lessons about respect, humility, honesty, courage, self-discovery. The list goes on forever. Your kid will listen intently when you're telling him how you screwed-up with him and why you owe him an apology, as long as you keep the focus exclusively on you, not on your child. Apologizing models, teaches, and heals both the child and the contrite parent.

So why don't we use it more? Ask Amy.

Amy stared at me incredulously after I told her to apologize to her daughter for forcibly drug-testing her and having the test come up clean. "NO WAY," she almost spit at me. "After all the hell Corinne's put me through, the lies, the deceptions, the 'let's do drugs' notes I found? Absolutely not! I was completely justified in testing her. She fits the profile of every drug-user checklist I've ever seen! What would you have done, Dr. Bradley? Just sit there and maybe have your kid overdose? I don't think so! This is ridiculous!"

Amy was very mad. I put my clipboard down, capped my pen, and leaned forward. "Look, Amy, this is not about what I would do. If you want me to answer your question, I probably would have done something dumb like your drug-test idea a lot sooner than you did. I'm not as strong as you are. I could never do the single-parent grind that you do every day. I know I'm not that tough, so if you think I'm judging you, be clear that I see you as way ahead of me in strength of parenting. I'm your mechanic, not your priest. I just tell you what works and what doesn't with your family engine.

"What works here is to apologize to your kid. Now! Especially while she's so mad and more likely to do something crazy. Were you parentally justified in making Corinne pee in a cup? Absolutely! And that's got nothing to do with why you should apologize. Is Corinne justified in being outraged that you made her pee in a cup? Absolutely! And that's got everything to do with why you must apologize, because you're going to sit down next to her, watch her angrily turn away from you, and watch her become filled with outrage. You're going to use her outrage as a way of connecting with her.

"You're going to tell her that you were way out of line in not respecting her word to you that she was not using. You're going to tell her that you are ashamed of your own behavior here and that if you were her you'd be furious, too. You're going to tell her how this is another example of how you attempt to control her too much, and of how you have problems trusting people because of what you went through with your own father and with your ex-husband. You're going to tell her that, at first, you were going to blame her behavior as your justification for the drug test, that your first impulse was to make this all her fault, and that you're ashamed of that, too."

Amy interrupted me, "But her behavior is why I did the test." I put up my hand. "Let me finish, Amy. You're not done apologizing yet."

Amy stuck her tongue out at me and we both laughed. "I know I'm pounding you too hard, too fast," I explained, "but we haven't got time for the slow version. Corinne's at a very critical point right now.

"You are not going to say 'but Corinne, you made me,' and you are not going to say 'but Corinne, you have to understand my position.' You're going to leave those very legitimate excuses out of your talk like leaving huge, empty holes in a picture. Corinne is not stupid. She knows very well how justified you were and how she was provoking you to do this, and she will be amazed at your strength in not saying these things to her.

"You're going to go on to say that you have a tendency to put all of the blame for your problems with Corinne on Corinne, and that it's very hard to sit down and confront ourselves about our own contributions to craziness. Then you're going to finish with a flourish and talk about how you violated her trust, and what trust means to you. Amy, what does trust mean to you?"

Amy sighed sadly. "Having been betrayed by both my husband and my father, I see trust as a delicate and precious flower that needs constant care and work, one that is easily killed and very difficult to grow again. And as I'm talking, I'm seeing a thousand connections between my distrust of Corinne and what I went through as a child, one huge one being that my father never, ever apologized to me for abusing me."

Amy sat back, exhausted but calm. "I'm also going to ask her what these things mean to her, and how I can start regrowing that flower." She looked up. "I get it now. I'm ready."

Like I said, Amy was a lot tougher than I am. While under the fire of her adolescent crisis and her own old personal one, she made this apology. That night she left a 2:00 A.M. message on my phone machine.

"I know you're not there, but I had to tell you about my conversation with Corinne, which just ended. I was so scared she'd see me as weak for apologizing. WRONG AGAIN! She was incredible. She opened up and talked and talked and talked. I can't believe it. She told me how much she wants to be like me, how strong I am, and how hard she thinks she's been on me. She admitted to me how she has sometimes violated my trust in her, and how she hates that feeling as much as I do. I told her I was going to have to drug-test the both of us now since we must be hallucinating—that there's no way we could actually be sharing like this. We laughed until we cried, and hugged. Just thought you'd want to know." I did.

Amy's story encapsulates all of the critical aspects you must include in a powerful apology. Make it heartfelt, make it self-disclosing, make it honest, make it humble, and make it focused only on *your* foul-ups. Make it everything you want your kid to be someday. Never contaminate your apology by demanding that your kid understands why you did something, or that he apologizes in return. If he does, that's a bonus. If he doesn't, it really doesn't matter, for the real art form in reaching difficult adolescents is quietly laying in small, important thoughts for them to mull over on their own time. The screaming invectives just bounce off their armor. The quiet, self-risking, embarrassing, and vulnerable disclosures of parents pass right into their tormented souls. Maybe this is nature's way of shaping us up to being honest before we're granted access to the hearts of our children. I don't know. I'm just the mechanic. I do know that if you want to reach your angry child, you could do a lot worse than apologize. And given some of the behaviors we'll discuss in this next commandment, you won't find yourself short on reactions that warrant an apology.

VIII: *Thou Shalt Honor Thy Child's Identity (Even Though It Maketh You Ill)*

This next rule is another one of those fundamental guiding principles you must incorporate into all of your interactions with your kid. Get ready.

Green hair, pierced tongues, save-the-unborn-chicken diets, pants with crotches so low that they need skid plates, and car stereo systems so loud they can shred brain tissue are windows into that wonderful, horrible, laughable, and frightening adolescent struggle called identity formation. All of that frenetic and seemingly insane behavior of trying everything and keeping nothing the same is actually the most critical challenge of your kid's teenage years. It is also the most critical challenge for stunned parents sitting on the sidelines watching their child take on personalities like some creature from a *Star Wars* movie. What you are watching in disquiet amazement is your kid doing her No. 1 job: She's trying to figure out who the hell she is, which is a very hard thing to do, particularly in this new millennium.

The importance of identity formation in teens was one of the casualties of the political wars against psychobabble. The sarcasm and anger poked at terms like "values clarification" and "identity crisis" caused this most basic and most important of adolescent developmental tasks to get de-emphasized and shown the back door in many discussions of parenting teenagers. But this is what your kid is doing, whether politically correct or not. She is clarifying her values because she doesn't know what they are, and she is having a crisis of identity because she doesn't have one.

WHAT EXACTLY IS IDENTITY FORMATION?

It is a process by which your kid tries on a thousand different hats to see how they feel, to see if any of them seem to reflect who he is. These hats may include clothing styles, hair styles, religions, foods, vocations, music (music?), sleeping schedules, sleeping locales, sleeping clothing, social activism, social isolation, selflessness, selfishness, drugs, politics, sex, aggression, nonviolence, peer choices, academic achievement, academic underachievement, and so on. In other words, all that the world has to offer as ways of being a human being.

If this seems foreign to you, be comforted in knowing that in the old days, many of us don't recall having had the time for identity crises. We were too busy just trying to stay alive or earn money for college. The fact is that many of us who didn't complete that adolescent process when we were teens ended up going through this chaos at 30 or 40. Sooner or later, we all have to figure out who we are and what we believe in. The ticket puncher of life forces you to eventually stand up for something. Take it from a late bloomer, this is done better earlier than later. You want your kid being crazy while you're still around to protect her.

Today this process of identity formation has become twice as hard as it ever was before. The options for experimentation are overwhelming in number and much more lethal in consequence (see Chapter 2). This is another example of how the adolescent world you knew is just an old movie to your kid. You must work that much harder at easing your kid's transition through this tricky time, for this is another way to inoculate her against the insanity.

WHY IS IDENTITY FORMATION SO IMPORTANT?

Identity formation is critical because everything that follows in your child's life hinges on the successful completion of this process. In short, knowing who you are is the key to all else that is good in life. When your child's identity is formed (or consolidated, as we like to say), she will find the end of that terrible time called adolescence. Almost magically, wonderful things begin to happen. Life looks much more positive and exciting. Levels of energy rise. Challenges are gifts to be eagerly sought after and mastered with an air of quiet confidence. Overwhelming teenage frustrations become the minor annoyances of adult life. Crazy drives for impersonal sex become lusts for true intimacy and commitment. Self-serving behaviors transform into healthy needs to serve others, to give back, to have children. This is how you got into the fix you're in now (raising a teen), and yet, for most of us, even with the trials of parenting adolescents, these demanding times show us at our best. This is the stuff of life—and it can't happen without identity formation.

HOW SHOULD IDENTITY FORMATION HAPPEN?

If I could bottle the ideal way to go through this process, I'd be on *Larry King Live.* This is another one of those maddening questions of balancing two contradictory concerns that will keep you awake at night. On the one hand, you want your kid to be trying out everything as much as possible to learn what fits for him and what doesn't. On the other hand, it would be nice if he lived to be 20, wouldn't it? The best I can tell you is that you want to have your kid do this experimentation in a safe, secure environment with parents who are supportive of his explorations.

Becky smiled as she sat down. This single mother of a difficult 14-year-old girl had not sat down and smiled in the 10 months we had worked together. "Do you remember when I first saw you about Lynne last year? Do you remember how I told you that one of the many things I wanted you to fix was her punkish appearance?" I nodded, suddenly realizing how much older Becky looked than at that first session. She didn't look bad, just like she had been through a lot. Her face also looked much more peaceful than I'd ever seen. She continued, "Check this out." She stood up and opened her coat. She was wearing an Ozzy Osbourne shirt that had been a battleflag when it was first purchased by Lynne. "We've had our first good month in over a year. It feels like we've got a connection again. I think as I stopped fighting over the nonsense, the nonsense became less important to both of us. As I became more supportive of these things, she stopped embracing them so passionately."

"And are you headed to Ozzfest?" I asked. "Not yet," Becky laughed. "I found all of her old wardrobe in our clothes basket for the homeless shelter. Lynne asked me why I had retrieved this shirt, since she was 'way past that immature phase.' I told her we didn't want to add to the problems of a homeless family by giving their daughter a shirt like this. We were actually able to share a laugh together. You have no idea what that means to me. I'm keeping this shirt to remember what is truly important. It's being able to laugh together."

The key phrase here is *became more supportive,* because if you are able to stay cool as you see scary things parade around in front of you in the guise of your child, your kid's explorations will usually stay low-level, low-risk, and short-term. Your child will respect you for honoring her differences, especially the wackier ones, and ultimately she will come to assume most of your moral-ethical identity features, anyway (see Chapter 7). In your kid's head, she will associate your values with qualities like strength, tolerance, and love. That's not a bad crowd to be associated with, a fact that won't be lost on your child.

The key is to balance this supportive approach to identity exploration with the goal of keeping her alive. We'll talk more in upcoming chapters about specific strategies to use in the life-threatening explorations, but for now, be aware of the dilemma and the elusive balance you must find to protect you child. DON'T JUST CLAMP DOWN.

If you become angry, controlling, and critical of these 30-day free trials of identity weirdness, his low-level explorations will become oppositional crusades and he will seek out the precise antitheses of your values and shove them up your nose. Your reactivity can take a vital developmental and usually harmless process and warp it into a terrible war of attrition between child and parent. He will become the opposite of you not because this is who he is, *but simply because this is who you are not.* You do not want this to happen. You can condemn your kid to a lifetime of terrible identity pain with consequences that can include intimacy problems, relationship failures, multiple divorces, broken homes for his children, depression, anxiety, poor career choices, and so on. It is an ugly picture. Remember it.

As I watched Dean and his dad sit down across from me, it was like looking at a photograph accompanied by its negative. Dean the father and Dean the son were almost physically identical in body features and almost completely image opposites in every other way. Dean the senior, true to his military profession, looked every bit the officer: clean-shaven, cropped hair, and wearing conservative and meticulously clean clothes. Even his belt buckle was exactly aligned with his pants edge.

The 15-year-old Dean was a little different: scruffy semi-beard, unwashed and matted hair, punk clothes, enough body piercings to qualify him as a lightning rod, and a bookbag sporting a bumper sticker that read "Join the Army: Travel the world, meet interesting people, and kill them!"

As if out of a *Star Trek* episode about reversed, parallel universes, I was further intrigued to hear the same voice come out of these two distinct, yet identical bodies. They presented the problem, the insight, and the answer all at once without knowing it. Dad went first: "My son despises me. He hates me, my job, my religion, what I stand for—everything. If I say white, he says black. This started two years ago with the clothes and progressed to last month when I turned him into the police for possessing marijuana. Look at him! He's completely out of control, failing school, running away, and now he's some freak pothead. And the judge sent us to you for family counseling? Doctor, my son needs a prison, not counseling. He's way past counseling."

Dean the son interrupted Dad. His voice was so similar that if I closed my eyes I might not be able to tell who was talking: "Yes of course, Colonel, even the judge couldn't know anything better than you. You know everything there is to know that's worth knowing, right, sir? Isn't that what you always say? Well once again you don't know what the hell you're talking about. 'Cause it was YOU who hated ME first. Nothing I did was ever good enough. Whatever I wore, you had a comment about it AND IN FRONT OF MY FRIENDS! Do you remember at my twelfth birthday party how you made fun of my baggy pants in front of everyone so bad that I had to go and change? AT MY OWN PARTY? No, sir, you probably don't, 'cause you don't give a damn about me. You never have."

Dean Junior continued: "And the drugs? That's right, Colonel. Me and grass, right up your ass! I intend to do every drug I can, whenever I can, and there is not one f'ng thing you can do about it…" Dad leapt half up from his seat towards his son, yelling "SHUT UP!" but he had trained his son well to never run away from a fight. Junior moved even closer. "Oh, that's real good, sir. GO AHEAD. YOU WANT TO HIT ME? TAKE YOUR BEST SHOT, OLD MAN, 'CAUSE YOU AIN'T NOTHIN' ANYMORE. PUNCHING ME OUT DON'T GET IT DONE NOW, SO WHAT ARE YOU GONNA DO? SHOOT ME? YOU'D BETTER 'CAUSE I'M NOT CHANGING AND YOU CAN'T STAND WHO I AM."

These two were the same even in confrontation. As they both struggled to do their best macho routine, the hurt, betrayal, and pain of love lost was crying out in both of them, but they were the only ones who couldn't see it. They were the same person sharing the same anguish and struggling with the same blindness towards themselves. The shouting faded to the sounds of only heavy breathing of these combatants who remained nose to nose. As I watched these two identical, yet opposite, faces glaring at each other I quietly intoned, "You guys ever watch Star Trek…?"

What's the strategy with your reverse mirror-imaged child? Pick your battles. In short, if it's not going to kill him, forget it. Wherever you can, get out of the way of these explorations and let the world teach your child as many lessons as it can so that you can stay supportive (*"Bad break, son, about your tech teacher not allowing you to wear kilts into the auto shop. The world is filled with these kinds of silly rules. I thought you looked cool in that skirt, I mean kilt."*). If the exploration dabbles in the "this might kill him" realm, don't rush to the ultimatums. Start backpedaling and thinking about other ways to sidestep or compromise on the issue.

If she's decided that backpacking alone through the Swiss Alps at age 13 is next on her list, support the intent of her idea, if not her expression of that intent. For example, you might wax on with her about how great that would be, and what an incredible girl she is to want to do something like that. Suggest that she might want to research this a bit to find out what park rules there are and how much preparatory experience she would need. She might start training in the local foothills with you or a group of friends. Perhaps she can save up for one of the many excellent adolescent wilderness adventure programs that exist today. Rolling with and supporting these scary identity explorations can lead to all kinds of growth opportunities for you and your kid.

Crushing an identity exploration by jumping up and yelling, "Absolutely not, are you crazy?" can lead to a missing 13-year-old hitchhiking to the Swiss Alps.

Keep terrible pictures of the consequences of incomplete or crushed identity explorations clipped on your mental visor. They may help you stay composed as you squint at his blindingly iridescent purple hair spikes and attempt to operate your mouth in response to his question, "Well, what do you think? Cool, huh? I had to really hassle the hair lady to get this done in time for Uncle Kevin's wedding tonight. After all, I am the best man. Dad? Dad? Are you OK? You don't look so good. Dad?"

IX: To Thine Own Self Be True

One of my shrink friends claims to have originated a phrase that I love. He says that adolescents are psychosis carriers: Contact with them can make you crazy. There's more truth than humor there as far as parents are concerned, for those difficult times with a teenager can slowly tear at the fabric of the parents' self-concept, causing them to begin to doubt their own worth and competence. We all joke a lot about adolescent acting-out behaviors, but we forget that somewhere a mom and dad are desperately soul-searching and self-blaming as they watch their beloved child act crazy. This pain and guilt can be quite intense, since we live in a culture that loves to gossip, judge, and assess blame.

Truthfully, when you see a teen yelling at his parents in a mall, don't you stare at them as they quietly turn and walk away, to see if you can figure out how they screwed up to produce a child like this? Don't you form bad opinions about those dispassionate, controlled parents, attaching labels of incompetence or weakness to them? I know I do, reflexively, without thought, and I'm the guy who tells parents not to rage back. But when I see this in action, part of me winces at this display of parental "weakness." It's just that old training, I guess.

These judgments are not lost on parents of acting-out teens. Reread the parent stories told throughout this book, but this time focus on the emotional state of these mothers and fathers. Those feelings of worthlessness and self-doubt can lead to another problematic element in the parent-child relationship: parental loss of identity.

Commandment VIII talks about how critical identity is to healthy functioning. Adolescents in crisis can assault your identity to its core, causing you to forget who you are. The screaming at home can become a contagion that spreads throughout your life to infect your work, your play, and your relationship with your spouse. You can forget that you're a successful, fun-loving, and competent adult. Slowly, you sink into seeing yourself as nothing but a parental failure. This leads to some bad consequences.

The first is that, as you feel worse, your ability to respond to your kid as that dispassionate cop erodes. As you lose that calmness, your outbursts of anger or despair only reinforce your kid's acting-out behaviors and bring on more of them. You'll also start to *truly hate your own child* for making you feel like this, and then you'll have more reason to hate yourself for having such terrible thoughts about your kid. This downward spiral feeds itself.

The second consequence of parent identity confusion is a tendency to try to become something we're not. At first glance, changing ourselves may seem logical. After all, if who we are is not good enough, then we must become something else, so we try changing.

On the surface, we might try to dress more hip, pretend to like their music (music?), or adopt their language. Inside, we may stop displaying our own values and try to act more cool about things we're not really cool with. We start to give up our rules and beliefs and, in general, we sort of apologize for being who we are, since our child clearly hates us. *These are not the changes that I'm encouraging you to make.* I know this may sound contradictory, so read slowly here.

It is most vital that you remain who you are *particularly* in the face of an adolescent crisis. Your kid needs stability around her as she gets tossed around by one insanity or another. Those outdated clothes of yours will become welcome signs of safe anchorage for her, even as she rolls her eyes at your hat. Those outdated values of yours become a critical counterpoint that she needs to see constantly, as she makes up her mind (forms her identity) about sex, drugs, and rock 'n roll. The changes I pound you with concern *how* you should present those values that define you.

It is critical that you hold firm to your values about sex, drugs, and rock 'n roll. Don't change that, but it is no longer effective to physically threaten your kid for doing sex, drugs, and rock 'n roll. Do change that. In the following chapters, we'll get into specific response strategies for all of these issues, but they are all predicated on you holding fast to those things that make you who you are. Without that, nothing else will work.

X: *Know Thou, This Too Shall Pass*

The tenth commandment is the most important of all: This too shall pass. I repeat this message throughout the book because of our tendency as parents of distressed teens to fall into that very adolescent life view of today as being forever. Kids really can't peer much further ahead in their lives than a day or two, so whatever's happening now becomes an eternity to them.

As an adult, you have the unique ability to remember that the sun will rise tomorrow, that the adolescent crisis in front of you will end, and that it will likely end happily. Adolescent upset is diapers, it's root canal, and it's getting drafted. It can really get messy, it can be quite painful, and it can be very scary. But these things all end, and to get through them sanely we have to keep our eye on the end of the dark tunnel we're in.

And as you wait for the dark time to end, keep your other eye trained on something about your kid that you genuinely like. Find an endearing, admirable, or unique quality that you can honestly and powerfully praise. Remember, your kid is painfully used to hearing about all of her failings, particularly from you. So always try to find something positive to focus on as you approach her. This can help you build one of those precious bridges to your child that could save your relationship and, possibly, could even save her life.

Congratulations! You've just completed your basic training. You have a set of basic rules you can apply to any situation you may encounter with your kid. Now we're ready to push on to advanced parent training and dive headfirst into answering those eternal, mystery-shrouded questions that existed before the dawn of time and will live on long after our race has died out. We'll be answering questions like, "Well, if I'm allowed to stay out until 9:30 on school nights, and 11:00 on nonschool nights, then why can't I stay out until 10:15 on nights before a half-day of school?"

Get ready for rules and regulations.

Chapter 10

MAKING AND ENFORCING
RULES AND DECISIONS

WE READ PARENTING BOOKS to find out (1) how to make decisions about our kid, (2) what kinds of rules are appropriate for our age child, and (3) how the heck we get our kid to abide by those decisions and rules. If the kid would just do what we asked, we think, the world would be fine. As Mitchell found out, it's not that simple.

"I don't ask a lot," Mitchell complained, "I just ask Jon to do a few chores, go to school, get decent grades, and not do drugs, but we fight constantly. Whatever I ask, it's too much for my son. Maybe it's me. Maybe I do ask too much. Doctor, I'm here because I need someone like you to tell Jon and me what demands are reasonable to have of a 14-year-old. I quit seeing the last psychologist because she was no help at all. She wouldn't tell me anything. She kept asking Jon what he thought. She was a complete waste of time and money. I don't think she knew anything about kids. I was told you're really good with teenagers, so tell us, what are some reasonable rules? What rules do you have in your house?"

I couldn't help myself. I shrugged my shoulders and looked at Mitchell's son. "Jon, what do you think?" Jon laughed, but Dad looked mad. I tried to explain. "Look, Mitchell, your first psychologist was probably doing exactly what needed to be done. Your problem is not what your rules should be, but that you guys are sitting here asking a stranger what your rules should be. I don't know what they should be. I'm not sure I know what the rules should be in my own house. They're not up to me. As a family, we sort of make them up as we go along. This works a lot better than if I were allowed to impose my rules on everybody else."

Mitchell was still not getting it, so I took another shot at explaining. "The point is that you must have *your own* process for figuring out *your own* rules. Does this make sense?"

I liked Mitchell. He was straight-up. He told you what he thought. "Sounds like a lot of work to me," he sighed. "Can't you just give us a couple of rules and let us see how they work out? I won't hold you responsible if they don't." "Mitchell," I laughed as I shook my head, "I bet you're a guy who hates movies with English subtitles. Am I right?" Mitchell grinned. "OK, OK!" he mock yelled as he turned toward his son. "I GIVE UP! JON! WHAT-DO-YOU-THINK?"

The shared laughter that followed was the start of their healing. It was the beginning of their own process for setting up their own rules.

Making Rules and Decisions

The truth is, like Mitchell, I don't like subtitled movies, either. I like things simple. When I do seminars on parenting adolescents, I often find lots of people who hate subtitled movies. They become disappointed when I take them through the same hoops I took Mitchell through. They're often mad they came, just like Mitchell was, when they find out I don't have rules to offer them. There's a common reason for this common disappointment.

Back before your child's brain exploded into adolescence, making rules and decisions was done simply. You simply told your child what to do and he did it. Weren't those days wonderful? They were for Kathy.

"Not long ago," Kathy narrated, "Luke just did what I asked. He hardly ever whined or complained. Times have changed now that he's a teen. Yesterday, I told him that he couldn't go out until his homework was done. He laughed at me." She shook her head slowly as if disbelieving her own words. "He laughed at me, sneered, 'Yeah, right,' got up from the table, stretched and yawned, and walked. . .out. . .the freakin'. . .door. I still can't believe this is happening. I don't even know what it is that happened."

What happened was adolescence. Gone forever are those days of parental dictatorship. Welcome to America. Today you rule by committee. The balance of power has shifted partially away from you and more toward your brain-challenged teen. You want to help this power realignment occur smoothly or you might have a Boston Tea Party in your harbor. And don't forget what happened to the British.

You also want to welcome your kid's demand for power sharing as a sign that you are doing your job properly, since this is what is supposed to happen in adolescence. A teen who passively permits full parental control of his life is a kid who would make most psychologists worry. A lot. There are many important reasons why you *want* your kid to get in your face and present an overwhelmingly good argument for being allowed to go to that concert (which you will never allow, anyway).

First, the fact is that there is no one universal set of rules or decisions that works for all teens. Children and families are all so radically different that the rules must be created to reflect the realities of each particular situation, and each particular situation changes constantly even within one family. This is how you end up in those head-scratching poses saying, "You know, she's right. Why are we giving her a 10 P.M. curfew when we never set any curfew for her older sister at this age?" It's because those two kids are different (in personality), the parents are different (in their evolving views on parenting issues), and the world is different (in its perceived dangers). Your kid's demand for power sharing ultimately helps you make better decisions, since the discussions that accompany power sharing address all of these differences, and make the resulting rules fit and work better.

Second, your kid's demand for power is incredibly therapeutic for her if you respond to it well. A family *process* of making rules and decisions is wonderful and effective on many different levels. It strengthens your child's sense of positive power and control (versus behaving like a lunatic to feel powerful), develops good negotiating skills (versus punching out walls), teaches the art of compromise, forges bonds of trust and respect between you and your child, and develops good decision-making skills. Most important, this rules-setting process helps immensely with that most critical of all adolescent tasks, identity formation (see Chapter 9). As you will see, a good rules process advances your kid way down that road of consolidating his identity by forcing him to confront who he is now and how he wants to live his life. It also acts as a prophetic mirror in which he will see the reflection of who he is becoming as a young adult. This process is much more important than just getting him in by 9:30 P.M.

Finally, unilaterally making decisions and rules (even those offered by experts) without a good process that involves negotiating with your kid is simply asking for more drywall repairs. Your child was not designed to exist in that kind of authoritarian atmosphere, and it can make her reactive in her identity exploration, something you now know to be disastrous.

So the bottom line is that your family must make its own rules and decisions. The bottom line is also that the rules and decisions themselves are usually not that critical. It's the *process* by which we arrive at decisions and enforce our rules that is the gold. Ironically, a good rules process eventually eliminates the need for most of its own laws because of the growth it produces in identity formation for your kid and the wonderful parent-child relationships that follow when your kid knows who he is.

To paraphrase a president, it's the *process,* stupid, which is really all about *identity.*

The Goal of a Rule-Setting Process: It's About Identity, Not Rules

Your kid comes with a built-in feature called limits-testing. The short definition of this is "locating the fences." It's finding the point beyond which parents are unwilling to compromise. As a young child, your kid would periodically take a run against the fence to see how strong it was, but typically she'd back off if she saw that the fence was solid and large.

As an adolescent, she is suddenly tall enough to peer over your fence and become entranced with what she sees on the other side. She's also big enough to just hop over the fence if she wants to, and she's strong enough to run right through it—so the nature of the limits game changes drastically. The fence used to be the containment tool. Your kid couldn't physically or mentally get past it because she was no match for you. In adolescence, the fence becomes only a boundary line, a symbolic representation of the limits. The fence itself, or the parents themselves, are no longer a match for the physical and mental skills of the adolescent, so for the limits to work, *your kid has to voluntarily agree to observe the out-of-bounds line.* This is as hard as it sounds. It's also much more critically important than you can imagine, because the whole intent of setting these boundaries has changed now that your kid is a teen.

When he was small, the purpose of the fence was to keep him alive and healthy. As he grows into adolescence, this purpose must be enlarged to include a whole new batch of goals whose common end is to enhance identity formation. This is done by allowing identity exploration with some element of risk, but within an open field of choices. He can sort these choices out, try some, and then embrace a few. This is how he learns who he is, and knowing who he is, is the best defense he can have against the insanity of the adolescent world.

The rules now have to accommodate this new goal of identity formation. Before we examine the specifics of a good rules process, be sure to enter this work understanding that the focus must be on your kid's identity needs, and not on your control needs. David found that this was easy to say and hard to do.

"Neil is a gifted tenth grade student. He's done fantastically well all through school and is academically ranked among the top 5 percent of his class. He's on a fast track to a prestigious college scholarship. At home, he's been pretty much a joy. Some normal bumps, you know, but nothing much until last week when he came home and asked us to sign a form allowing him to go to tech school to major in cooking. COOKING? We were stunned. When we told him absolutely not, that this was a crazy idea, he went nuts. He said we've never allowed him to make any choices in his life. That's not true. We've let him decide which sports to play, which academic courses to take, and so on. But we're not budging on this one.

"Now he's saying he will not go to school unless we let him do this tech school thing, and let him ruin his life. I know you've only met him one time, but tomorrow they close tech enrollment and Neil says if he's not signed up, he's not going to school at all. I know you can't tell us what to do, but I've got to ask, anyway. What should we do? What would you do?"

I hate that question. It always makes me have to muddy the waters by complicating the issue. I also hate it because it reminds me of how human I am. "What I'd probably do, David, is be crushed like you that my son might not become the academic superstar that I never was.

I'd probably go to the mat on this and refuse to sign." David looked relieved, but not for long. "And I'd be screwing up by doing that. David, your son is a fine young man. You've done a wonderful job raising him. Neil speaks very powerfully about his fascination with cooking and his desire to be a chef. He really loves that dream." David interrupted impatiently, "Yes. Exactly. It's a dream. Silly, stupid, and short-sighted. He wanted to be a neurosurgeon, for Christ's sake. And you're telling me to let him be a cook?"

I sat forward to let David know that I knew this wasn't going to be easy to hear. "No," I replied, "I'm telling you to love your wonderful son enough to respect his dream, even though you may have misgivings about it. He needs to decide this vocational question by himself, but more important, he needs to feel that you'll support him no matter what he chooses. If you don't, you could lose a lot more than just the neurosurgeon. You can lose the son."

David was upset. Sarcastically he asked, "Well, how many happy cooks do you know?" I laughed. "Neil asked almost the same question. He asked if I knew any chefs, if I knew any physicians, and were they happy or unhappy. The answer to all those questions is yes. There are chefs and physicians who love their work and there are chefs and physicians who despise their work. The secret is figuring out which would be you. The way we do that is by trying these ideas out. It's called identity exploration."

David said nothing for a long time. Finally, in a much softer voice, he began, "I know this doctor idea is largely my dream. All my life, I've had to struggle and put up with crap from bosses I was always smarter than just because I dropped out of school. It would kill me to see Neil piss away this chance at success." "David," I asked, "Why did you drop out?" David looked ashamed. "Because I didn't have the discipline to study. I just wanted to have fun, do drugs, and screw around. And nobody, including my father, could talk to me. I was too muleheaded. I just ran away."

"David," I said pointedly, "your son is not running away from anything. He wants to run towards something that he may truly love—or that he may truly hate. But he's been thinking this out pretty well. He says if he hates it, he'll have to do summer school classes to catch up and he told me he's willing to do that if need be. If he loves it, then you will have to come to grips with what your son wants to do with his life.

Either way, Neil will learn more about himself—which maybe is what you were never able to do?"

David paused and thought. "I guess who I've decided I am is Neil's father, which means most of me is wrapped up in him. Maybe too much?"

It's very easy to mix our own struggles and needs with those of our teens. Even after setting your own needs aside, making these identity exploration decisions versus future life impact decisions can feel like juggling chain saws with your child. You hope he doesn't get crippled in the act. This is another example of excruciating balancing, where you earn your parent salary by attempting to weigh his needs for identity exploration against your concerns for his welfare. As a parent, you are trying mightily to prevent your kid's life from getting screwed up by bad decisions.

The best defense against making bad decisions is developing good decision-making skills. And the best way to develop these in adolescents is to allow them to make their own decisions, both good and bad ones. The best decision-making scenario is a cooperative effort between child and parent, where your teen can feel at ease in open discussions of her choices, and feels confident enough to incorporate *some* of your older, wiser views in her process. You may have noticed this not happening too often recently, with many decisions ending up in "my way versus your way" standoffs. It takes a lot of work to get to that ideal cooperative situation, which can only occur when your kid has consolidated her identity—when, for the most part, she knows who she is. So in the interim, what should you do with the standoffs? First, redefine success. Winning here may mean *not* getting your way, even though you're sure that your choice would be so much better for your kid.

Ironically, your child will learn more about decision making and identity formation from being allowed to make a bad decision in a good way, than if he is forced to make a good decision in a bad way. He will learn more from being allowed to choose badly, because handled properly, a bad decision can teach your kid a lot about many important things—like the need for proper research, the obligations of self-responsibility, frustration tolerance, impulsiveness, delayed gratification, and last but not least, the wisdom of experts (parents) who *advised* versus *compelled* another course of action.

A good decision made badly can teach little that is positive and much that is negative. A successful outcome may not feel successful to a child who was forced to make the "right" decision.

> Bobby waved off my congratulations on making first honors. "That's probably all they told you about when they met with you, right? My first honors and my smoking dope. Right? That's all I am to them. You should go and congratulate them. Those honors belong to my parents, not to me. I didn't have any choice in the matter. If I miss honors, I get grounded until the next interim report." He snorted disgustedly. "You think I give a rat's ass about school? It's a joke! If it weren't for my friends being there, I'd be long gone. But the dope, yeah, that's all mine. You can congratulate me on that, dude."
>
> Bobby's parents never came back after I suggested that they needed to rethink the honors-for-no-grounding type of rules. Two years later, a hospital called to arrange follow-up treatment for Bobby who had just been released from his second drug rehab for heroin addiction.

Rules, regulations, and decision making with your teen must be geared toward self-sufficiency and identity. Rather than just giving her the loaf of bread, start giving her the seeds and tools to begin making her own. Be it bread or decisions, the more she makes on her own, the more her identity will consolidate. Remember that identity formation is your long-term ace-in-the-hole against adolescent insanity, a goal you may have to choose over your needs for short-term compliance by your kid and shorter-term peace of mind for you. Keep the big picture in sight when making decisions. Don't toss in your future-securing ace just to get a pair of 10s now.

And while you're playing cards to form your kid's identity, keep in mind that ultimate game of making good and peaceful decisions: negotiation.

NEGOTIATING WITH YOUR TEEN:
WHERE THE PROCESS BECOMES THE RULE

One universal rule you should have for your child as being absolutely nonnegotiable is negotiation. You must unilaterally declare this as the means for decision making with your kid. Everything else should be negotiable. Yes, I mean *everything*. No, I do not mean that your kid gets to do whatever he wants. On the contrary, I submit that insisting on negotiation as the process for rules and decision making makes it far more difficult for your kid to act on those crazy impulses that zing through that temporarily unstable brain.

How can I take this radical a position? From having worked with so many teens for so many years and seeing how much better this process works out in the long run. Before you get upset thinking that I'm suggesting Harold gets to decide if quitting school at 14 to work on a tramp steamer is a good idea, let me define negotiation.

Negotiation means open-minded discussion. It means allowing your kid the opportunity to present a viewpoint without prejudgment or interruption, no matter how bizarre that view may seem. *Remember that confrontation, ridicule, and ultimatums only reinforce those bizarre adolescent thoughts and entrench them into your kid's identity.*

There is a series of steps in this process that you might want to follow, depending on the nature of the issue being negotiated. The steps might occur over one meeting or be broken up into a series of conferences. They include:

- Opening premise: The presenter (you or your kid, whoever wants something decided) gets to say what she wants to see happen.
- Opening response: The audience (you or your kid, whoever needs to be convinced) initially reacts to the proposal, without saying yes or no. If you are the audience, you always acknowledge some respect for your kid's position (sometimes with a churning stomach).
- Delineation of potential problems: First, the presenter tells the audience what possible problems she sees in the request. Then the audience adds his (their) own issues.
- Problem solving: Both parties now develop solutions to the problems raised. This step may involve research or gathering more facts needed for the decision.
- Summation and clarification: Both parties state where they are in the process. If there's agreement, shake hands. If not, go to the next step.
- Compromises and alternative seeking: If the parties can't agree outright, possible alternative positions are developed. If still no agreement is reached, go to the next step.
- Final options: Here the irresolvable differences are summarized as

objectively and respectfully as possible. Options for re-evaluating the situation at a later date are discussed, along with conditions that might allow for a different outcome in the future.

WHEW! Why in the world would you want to go to all that trouble when a simple "NO, BECAUSE I SAID SO!" would suffice? First, because if you look closely at that tedious process, you'll see the ultimate judo principle of turning your opposition's momentum against her. In kinder terms, you'll see how opening up everything to negotiation forces your kid to work on identity consolidation and learn some great skills in the bargain. Plus, all of that work involved in those negotiating tasks lets you take advantage of one of those rare windows of opportunity to mess around in your kid's head.

Remember that most of the times you approach him for a "parent-moment" talk (as my son likes to call them), he's often closed down. But if your child approaches you for a rule modification, that brain is suddenly open to your input. He wants something, and you're going to make him pay dearly for it—you're going to make him think, learn about himself, and grow.

Second, that tedious list helps you to deal with those frustrating complications that the individual differences of children can have on setting rules and making decisions. All of those factors that make a particular situation unique usually get raised in a good negotiation. Understanding and appreciating your kid's individuality is critical to a good rules process.

ABOUT THOSE INDIVIDUAL DIFFERENCES:
MEET *CAPTAIN EVENTUALLY*

Since you volunteered to become a parent of an adolescent, you must have a fatal attraction towards impossible tasks. A winter climb of Mount Everest is nothin'. If you like truly daunting challenges, try adjusting your parenting style to meet the individual needs and differences of your kids. That is precisely the goal you must try to reach. Like many parents, it drove this one crazy:

"My son is a slob. Actually, he's not what I would call an active slob. He's kind of a passive slob. He just has this vision problem opthamologists have never heard of, where items like food wrappers, unmade beds, popcorn bits, laundry on floors, and breakfast trays cannot be seen in his field of vision. He also has this audiological problem the ear docs have never heard of, where he acknowledges being asked to clean up, but then has forgotten that request 30 seconds later.

"He's also a wonderfully loving, affectionate, kind, giving, and compassionate young man. I love and respect who he is. I know that his messiness comes from being so keenly focused on the million other things in his world that fully absorb his interest. My clean-up requests just don't get into his brain wiring. He acknowledges this characteristic and jokingly refers to his disorganized self by announcing, 'What's THAT, you say? Clean up my room? THIS looks like a JOB for CAPTAIN EVENTUALLY.' He makes me laugh and I know this behavior is not intended to defy me, yet it gets me mad. When I'm racing around the house in the morning trying to get out on time and I find all these little messes, I start to boil. I used to be in the army, and the only part I liked was the neatness of barracks life. I know I'm neurotic on this, but I worry that my son's disorganization will cost him dearly as he advances into more difficult schoolwork. He's mentally gifted and does great academically, but I fear that his messiness will keep him from getting into challenging schools where his gifts can be used.

"I've tried incentive programs and charts and so on, but nothing really works. So what should I do? Should I get mad and start to blast him when I know that will hurt his self-esteem and cost us a lot in terms of our closeness, or should I shut up and watch him possibly take it in the teeth in school? Which is the act of love?"

Excerpt from the personal journal of Dr. Michael Bradley.

If you have a suggestion for me, please forward it. I'm always open to debate on these calls, as you should be on yours. The fact is, there are no clear answers to these parenting dilemmas, and we often end up choosing the lesser of two evils. You just can't have it all, so you have to pick your battles based on what you think is best for your child. This is an art that starts with trying to learn who your kid is (her present identity) and ends with lovingly accepting your child for who she is, warts and all. You always dispassionately reference the warts, hoping for some changes, but you don't go to war over them. You don't push hard at these things because you understand that your loving, respectful relationship with your child is not worth damaging over spilled popcorn, if that popcorn is just popcorn.

But if that popcorn represents a sneering, arrogant, willful disregard of rules intended to provoke and hurt, then the popcorn becomes important, not for its own sake, but for what it symbolizes: a deeper anger and control issue that must be addressed in discussions and negotiations before it spreads to everything else between you.

Some kids just can't make their beds. Move away from these issues. Others can and won't just because you're asking them to. Move closer towards these issues.

TIPS FOR NEGOTIATING RULES AND DECISIONS

Here are a few general tips for these discussions. In later chapters, we'll flesh these out with specifics as they apply to different situations like school, drugs, and so on.

1. *Keep it dynamic.*

Your child is constantly changing and growing, and so should your rules. As he rightfully and passionately demands more autonomy from you, you should rightfully and dispassionately request more responsibility from him. View the rules as two concentric circles around your child that grow ever larger. One represents his amount of freedom and the other shows his amount of responsibility. They must always grow together in the face of mature behavior or shrink together in the face of irresponsible behavior. View the area within those circles as identity exploration space.

2. *Start shifting the power from you to him.*

Stop assuming control and giving fast answers. Act confused (this should come naturally) and in need of information. Once you give an answer to a request, that window into your kid's brain slams shut. Avoid answers as much as you can. Rather, pose questions to your kid to force him to keep talking, thinking, and negotiating as long as you can without creating too much frustration in your child.

3. *Provide options for her to choose within a set of parameters.*

Whenever possible, wrack your brain to come up with multiple choices for her to evaluate and select. This gives her some power of choice in a situation in which she may rebel if you impose one option on her. "I'm afraid that staying home alone won't work, but you can come with us on vacation and bring a friend, stay at Gramma's, or maybe try one of those adventure camps. Let us know what you decide."

*4. Know where your boundary lines are, and keep these clear
in your head and in your child's head.*

If you don't already have a clear idea of the nonnegotiable fences you want to establish around your child, you're in trouble. Two unrelated parents in my township have been sentenced to jail in the past month for providing beer to their underaged kids at home parties, which led to some of the kids running their cars up a few trees. These parents were so sure the kids would honor their promises not to drink and drive. We buried two of the children. Being vague about rules on life-threatening activities is a life-threatening activity. As you read the scarier parts of this book, you might want to keep a list on the back page titled "My Nonnegotiable Fences." Nonlethal issues like curfews are always open to modification. Things that might kill your kid must always be out of bounds, even though they are open for discussion. ALWAYS. Sex, drugs, and rock 'n roll are a few examples. You may not be able to stop these actions, but to your child, you must (like the cop) be dispassionately, but unequivocally, clear that these things are not OK with you. When you discuss them with your kid, make very sure he knows that they are not somehow permissible simply because you're willing to talk with him about them. Remember that negotiation just means open-minded discussion *to maintain some access into that brain-challenged thinking.* It does not mean caving in to outrageous demands. The fact that you are against teen sex should be no secret to your child, yet you should always be willing to discuss the topic. Talk to him about his demand to be allowed to have sex with his girlfriend *in order to get him to hear your concerns about teen sex that he would not hear in the form of a random one-way lecture.* Let me sketch an example:

Teen: "I want to spend the weekend down at the shore alone with my girlfriend."

Parent: "You know how I feel about that, but tell me why you think this is OK."

Teen: "Everybody does it. It's no big deal."

Parent: "Do you feel like this is a girl you'll have a long-term exclusive relationship with?"

Teen: "Nah, we're just, like, friends."

Parents: "Are you sure that's the way she sees things?"

Teen: "Why shouldn't she?"

Parent: "Well, sex is a lot different for girls than it is for boys. She might have much more emotional investment than you think. You might want to check it out. Do you feel OK maybe really hurting her feelings? And what if she gets pregnant?"

Teen: "We'd use protection, and besides, if she had to, she'd just get an abortion. No big deal."

Parent: "Abortion might be a much bigger deal than you think. Do you know any girls who've had one? You might want to ask them if it was no big deal."

Teen: "Well, can I go or not?"

Parent: "Sorry, son. I heard what you said, but I worry that you're not thinking about how much pain this could cause everyone. I'm still opposed to it, but I'd be happy to talk more about this whenever you want."

If he pushes you with threats of disregarding the boundary, keep in mind this next tip.

5. *Never disclose your enforcement options.*

Be very clear and succinct about your limits, but insist on not talking about punishments in advance of a crime. Don't end up with your kid weighing whether drinking at her prom is worth a month's grounding. Like that dispassionate cop, you're always trying to find another way of handling disagreement without referencing the gun on your hip. If the discussion becomes a test of limits, immediately and dispassionately state those limits with the footnote that you'd rather not talk about what you'd do if she jailbreaks, but let her know that boundaries exist and they will be enforced if need be, but you'd rather talk about another way of handling the situation. In a moment, we'll talk more about how to handle these ultimate enforcement discussions, but for now, if your kid demands to know what you'll do if she disobeys, refuse to answer. Specifying punishment threats in advance of a jailbreak turns a discussion of values into a game of chicken. Don't go there. Have you ever played the Yankees in Yankee Stadium? It's tempting to think that promises of pain will dissuade your kid from being crazy, but in the long run this is a losing tactic.

6. Deal like Honest Sam, the Used-Car Man.

Money talks, nobody walks. If the deal is about a nonlethal issue, you don't let her walk off your car lot without putting together a package for her to consider. Always offer to swap increased autonomy for increased responsibility, and sweeten the deal with incentives wherever you can. Keep her talking, negotiating, engaged, and thinking. For example:

Teen: "I think I'm ready to have my own car now. I have enough saved to buy Uncle Bill's Jeep."

Parent: "Great." (liar!) "First, I'll need your end of the insurance money."

Teen: "How much is that?"

Parent: "I don't know, but here's the number you can call to find out."

Teen: "Can't you call?"

Parent: "Sorry, honey, but being old enough to own a car means being old enough to do all the work involved. How much do you have set aside for maintenance?"

Teen: "I don't know what you mean."

Parent: "You need to call Uncle Bill and find out what it costs to keep a Jeep running every year. It would be sad to have a car parked out front that you couldn't afford to fix or insure. But lemme tell ya' what I'm gonna do. You do A and B work at school this semester, and I'll post half of your insurance money. Do we have a deal?"

7. Let him make some scary decisions.

On nonlethal but important issues, err on the side of letting him try. Properly handled, those failures can be wonderful ways of building decision-making skills and inoculating your kid against the insanity.

8. Have clearer and fewer rules.

The research nerds have repeatedly shown that parents who maintain a relatively low number of consistent, reasonable rules that are formed in discussions with their kids tend to have teens with high levels of self-worth, self-control, and moral-ethical values. Conversely, kids from over-controlling, angry, and inconsistent homes tend to act out, be self-centered, and generally hate themselves. How can fewer rules lead to better kids? Because of Tip Number 9.

9. Build rules with respect, not with contracts.

If you forget all the other tips, use this one and you'll still do OK. Ever wonder how people who work with youth gangs manage to sometimes stop gang wars? They tell me that rule one is to show respect for the position of the kids. Once the kids feel respected, they become more interested in negotiating like reasonable adults and less inclined to load up the AK-47s. If the gang kid smells disrespect, you can hear the rounds being chambered. Your kid is not that dissimilar. Showing respect for her position draws her closer to the safer, calmer path, even if she ultimately doesn't get what she wants. Having you respond to her as a young adult (being willing to negotiate and discuss), can be addicting for her. Your act of listening well even to her failed argument can build respect, and respect turns out to be the key factor in making good decisions. We find that the more mutual respect exists between parent and child, the fewer rules they need. Conversely, without mutual respect, there is no set of rules that will work.

> Dad slapped a five-page document into my hands. "These are my rules for my 13-year-old son Frank. You'll see that we both signed each page, and now we've both initialed each line. That's because he's a goddamn liar and can't be trusted to say he read each page. You'll also see that I've got lots of subparts to each rule, where I've been trying to eliminate all of the loopholes the little bastard keeps finding. I got this idea for writing a contract out of a magazine, but it doesn't seem to be working. If you read over that contract, you'll see all the things that are wrong with my kid."
>
> "Mr. Alper," I inquired, "what is right with your kid? What do you respect about him?" "Not a goddamn thing," he responded angrily. "My kid is nothing but a foul-mouthed, sissy punk, cursing at his mother and punching out walls when I'm not there. He doesn't have the guts to get in my face because he knows where that would go. He's nothing but a candy-assed coward. I'm ashamed to be his father. I've told him all this, I've screamed it at him and dared him to swing at me if he had the backbone, but it does no good. He just skulks away crying

like a little baby. I don't hit him much anymore, but maybe I should. I don't want to tune him up, but he's really getting to me. What I need is a better contract, but I can't seem to get one to work."

I had to hit Dad over the head. "What you need is to have some feeling of love and respect for your son. I've never seen a contract that will give you that. Can you find any in yourself?" "Sure," Dad scoffed, "the day he starts acting like a man." "Maybe that's what Frank is doing," I said softly, guarding against my own anger. "Maybe he's learned that being a man is being angry, sarcastic, and bullying smaller people."

Contracts can be helpful, but in a respect-free environment, there is no contract that will work. Good decision-making processes arise from mutual respect, and when we have high levels of respect, we need far fewer rules. So put your time into building respect and the rules will follow much more easily.

There you go! Now you have all the tools you need to develop that critical process to create a wonderful set of rules and decision-making skills all carefully tailored to build your kid's identity and keep him alive. Now that you're feeling so confident, let's move on to the second half of this chapter and talk about what to do when all of those wonderful rules and skills come crashing down around you: enforcement.

Enforcing Rules and Decisions

Your kid is going to break rules. I'll bet you already knew that, but what I'll bet you didn't know is that you *want* your kid to break some rules—the ones that don't threaten her life. As much as we hope and pray that she doesn't, she has to do this, because breaking rules can be as much a part of the identity-building process as the cooperative setting of rules. I'll elaborate on this point in a minute, but I'm telling you this now because I need you to reframe in your head what a rule violation is: It's a *learning opportunity* for your child. It is *not* an indication of failure—on your part or your kid's.

This is probably not what your childhood training taught you. If you went to the school of fear-based parenting, what you learned from your folks may have been that rule infractions were catastrophes, mortal sins to be punished with the fires of parental anger and fury. As we've discussed already, that approach may have worked in the past, but these days, it is as effective as flipping a finger at a road-raged driver to teach him some manners. Just as you needed new training in setting rules, you need new training in enforcing them.

In the next part of this chapter, we'll take a look at the general principles you should use in enforcing adolescent rules and decisions. We'll expand on and discuss how they apply to specific situations in the chapters that follow. First, let's look at another one of the many things that has contributed to your own feelings of insanity since your kid got zits. It's that Catch-22 of setting limits for adolescents: damned if you do and damned if you don't.

THE GREAT LIMITS PARADOX: I'LL HATE YOU IF YOU LIMIT ME AND I'LL HATE YOU IF YOU DON'T

Another experience you've probably had by now is being told by your teenager that your unreasonable restrictions have caused him to hate you for ruining his life. The hating-you-for-your-limits has been made perfectly and loudly clear to you. It's that flip side, the hating-you-if-you-don't-set-limits, that may bear some explaining.

As your kid transitions through these adolescent seas, he starts off desperately needing your appropriate limits—you know, the ones he hates you for. The reason (which he will take to his maker with him) is that he knows that in early adolescence he is way too crazy to be in charge of himself. In fact, he gets terrified in situations where he's on his own, but not ready to function without your limits. I'm not kidding. That large, angry adolescent who seems ready to go to the wall rather than accept a restriction is the very same one who needs that limit.

Parents often get confused and exhausted by this paradox, and tragically, many of them end up leaving their kids largely unsupervised, thinking this is what the kid wants (see Chapter 11). Being home alone may be what he says he wants, but it's not what he needs.

The limits set the boundaries for identity exploration. Having this structure, particularly in early adolescence, calms and protects your kid by taking decisions out of his hands that are too complex for him now. Further, the limits provide a safe zone within which your kid can experiment with identity explorations. As he gets older, these limits can become those voluntary boundary-markers we discussed earlier. He will, hopefully, embrace these as his own identity as he matures, but particularly in today's adolescent world, you must have fences to make sure this identity process is as gradual, productive, and healthy as possible.

Bernadette was astonished by the first part of my diagnosis of her 13-year-old son. We hadn't even gotten to the second part yet. "Connor?" she snorted sarcastically, "My sweet little Connor, depressed? No way! He gets everything he wants, he has no rules, he goes where he pleases, he stays out all night whenever he wants, he doesn't give a damn about ever letting me know where he is, and he's certainly not depressed when he's screaming at me for being a retarded bitch. He's conning you, doctor. He just wants to get some more pills to get high off of or to sell."

I knew this was going to be very hard on her. "Bernadette, depression can look different than you think. Sometimes the only part a parent might see is the screaming part. Connor is not sleeping and I don't think he's really eating. He has no joy in all that freedom you describe. His thinking is focused on death and dying issues, and he's given up most of his friends. He's lost, scared, and very, very sad. I agree that he shouldn't just be given pills right now because he might try to overdose on them. I think he needs to be hospitalized immediately to keep him from hurting himself."

Bernadette stared at me. "Suicide? Connor?" I just nodded. "Well," she stammered, "even if it were true, there's no way he'll agree to go to a hospital. What am I supposed to do, hold a gun to his head?" She closed her eyes and sighed at her inadvertent black humor.

I shook my head slowly. I didn't know how to make this any easier for her. She was ashamed to be so far out of touch with her son, and I was about to devastate her further. "He's already agreed that he needs to go to the hospital. Luckily, he's still scared of dying, but he's only afraid that it might be painful. He does know that he needs someone to take charge of his life. For now, that must be the hospital, but afterwards, that must be you. You've got to be ready to do this, and it's going to be very hard. You need to decide tonight if you are up to this. I'm sorry to be so blunt, but your insurance company will probably force the hospital to discharge Connor in about a week. We don't have any time. So I need to know, are you up to this?"

Her eyes blazed with fury at me. She gathered up her coat and started to walk out, muttering that this was all too f'ng crazy. She stopped and turned at my door. "Connor really said that to you?" she asked with a tight voice, "the part about he'd kill himself if he knew it wouldn't hurt?" I could only sadly nod yes.

Her back shook the door as she leaned against it and started to sob. "My boy, my boy, oh God, what have I done? Oh my God, oh my God. . ."

Teenagers need fences to stay alive. The older ones may be able to erect their own as their identity forms. The younger ones, like Connor, need parents to build those fences. Without those limits that they hate, adolescents can be depressed, angry, and even suicidal. The structure of limits helps teenage life become more predictable and less stressful, a healthy lifestyle that your child will mock as "boring." But ultimately, after all the yelling quiets down, your kid tells me that she sees the limits as an expression of your caring. She'll often admit to me that she does know a kid who has no limits, and that she can see that those uninvolved parents don't really give a damn. Sometimes, if she's sharp, she can even see the resulting depression that occurs in her friend who is limits-free.

But you'll never get to hear any of this because kids also need to protest those fences that keep them alive and feeling loved as part of their identity exploration. Just embrace this paradox for the Catch-22 that it is. Don't try to solve it. It's a part of nature's mysterious plan.

Another part of the mysterious plan involves a second great paradox of parenting: having your kid violate your trust to learn about trust.

TRUST ISSUES: TURNING LEMONS INTO LEMONADE

Trust is another one of those words we preach about a lot to our kids. Over the years, they get to hear it so much that many kids have no idea what it means. Often, it just becomes background noise to arguments over rules. Many young teens see the concept of trust as a spending limit on a credit card, something that parents arbitrarily won't grant that limits their freedom (*"Mom won't let me go. She doesn't trust me"*). And yet trust, like respect, is one of those very few, very critical, and very complex concepts we absolutely must teach our children. It is so important that we must separate our child's violations of trust as aspects of behavior completely apart from the lesser misdemeanors. In other words, it's not the violation of curfew that is the big issue, it's the *lying* about the violation that is the big issue. So how do we effectively teach trust to those same kids who don't say more than a single, five-word sentence to their parents each day?

The best way to teach trust is by modeling (see Chapter 7), not lecturing. Modeling is walking the walk. It's quiet and effective, and it builds respect. Part of that modeling involves always extending trust to your kid, even when you have a hunch that it might get violated (but only in nonlethal situations). Why do you want to extend credit to a risky person? Because it's a win-win outcome for you and your brain-challenged child. If your kid honors the trust, then you both learn that the circles of responsibility and autonomy might be due for enlarging. If your teen betrays your trust, congratulations! You now have another rare window open into that challenged brain, this time into that shaky set of neurons where your kid houses his concept of trust.

Don't screw up this surgery with your anger. Yelling and raging are not the best options when your child's brain is exposed. Remember that dispassionate cop model and use your child's betrayal as a teaching tool. Here's how.

1. *Don't get personally wounded by an adolescent's betrayal of trust.*

Remember that she's nuts right now. This is not your spouse; it's your child. She's just learning what trust is really about. View the betrayals as similar to her first attempts at feeding herself. She had to fail at this a lot until she got the hang of it. One of the problems was that she did not understand the value of cleanliness, so throwing food around was not a bad thing to do. Your child may not really understand the value of trust. Set high public goals and low private expectations so that the failures don't sting quite so much. This will help you keep your cool for the next step.

2. *Separate a trust violation from other rule infractions.*

Shortly, we'll chat about how to handle other rule infractions with consequences. Trust issues should be viewed entirely differently. Calmly let your kid know from the get-go that a betrayal of trust is a unique and serious situation that goes way beyond assessing simple consequences for something like coming home late. Let him know that keeping trust in your relationship is so important that simply paying a fine doesn't get it done. If you're really seething, your initial response to your child should be one of delay. Tell him that you are too upset to talk right now, but agree on a time to talk soon.

3. Ask your child what she thinks should occur following a betrayal of trust.

She'll really hate this one. She'd rather you just smack her and get it over with, but keep on repeating that trust betrayal has to do with values and character and respect and all those vague identity issues she needs to deal with, so you're not quite sure how to handle it. Ask her to think about it and get back to you tomorrow.

4. Keep your kid's focus on the nature of trust, not on the nature of punishment.

Make him think. If this feels like a weak response, be comforted by the fact that it's probably the worst thing you can do to him, anyhow. When he comes back and proposes that he should be grounded for a week, respectfully decline. Dispassionately tell him that you appreciate his offer, but you're not sure that he fully understands what happened when he betrayed your trust. Ask him what he thinks happened, don't tell him. What you want to hear is an adolescent version of trust being a beautiful glass mosaic, built with thousands of deeds of love, caring, and respect, that can be shattered into bits with one thoughtless act. And that rebuilding this priceless treasure can sometimes become impossible if it gets crushed once too often. If he comes back and offers two weeks, decline again. Tell him you're still not sure that he understands, and ask him to think some more, or maybe write about it. Act as if everything else gets put on hold until you resolve this present crisis.

5. If he speaks honestly and from his heart about the nature of trust, then you're finished.

Don't add a single word to his words. Give him a hug and walk away. When he asks how long his grounding is, say there is no grounding that teaches trust and that his words rekindled your trust in him, and that's all you wanted.

For most kids, you can expect to repeat this teaching sequence a number of times before the lesson sticks, but it's important to maintain your discipline in always handling the trust aspects of misbehavior with this drill. If you just punish, then you teach your kids that there is only a fine to pay for violating this thing called trust, and they never learn the real lesson.

If you find that your trust gets broken constantly, get help. Something else is going on that needs to be addressed quickly. These incidents may accelerate into the potentially lethal zone if you don't get to the root of this behavior.

Now that we've trained you for handling the felonies of adolescence—the breaches of trust—let's look at the systems parents use for the misdemeanors: punishments and consequences. As it turns out, these two are very different and, sadly, they are used interchangeably by some parents, taking them further from their goal of raising a healthy, wealthy, and wise child.

Punishments and Consequences

The most important difference between punishments and consequences is your goal for your child in handling a misbehavior. Punishments are intended to stop a particular behavior fast by hurting your child physically or emotionally. Consequences are designed to *encourage* another related behavior to eventually take the place of the undesired action. Punishments control kids, temporarily. Consequences teach kids, forever. Punishments seem fast, efficient, and effective. They are, but only in the short term. In the long term, they are ineffective. Consequences seem slow, complex, and time-consuming. They are, and they're also a wonderful way to help shape your child's identity for the rest of his life.

Punishment is a simple process that is very appealing to us time-pressed parents. You hurt me and I hurt you back. You curse and I slap your face. You neglect a chore and I humiliate you in front of your friends. You come home late and I take away that guitar you love. Punishers argue that this is effective parenting in that it associates an undesired action with a painful outcome, thus discouraging that action. I argue that this is short-sighted and ineffective parenting, and it also serves as a dangerous outlet for our own anger and frustration. Punishments are intended to hurt. The outcome of a good, hurtful punishment of an adolescent is to have your kid lying quietly on his bed staring at the ceiling and thinking, *God, how I hate my parents. I'd love to see them crushed and hurt like they hurt me. How can I get back at them? Maybe I can really piss them off tomorrow.*

A consequence is something you carefully craft that, ideally, results in your kid lying quietly on her bed staring at the ceiling and thinking, *What is wrong with me that I would do that? I don't want to do that and I intend to try and not do that ever again. That is not who I want to be.* In other words, a consequence is designed to teach, build maturity, and form identity, not just to stop a behavior. The most critical goal for a consequence is for your kid to be learning *what to do* versus *what not to do.* Heady work, not easily done, but well worth the effort. Let's look at some examples to see how punishments and consequences differ.

Remember those tickets you got from those two cops in Chapter 9? That angry cop was a punisher whose primary intent was to give you pain. She was yelling, threatening, and humiliating, and seemed to go far out of her way just to stick it to you. Her actions did little more than to make you even angrier in return, and tempted you to somehow strike back at her. I will agree with the punishers that if that raging cop were frightening enough, you might not ever again commit that same offense in front of her. But what did you learn? Did you contritely reflect on your poor behavior in such a way as to reduce the odds of it happening again? Did you resolve to try to become a safer driver, whether or not a cop is watching? If you answered yes to either of those questions, you are likely not human. The essence of punishment is to intentionally inflict pain on a person. That experience of having someone intentionally hurt you creates a dark, seething anger that feeds a desire for revenge. Your immediate bad behavior may stop, but seeds have been sown for 10 other acts of striking back. This is even more true for adolescents.

That second, dispassionate cop wanted a lot more than to simply hurt you for missing the stop sign. He wanted to give you a consequence. He wanted to figure out a way to get you to be more careful with the 10,000 stop signs you'll encounter when he's not around. He wanted you to think about your behavior and resolve to be better. *He wanted to teach, and he wanted you to change part of you,* so he used a system we call administering consequences. He did this first by specifying your restitution to society for your unsafe driving: He gave you a fine. Second, he made you think about your actions by pointing out the crazy, unnecessary driving risks you were taking that could devastate your loved ones. And third, he did all of this while remaining calm and *even sympathetic* to your situation. It felt like he was on your side, calmly trying to help your life to be better. He didn't distract you by inflicting intentional pain. He left you feeling somewhat abashed, but with no one to be mad at but you.

To decide if you want to use punishments or consequences with your child, think about the outcome you want. Which of those two cops had the most positive impact on your identity? Do you want to simply stop one behavior in your kid, or do you want to alter your child's identity in a way that will live on forever? If you chose Door Number 2, welcome to the world of consequences—but bring your new training. You're gonna need it. And forget your old parenting-by-punishment training. You need to lose it. Consequences are a lot more work.

As the dispassionate cop demonstrated, a good consequence has two parts. The first is material restitution. Material restitution is easy. Your kid has to repair whatever damage he caused. If he threw a rock through the old widow's window as a prank, he needs to replace the window. That's the easy part. It's that other type of restitution, the emotional/moral/spiritual kind, that's tough. Ironically, as parents, we often think the job is done when the kid pays the window guy, mumbles "sorry," and runs off to his rock concert, but the fact is that the job has only just begun. The learning (and identity formation) occur with that second type of restitution, which is intended to heal not only the victim, but the *perpetrator* as well.

The second type of payback, the emotional/moral/spiritual restitution, is hard, but it's essential for your rock-thrower, and you need to require it as part of his overall restitution. The way he'll learn is for you to ask him to come up with answers to some very difficult questions that you'll dispassionately put to him. Questions like: "How do you replace that vulnerable woman's peace of mind? How do you restore her trust in teens? How do you repair the spiritual damage to a person already coping with loneliness and fear?" Both you and your kid will hate this questioning. Both you and your kid will wish that you could just smack him and get it over with. It's a lot of work, and it makes your head hurt, but aching heads are part of what happens when we grow in important ways.

Engage your kid a lot in this process. Be clear with her that you have the ultimate veto power on inappropriate consequences, but that she can have lots of impact on the outcome. Keep her involved, not steaming in the next room while you decide her fate.

What are you looking for in your kid? You want something said in teenager dialect that demonstrates some awareness on her part of the importance of emotional/moral/spiritual restitution. You'll know it when you hear it. With the elderly widow, it might be your daughter talking about how she must have terrified that woman, or how ashamed she feels. It might be her heartfelt apology or her tears of sorrow for her victim. But you'll have to restrain your old training and shut up if you ever want to hear these things, because these priceless jewels evaporate in the face of parental moralizing or rage. You must provide a quiet space for these bits of learning to come out of your kid.

If you're not hearing good answers, dispassionately keep posing the questions to your child until she gets it. Once you hear those magical words of insight and responsibility, ask her what she needs to do for that second type of restitution to complete her consequence. For example, in addition to fixing the window, she might want to wash the neighbor's other windows, and thus spend time with her. She might cook a meal and take it over and share it with the woman. Both consequences would force your kid to see the victim as a human being who can be terribly hurt by a thoughtless deed far beyond the cost of a window. These paybacks can foster wonderful maturity that a grounding ignores and a smack across the face destroys.

Here are some other tips for rules enforcement:

1. *Be that dispassionate cop.*

Raging at your kid just diverts his attention from his own behavior to yours. If you're seething, now's not the time to deal with the situation. You don't get any points for handling crises immediately. Don't hesitate to put off talking about a problem until later that night or the next day if you're really mad. We do much better thinking when we're rested and calmer. The judges got it right. They don't hear cases when they're mad, tired, or scared. Don't discipline a kid who stumbles in high at 2:00 A.M. I can guarantee you will not be at your best.

2. *Separate the fact-finding discussion from the consequence one.*

Steal another trick from the judges. They'll find you guilty on one day and tell you to come back another day for your sentence. They separate the passion of the trial from the objective consideration of a sentence. If you issue consequences on the spot, you will either be stuck with poor consequences that you'll have to live with, or you will end up rescinding your decision—and both options are very bad.

3. *Use probation on minor first offenses.*

Your kid is nuts. Don't personalize her behavior. That expanding, impulsive, and judgment-challenged brain is going to do and say things that will astound her as much as you. Jumping in with a formal consequence for a minor, one-shot event can be counterproductive. Look for real regret and owning of responsibility in your child. If they are there from the get-go, close the book, you're done. Just keep your eyes open for any pattern of behavior that needs to be addressed. Remember, giving your kid a pass on a first offense looks like power to her, not weakness (see Chapter 7).

4. *Avoid life sentences.*

Always provide light at the end of any tunnels you construct. Give your child some reason to want to do better. If you end up curtailing curfew, don't leave the duration open-ended. Lifers are dangerous prisoners because they have little to lose. Set a time frame for the consequence: "We'll do this for a month and then see if you're ready for the responsibility of the later curfew." Don't put the focus on the penalty by saying, "That's it! You're in at 9:00 P.M. from now on!" Do focus on the road to freedom: "If you do well with 9:00 P.M. for a month, then we'll go back to 10:30 P.M. Fair enough?"

5. *Never acquiesce to terrorism, but don't react harshly to it, either.*

If a consequence impasse pops up with your child saying something scary like, "You'd better watch out if you make me come in at 9," hold on to your dispassionate-cop training. Don't rise to that bait of a challenge from your kid. Again, he's nuts and can't edit some of the things he hears himself saying. Deflect if you can (*"Why don't we pick this up again tomorrow"*). If he won't give it up (*"Well, I'll run away tonight"*), never change your position to accommodate a threat (*"Well, I hope you don't run away, but since I love you I can't let that change what I think is best for you"*). Resist that overwhelming urge to threaten back (*"OH YEAH, well, I'll have the cops on your butt so fast it'll make your head swim!"*). He knows better than you do the enforcement powers you have, but they are much more powerful to him when they remain unsaid.

There is one more behavior-enforcement technique that I want to pass along to you as a gift from another parent. It struck me as a powerful contrast to our present society that has lost so much of its sense of community. Lydia made me dream of how life might be for all of our children if we all had her courage.

> Lydia spoke a little sheepishly as she narrated how she responded to discovering that her son and his friends were stealing beer from neighborhood garages. "I don't know if I did the right thing," she confessed. "I never read this in a parenting book or anything like that. I just kind of reacted, you know? I picked up the phone and called all of the other parents and asked them to come to my house that night with their kids. We sat our children in the middle of the room, and the parents formed a circle around them. Somehow we parents all ended up holding hands like a ring around the kids. I didn't mean for that to happen. It just did. Parents started to say things one at a time. It was like we shared the same thoughts. We said we were just not going to let this stuff happen here. That we couldn't change what was going on in the world, but we were not going to let this craziness go on in our neighborhood. We told them that we loved them so much that we were going to fight with them whenever they were bad. We told them that we were now a community, and that meant that each one of them had to deal with all of us."
>
> Lydia paused here, looking at me as if waiting to be criticized. I was stunned by the elegant, simple genius of this. All I could say was, "What happened?"
>
> "I'm not really sure," she replied, "These big, tough 15-year-old kids just sat there quietly for a minute and then one started to cry. Suddenly everyone was crying, kids and parents, and we all rushed in together to hug the kids. I don't know exactly what was going on, but it was like a huge release of fear, pain, and helplessness for everyone. This seemed to go on forever until my son, the clown, couldn't stand

it anymore and yelled, 'GROUP HUG!' Then we laughed and cried and went out for ice cream. I've never seen a group like ours at an ice cream stand."

Lydia paused again, then asked, "Well, what do you think? Was that an OK thing to do?" I shook my head with admiration and said, "Lydia, I'm writing a book about parenting adolescents and I was wondering if you'd mind if I..."

Now that you've mastered the guiding principles and philosophies of parenting adolescents, you've finally earned the right to enter Chapter 11. This is where you get to do what I always do when I'm at a party with some child psychologist. I wander over, look for an opening, and sheepishly inquire, "I hope you don't mind if I ask you a parenting question, but what would you do if your kid..."

Chapter 11

PROBLEM-SOLVING STRATEGIES:
WHAT TO DO WHEN YOUR TEEN...

NOW THAT YOU HAVE BASIC TRAINING in establishing rules, making decisions, and enforcing them in ways that build identity, let's take a look at how we apply these skills to some common struggles with teens. The strategies described in this chapter are based on the training provided in the previous chapters. If you've jumped ahead, stop and go back. These "how-to" techniques will be of no value to you unless you incorporate all of the training offered up to this point. There are no shortcuts to effective parenting with adolescents.

The guidelines that follow are designed to help stimulate your own problem-solving thinking. They're listed alphabetically so you can easily flip to specific topics as you wish, but read all of them to give yourself a good overview of general problem-solving techniques. These are not necessarily the best options for your family. The best responses are the ones that you create based on your knowledge of your child, who you are, and the training you've had so far in this book. You must assess those individual differences that make your kid unique before using any specific tips you'll see here. Some of these techniques may work for you, others will not, but they will at least encourage you to become creative in your parenting. The more complex areas of struggle, namely drugs, sex, and rock 'n roll (rage), are discussed separately in later chapters.

Aggression

I'm rarely confused about why adolescents are aggressive. I'm always fascinated by teenagers who are rarely aggressive. These increasingly rare kids have somehow found ways of living peacefully in a rage-focused society (see Chapter 2) within a rage-obsessed subculture of adolescence. And they manage to do this while surviving the onslaught of neurological, hormonal, and physical changes that urge them to act out aggressively. Pretty impressive. Most adolescents make up the middle-ground between always angry and rarely angry, but anger and aggression clearly take up more space in a teenager's world than ever before. So here's another place where you want to publicly keep your goals high, but secretly keep your expectations low.

Cherish your teen's peaceful, non-aggressive moments as special gifts to savor, and understand that his aggressive, in-your-face behaviors are normal to some degree. If these escalate into physical contact, they're not normal (see Chapter 13), but if he's yelling, sarcastic, and even occasionally physically challenging (without contact), you must find some way of depersonalizing his anger and not allowing it to wound you. This is easier said than done. This is your beloved child, your flesh and blood, treating you so terribly after all these years of closeness, but you need to have this mindset or you'll never be able to react to the aggression in ways that will reduce its frequency and minimize its impact on your family.

Try to reframe that screaming 14-year-old face with your memory of her tantrumming when she was two. This is largely the same kind of process, just bigger, louder, and scarier. Perhaps try viewing her swaggering, semi-intimidating behavior as a kind of seizure disorder. *She really doesn't mean it and she really doesn't enjoy it,* but like a great actor, she starts to believe in her own made-up tough character as now being real. You must trust me when I tell you that the odds are huge that she wishes she wouldn't act that way, but she can't find ways of disengaging, of getting out of character when she's in the middle of one of these brain-dysfunctional, hormonal, physical, societal, and cultural snits. As hard as it is for you not to take these snap-outs personally, it is twice as hard for her to control her aggression at times.

So what do you do? You don't become aggressive back. Using aggression against aggression is called war. That's what you'll have in your home if you go that route, and you'll be hard-wiring that initially explorative, typically short-lived behavior into your kid's head to ensure a long, bitter, and protracted conflict.

The best response is whatever version of that dispassionate cop (see

Chapter 9) works for you. You might stand calmly, hands at your sides, while your kid blasts you nose to nose, wait until she's done, and then quietly note, "No one's yelling at you," and turn and walk away. Another response is, "OK," as you walk away. A third might be, "Is that the way you want to speak to me?" again, with your withdrawal.

Why walk away from a fight? If you stay and slug it out verbally, you're telling your kid that this is a parentally approved method of dispute resolution. Walking gets the point across that you'll have nothing to do with that type of exchange, and that if your child wants something, she'll have to come up with a better approach. Even more important, leaving the room as your kid's epithets are echoing off the walls gives her the break she needs to try to get herself together. If the last words of the exchange were your calm, tolerant ones and her crazy, insulting ones, those are the words you want stuck in her head as she sits there and stews. Let her finish her sentence before you respond quietly. The contrast between her fury and your control will be dramatic and instructive for her.

CRITICAL DOs

◆ Stay calm

◆ Let her finish her diatribe

◆ Walk away with a quiet response

CRITICAL DON'Ts

◆ Take it personally and rage back

◆ Interrupt to gain control

◆ Discipline on the spot

Appearance: Clothes, Hairstyles, and Other Pointless Battles

The best insight into the relative importance of appearance is the perspective of parents who decided to go to war over clothes. I can recall many who initially thought it was a good idea to forcibly dictate their teens' appearance, but I can think of none who walked off those battlefields still believing that.

"You should tell parents," Art instructed, "to forget about all the small, stupid things when their kids become teenagers. If I had any idea then what it almost cost me now, I wouldn't have said word one to my kid about his appearance." Art shook his head thoughtfully. "Jim is back with me now. We talk, we share, and we relate, all without screaming about his clothes or hair, or what a son-of-a-bitch I am." He paused, and then proudly he added, "Want to hear something weird? I couldn't even tell you what he's wearing today. But I can tell you some of what he's thinking about today. I guess I've learned to look past the clothes into the child."

I can't add much to that thought. I can tell you that fighting over appearance issues hands your crazy kid a perfect excuse to get crazier. You will look truly arbitrary and fascist to her, thus wiping out your ability to talk with her about the really important issues that can kill her. Save your ammo (your respect chips) for the big fights.

Piercings have become the latest twist to push previously tolerant parents to the edge of enrolling their kids in military schools. You might be cool with green pigtails (his) or staggered buzz cuts (hers), but spikes through the tongue, navel, and nipples make most parents think of Inquisition torture techniques (*"NO ONE EXPECTS THE SPANISH INQUISITION!"*) and antibiotic-resistant infections. After this book has sat on your shelf for a year or two, piercings will be passé and some other eyeball-popping fad will take its place. In that event, scratch out the word "piercings" in the following paragraph and insert the new fad word in its place.

The hair, clothes, and piercings are all psychologically harmless expressions of identity exploration that are actually critical steps in your kid's journey to figuring out who she is—which is a journey that can keep her alive. Don't start wars over something that just embarrasses you.

Here's another example of using your kid's momentum against him. As he tortures you to sign the piercing permission slip, bargain. Tell him you're uneasy about this and need more information. Schedule a trip to the physician to get her opinion about the risks and proper care of a piercing. Say that ultimately you're opposed, but that if his behavior continues to be good (or improves in some way), you can't deny him his young-man rights to decorate his body as he sees fit, if it is done responsibly. In other words, use these struggles to build both your kid's identity and his level of responsibility.

I've been in this business too long to give any credence to my personal reactions to a kid's appearance. I've known straight-edge kids (adolescents who don't do sex, drugs, or rock 'n roll) who looked like drug-dealing gang members, and I've known teenage heroin dealers who look like they attend an exclusive private school. If you think that a kid's appearance is the reason he goes bad, you're looking in all the wrong places at all the wrong things. Focus on what's important: the heart of your child. The rest is all a passing illusion.

Chores

Having responsibilities for doing chores around the house is vital to developing your child's character and identity. Even more critical is how you engage your kid on this issue. Threatening or yelling will only turn the chore into another contest for power and another fight over your child's autonomy. Don't go there.

Try to make chores a voluntary commitment for your kid. Give him a list of all of the jobs that need to be done in the house, and ask him what he thinks is fair for him to do. What's fair depends on your situation in terms of total number of chores, number of adults to handle them, free time, financial conditions, and so on. The length of the list will astound and impress your kid, and his freedom to choose will make it easier for him to sign on.

Bribe him. That's right, I said bribe him. There's nothing at all wrong with paying your kid to do chores. You can bribe with increased freedoms, money, privileges—whatever works. The anti-bribing crowd hates this concept, saying kids should do chores out of a moral commitment to the family and so on. That's a nice thought, and if that's already happening in your family, congratulations, but if it's not, try bribery in a controlled form. For example, set up a chore chart that tracks accomplished chores and lists the earned rewards. If you go this route, be clear in your negotiations that you are no longer running a welfare system. All money and privileges have to be earned according to the agreement your kid inked. Of course, this implies that if the chores are not done, there is no money doled out for the Friday-night movie and, perhaps, there's no time earned to go out. The key difference here is that your kid suffers a *consequence* for not doing chores he agreed were appropriate, versus *punishing* him because you decided he wasn't being responsible (see Chapter 10).

Do the anti-bribers have a point? Absolutely, but they forget that they get bribed every day, as we all do. Initially, we all honor our responsibilities in order to get rewards like money or freedom. These are *extrinsic* rewards, based on payoffs that are outside of ourselves. Over time, we grow to enjoy being responsible and doing what we believe is right because we develop the internal moral character that gets rewarded when we are consistent with our beliefs. These are the *intrinsic* rewards that bribe us to do good things, even without an extrinsic payoff. The extrinsic rewards can help start your child down the path of learning the higher values of work and responsibility.

What if you come home exhausted after working late and the trash is still in the garage and the kid is still on the couch? First, stay in your car, tune to that easy-listening radio station, take three deep breaths and wait for the boiling to subside. Remind yourself that you are a parent. You have to learn how to deal with constant failure. You're not running a Fortune 500 company. You are rehabilitating brain-challenged people. This is much harder.

When you're back in control, *you* do his job as obviously as you can so he sees it, *but without saying a word.* He may continue watching *Gilligan's Island,* but I know that he's feeling like a jerk inside. Occasionally, feeling like a jerk is very therapeutic for all of us. Getting your kid to feel like a jerk is a much worse consequence than any yelling you might do. The yelling will only divert him from the real issue and let him off the hook. I know this is impossible to do when you're tired, mad, and stressed. Just do it. If you're successful most of the time, you're doing great. More important, your kid will be doing great, too.

As a final thought about chores, I have to reinforce an important concept. You are in the failure business, which means that your kid is not yet a professional person. He's an amateur, still learning the ropes. If you want perfect theater, go to Broadway. If you want the excitement of seeing people learning their craft, yet making mistakes, go to summer stock performances. If you demand perfection, adopt an adult. If you want the thrill of watching someone developing into a fine human being while screwing up a lot, become a parent. Personally, I don't think you can beat the suspense of summer stock. The challenge and risk make the outcome all that much better.

CRITICAL DOs

◆ Involve your kids in chores

◆ Give them chore choices

◆ Bribe them

◆ Expect imperfect execution

CRITICAL DON'Ts

◆ Let them do nothing

◆ Mandate tasks without discussion

◆ Expect adult responsibility

◆ Snap out over failures

Curfews

You might think that curfew should always be an easy rule in the house. It's not, because curfew, perhaps more than any other rule, so concisely and daily embodies that basic dilemma of parenting adolescents: adults trying to keep their children alive and children trying to prove that they are adults.

When an inevitable parent/teen struggle flares, the first testing ground is often a curfew violation. Knowing this, the wise parent might not focus on the first curfew violation as a challenge, but take it as an invitation to talk in general to see if it's time to enlarge the autonomy /responsibility circles (see Chapter 10). Sidestepping challenges whenever possible is a very powerful thing to do in the eyes of an adolescent.

Whatever your strategies are in dealing with it, there has to be a curfew, and it must be generally respected. Unless your kid is a rare self-regulator, abandoning curfew enforcement is like deciding it's OK to do trapeze work without a net, since curfew serves so many purposes so well.

First, curfew is a speed governor on your child's over-revving teenage brain. Those wild impulses often become scheduling impossibilities if she has to be home by 10 P.M. Second, curfew gives your kid exactly the excuse she may need to artfully pass on joining in someone else's weird impulse (*"Gee, nude midnight skiing sounds so cool but I, like, have to be in by 11"*). Third, it helps stabilize sleep patterns. Left on their own, many adolescents find their sleeping patterns (sleep clock) inverted, so that they're up all night and sleeping all day. Part of this may have a physiological basis, but most studies of controlled sleep environments (military schools, sports camps) suggest that working hard in the daytime and being forced to wake up early in the morning causes even adolescents to maintain a more normal sleep clock.

Perhaps most important, maintaining a curfew is maintaining a critical symbol of the parent/teenager relationship that reminds everyone every day that the *adolescent is still a child*. This is something we tend to forget in these days of parent-sponsored teen beer parties and 11-year-olds being criminally prosecuted as adults. These teen years are transitions to adulthood. They are not adulthood. And holding to a reasonable curfew can set the tone of similar negotiations on rules and decisions. Ultimately, the teen is not ready to be fully autonomous, but everyone's number one job is to prepare her for that time of adulthood, which is coming fast.

Be forgiving of legitimate infrequent curfew lapses. Remember that you always want to be modeling flexibility and reasonableness to your kid. If the frequency worsens, you might consider the "time-and-a-half" rule, where Junior owes you time, and he has to come in early tomorrow for tonight's infraction. If violations of reasonable curfews agreed to by your child are nightly battles, something else is going on. It might be time to call for help.

CRITICAL DOs	CRITICAL DON'Ts
◆ Have a curfew	◆ Let this tough task slip
◆ Negotiate hours	◆ Unilaterally impose hours
◆ Forgive occasional lapses	◆ Ignore chronic lapses
◆ Trade hours for hours	◆ Flatly refuse to talk about new increased responsibilities

Driving

If this subject scares the heck out of you, take comfort in knowing that it should. Providing high-speed mobility to that questionably functioning brain should be scary. I don't have to quote you the statistics that suggest that this is a bad idea. Most parents of 16-year-olds are pulled in two directions on this issue. The cons include safety concerns like speeding, drug use, and sexual possibilities, while the pros center on increased autonomy and no longer having to provide 458 rides every week. The bottom line is that it is one of those areas of calculated risk that, so far, our society seems inclined to accept. You probably just have to make the best of it.

On the bright side, I have a list of all those kids I knew for whom driving was a great bribe to bring them back to the family negotiating table. The pitch we use with much success is that driving is a huge responsibility and, as such, a teen must *first* demonstrate qualities such as good judgment, emotional control, personal responsibility, and even proper sleep patterns (*"You can't be driving to school at 7:00 A.M. if you're on the Net at 3:00 A.M."*) before he can drive.

Once licensed, the new driver has to grow into such additional responsibilities as working to pay for insurance, upkeep, and fuel. If you're on a roll, you might even get the chance to teach her how to change her own oil. These things have a way of filling an adolescent's life so that there's less space left for the craziness.

Keep closely attuned to driving rules. Violations here must be met dispassionately but very firmly, particularly in any instances where either driver or passengers use drugs (including alcohol): "It's clear you're not ready for this much responsibility yet, so we need to hang up your keys for a month. Then we'll re-evaluate your situation to see if it looks like you're ready." Keep your kid's sentence on the short side to give him a reason to try harder. Remember that life sentences promote jailbreaks.

CRITICAL DOs

- Accept driving as a scary reality
- Trade driving for responsibility
- Monitor for compliance to rules
- Temporarily pull back privileges if rules are violated

CRITICAL DON'Ts

- Outlaw driving without just cause
- Just hand her the keys
- Set forever punishments

The Internet

In Chapter 3, I talk about the Internet as an issue of peer relationships with similar benefits and hazards. Most teenagers will use the Internet like the telephone of yesteryear. It becomes *the* way of fostering those peer relationships that kids rank just above air as a basic survival need. In some respects, those group chat rooms have become the malt shops and hamburger stands of earlier generations—places where kids can hang out without adult interference. Overall, this is not to be feared, but sometimes the Net can become a distorted and frightening universe that draws kids away from the real world into insanity.

Excessive and obsessive Internet use are new phenomena that have been linked to teenage depression, isolation, emotional immaturity, and even suicide risk. The much-publicized risk of predators on the Net is relatively small. If your kid has a problem, it will much more likely be with excessive use of the Internet and consequent social isolation.

You must view these .com relationships just as you would real ones. Mocking this activity will drive your child further into the cyber relationship out of rebellion, and further away from you and the real world. You want the opposite outcome. You want to be as involved as possible in his Net life.

Remain at least neutral about any computer love relationship, much as you should with a real one. Rejoice that your kid is talking to you about this, even if it seems crazy to you. What is most critical is to maintain your connection with your child, so that you can be there to catch her when problems occur. The more neutral you can be, the faster the cyber love will fizzle out. Nothing bonds cyber lovers more intensely than parents who don't understand.

If you see your child beginning an obsessive Net phase, first stop and get hold of your own panic. Knee-jerk restrictive edicts may push your kid away from you and into the arms of the Web (aptly named?). Try to quietly and succinctly outline your concerns to her (dispassionate cop stuff). Don't argue with her responses. Just acknowledge that you may have differing points of view, and she might well be correct in thinking that this is harmless. Negotiate (versus mandate) some Net time allocations. Ask her what she thinks is an acceptable time limit per week. Then when she violates that limit, simply ask if she thinks it may be becoming a problem since she couldn't honor her own time commitment. Let her mull it over for a while. Don't hammer your point of view. Try to bargain real-time activities (school clubs, dances, movies) in exchange for time on the Net. Be patient. If you can keep your cool, she will likely begin to see that the real-world stuff is better than the screen stuff. However, if your child repeatedly starts staying up all night on the Net and begins totally shunning the real world, get help fast. We are also beginning to suspect that the Net may be a powerful addiction for some adolescents.

CRITICAL DOs

◆ Take your kid's Internet life seriously

◆ Pay close attention to Net activity

◆ Foster real-world activities

◆ Stay calm (*"it's a phase, it's a phase"*)

◆ Trade off Net time for "real" time

CRITICAL DON'Ts

◆ Laugh off or mock Net relationships

◆ Assume Net time is harmless

◆ Ignore massive Net use

◆ Angrily cut off all computer use

Music (Music?)

In life, it's much easier to find a simple cause for a terrible problem than to admit to complexity, which makes our heads hurt. If we find a simple cause, then we can find a simple solution and get back to watching our football game. Such is the way with music, adolescents, and scared parents.

If I had a CD for every parent who was sure that accidentally microwaving their kids' CDs would eliminate their kids' insanity, I'd have more CDs than my son. I wish adolescent insanity were this simple.

Is much of the music of today's adolescents outrageous, disgusting, evil, racist, chauvinistic, violent, and poorly harmonized? Without a doubt. Does it cause kids to become outrageous, disgusting, evil, racist, chauvinistic, violent,...and poorly harmonized? No, it doesn't. Is it part of the problem? Perhaps, but, more likely, it's just another expression of the larger, more complex issues.

But before we get self-righteous about "our" music versus "their" music, I might ask you to play one of your old albums and place yourself in the position of a parent in 1973 listening to Jim Morrison lyrics. My point is that music, whether by The Doors or one of today's music (music?) idols, doesn't cause bad behavior, but it can be another one of those windows into the culture and soul of your kid that you cannot ignore.

You are probably complaining that there's no way to compare Jim with one of today's music (music?) stars, and you certainly have a case there, but not in the way that you think. A kid who chooses to listen exclusively to the vile ooze on a heavy-metal CD over and over, who fantasizes about doing those things he hears, and who withdraws into that evil world, is no worse off than the kid you knew who played that Morrison track over and over. What's changed is the world around these kids (see Chapter 2). The soul of those two different adolescents from two different worlds is in the same condition: troubled.

The influence of a kid's music on his life all depends on the kid. As background noise, does it subtly shift his tolerance towards these forms of evil? Maybe, but we don't really know. Does this music represent part of a larger societal shift towards rage and aggression? Likely, yes, for we see it everywhere we look in the things that reflect who we are as a people in this culture. Do those lyrics get him temporarily charged-up and aggressive at times? Possibly. But does that horrid CD alone make your kid do crazy things? Nope. Sorry, but our parental task is much larger than CD-smashing. If your child is in such bad shape that a CD really appears to be a threat, then there must also be many other indicators that you need to get expert help, and quickly.

So what do you do in the more normal situation? You do the individual differences drill. You engage your kid in discussions about who she is and what the music means to her. Don't hammer her with what the experts say it does to all kids. Don't smash the CD or you'll smash another one of those precious windows into that kid's head. Bargain with her. Tell her she can have the CD provided the two of you listen to it (gulp!) together and then chat. Ask her questions about what she thinks of those lyrics, if she thinks they do inspire insanity or just parental fear and market shares. Ask if she'd let her little sister listen to it, and why not? Engage your kid in dispassionate debate, raise the counterpoint, and make her head hurt just like yours by making her think.

If the music is so offensive, tell her it can't be played aloud in the house, but she can use her earphones. Perhaps, also let her know that if it is left out where a younger sibling can get it, then it must leave the house. With adolescents, try at all costs not to just forbid music, or you'll make that stupid CD the battleground for endless fights that will use up much of the precious parent ammunition you need to save for the big fights (sex, drugs, and rock 'n roll).

Try trading off the music for increased responsibilities. Tell him that if he can do better with his temper, then maybe you'll be more inclined to have to accept his argument that the music does not increase his aggressiveness. And if not, maybe the music has to wait until he's more mature.

Remember: Inoculate, don't mandate. The last laugh might be on the offensive music, because if you can use that fertilizer (CD lyrics) to get your kid to worry and think about our violent society, then he will carry that protection and wisdom with him wherever he goes. If you just forbid the CD, you may make the music more important than it really is in your kid's head—another thing you don't want to do.

CRITICAL DOs	CRITICAL DON'Ts
◆ Allow him free choices with conditions	◆ Censor his music and create martyrs
◆ Monitor your kid's music content	◆ Let the scary lyrics go unchallenged
◆ Trade off bad lyrics for responsibility	◆ Lose windows of opportunity to talk
◆ Inoculate	◆ Mandate

Peers

In Chapter 3, I gave you a basic understanding of what peer influence is all about, that it is not the terrible menace most parents fear will recruit their child into a life of drugs. Connel put this very well to his mother.

Ruth looked scared after finally asking Connel, her 14-year-old son, if his peer group used drugs. "Yes," he responded truthfully. Mom's terror grew as she framed her next question. "Do you use drugs?" Connel's dead-on gaze was convincing. "I tried marijuana a couple of times years ago, Mom, and that's it. I really just don't feel like doing any of that stuff." Ruth's fears blossomed into confusion. "Well, Connel, what do you do when you're hanging with your crowd at a party and they want to do drugs? Don't they try to force you or make you feel weird if you don't?"

Connel thought this over and gave a response that was so good, I wrote it down. "Mom, do you know any people who do drugs at parties?" Mom looked at me as if asking if she should tell the truth. Interesting parental dilemma, I thought, as I shrugged my shoulders to let her know she was on her own with this one. She glared at me like I wasn't earning my pay and then slowly nodded yes. Connel wasn't done. "Do you do drugs, Mom?" "NO!" Mom snapped, and then she stammered, "Well, I-I drink some wine sometimes, but that's not the same thing. And because I do something doesn't mean it's OK for a 14-year-old. . ." Connel nicely interrupted his flustered mother. "That's not what I meant, Mom. I just wanted to know what you do when your friends start using drugs at their party." Mom hated losing control of a conversation with a lowly teenager. Boy, do I know that feeling!

Ruth paused and gathered herself. "Well, I guess I just say that I don't want to do that and the drug users don't bother me about it, they just go off on their own to do whatever. They don't really care if I use or not. Sometimes if I'm uncomfortable, I'll leave the party. And they're not like heavy drug users; they usually just smoke some marijuana. It's not as if my friends do heroin or anything." Connel nodded vigorously. Ruth didn't get it. "What, what?" she asked. Connel kept nodding. "What you do with your friends, Mom, is exactly what I do with my friends. Is that OK?" Ruth again looked back at me. I continued to not earn my pay.

I kept quiet because I couldn't have added anything to Connel's response. Kids *are* prone to impulsive behavior and may be more susceptible than adults to peer suggestions like doing drugs, but the answer to that problem is to help them develop their identity so that they can make better choices (inoculating). The paradoxical facts are that (1) part of that identity-building is done by allowing your kid to make her own peer choices whenever possible, and (2) exposure to troubled kids can be a critical part of her learning about good choices. Short of allowing her to run with an acknowledged sexual child predator, your best long-term option is to grin and bear the dubious choices in friends—but do this proactively.

Keep *dispassionately* but effectively involved in your kid's life, including his peer choices. Push hard to have his friends visit a lot under your gaze. Encourage sleepovers and parties at your house. Find fun outings that you can sponsor to engage these kids. Talk with his friends a lot. Hang out with them as much as you are allowed. You'll be given much more access to his peers if you keep your criticisms and ultimatums to yourself.

If you are really scared of a peer group that refuses to have any contact even with supportive parents, first try negotiating with your child. Be dispassionately direct about your concerns and see if he's willing to compromise by allocating some hours to other pursuits like family time or school activities. Be more conservative about allowing unstructured time with scary kids, holding on to supervision rules (see Chapter 10). If you run into brick walls, something else might be going on between you and your child that bears getting some professional help.

The answer is not to pick her friends. Mandating who she can and cannot see is a great way to invert your choices in your child's head. To her, the good kids will look really bad and the bad kids will look really good. If you can master your own panic and give it some time, and if you're doing OK with your child otherwise, those good kids will eventually look like better choices to her. That's the gold for which you take some risk.

CRITICAL DOs

◆ Allow her peer choices with conditions

◆ Monitor your kid's peer choices

◆ Engage your kid's friends

◆ Inoculate

CRITICAL DON'Ts

◆ Censor her peers and create martyrs

◆ Let your kid run loose

◆ Lose windows of opportunity to talk

◆ Mandate

Religion

Freely and lovingly embraced, religion can be a wonderfully enriching aspect of an adolescent's life. It can convey many identity-building experiences that include shared family activity, religious/cultural/ethnic histories, social responsibility, and moral/ethical awareness.

Unilaterally dictated and compelled, religion can become a terrible teen battle that can severely damage otherwise healthy family relationships and contaminate many areas of parent/child function. There are not many other issues that create as much passion as a child rejecting the religion of the family. From the parent's perspective, you might view your religion as the glue that binds your existence, and the thought of your child being outside of your faith may seem unfathomable. You may believe that you are fighting for your child's eternal soul. How can you give in on such an issue?

From the teenager's side, the view can seem quite different. She may simply not believe what you believe. She's now able and, in fact, required to think for herself and she feels she is able to make such a decision, particularly a decision as intensely personal as choosing her religious faith.

I think the what-to-do decision is implicit in that description of the religion struggle. Forcing your kid to walk into the building most likely ensures that he will grow to hate whatever wisdom is offered there. Just as this nation recognizes that religion cannot be imposed, so too must parents appreciate that religion must be lovingly embraced to have meaning. The confusion arises from the early years when you were able to get your kid to attend services with you because you said this was a good thing to do. The attachment of a young child to a religion is not that of an adult. The young child gives the concept of God pretty much the same significance as Santa Claus. It's all that brain is capable of processing.

But in these years of adolescence, that brain develops and begins to ask theological questions that are impossible to answer definitively in the scientific sense, and insisting that the teen accept such a huge concept on faith alone is asking too much.

Your best defense of your religious values is to live them and display them to your child. Those qualities such as patience, tolerance, understanding, and open-mindedness will go a long way towards teaching your kid the value of your faith. If this is how your child sees your religion, he will be more open to dispassionate discussions of religious issues. As he explores who he is, these are the concepts you want him to associate with your faith in that expanding brain. This is simply the only good option open to you.

CRITICAL DOs	CRITICAL DON'Ts
◆ Allow him to make his own religious choices	◆ Compel a process of love
◆ Model your faith as tolerance	◆ Lose windows of opportunity to talk
◆ Inoculate	◆ Mandate

Running Away

The term "running away" is used by parents to describe three very different types of fleeing behaviors, each of which has different causes, outcomes, and suggested responses.

The first would be the "I've had it with this crap," 100-yard sprint out the front door, which gets slammed against the wall. BANG! I call this the door-bash dash. It usually occurs spontaneously in the heat of a fight, with your kid back within a couple of hours. The door-bash dash feels really bad to parents who see it as a representation of their loss of control and emotional connection with their child. The reality is that the door-bash dash can be a very helpful device in reducing chaos in the house by allowing your brain-challenged child a great way to blow off excess steam. Front doors and sidewalks can take a lot more physical punishment than drywall and parents. And, often, parents terribly regret attempting to restrain a kid from running out the door.

Don't get into a game of chicken by forbidding your kid from dashing. Instead, view her running off as a safety valve that keeps the situation from getting too far out of hand. The door-bash dashers are almost always back in the house within hours, so go make some tea and rehearse your dispassionate-cop responses for when she returns. She may come back and ask that you not talk further, usually because she is embarrassed that she lost her composure. Agree to this if she agrees in return to setting up a time later to finish the discussion. Try not to view the door-bash dashing as a punishable offense, but as something that brain-challenged people do when they get overly stressed. Your kid will respect and love you for not focusing on her loss of control (see Chapter 7).

I call the second type of runaways the weekend warriors. These are kids who usually take off semi-spontaneously in response to issues of chronic conflict that have been simmering for some time. They might leave in the heat of a fight or just disappear after school one day. This behavior is more like an act of civil disobedience—a kind of generalized protest designed to make a political statement. The kids call this "being on the lam" to distinguish it from the more serious forms of running away. Typically, kids who do this maintain the other aspects of their lives, including work and school, and usually bunk at a friend's house where those parents get to hear about how horribly unfair you are.

For pained parents who lose their child to weekend retreats, keep in mind three key points. The first is that what appears to be a fun-filled vacation is actually a pretty lousy excursion for your kid. Living in a strange house without all her stuff is not easy to do. And watching this other family getting along well and loving each other makes your kid homesick (I know you don't believe that this could be true, but I'm telling you that this is what your kid tells me). She'd rather be home.

Second, the weekend warriors are really just doing something that we encourage adults to do all the time: go on retreats. These respites from the rigors of daily routines help us to think about our lives, our families, and ourselves. When that weekend warrior is out of your vocal range for a few days, he becomes less able to focus only on your "unfair" demands, and gradually comes to do some very mature things, like considering your point of view.

The third point to keep in mind is that 95 out of every 100 weekend warriors are back home within three days, and the majority of them let you know where they are staying. Typically, they run to safe environments. These facts should dictate how you respond to the three-day junket.

Your first response should be to locate your kid. If your child doesn't call in by curfew and you can't locate him by phoning around, you must call the police. He'll go nuts that you did this, but you don't have any choice. Let him know that if he goes to a safe place, you won't immediately send out the cops as long as he's responsible enough to let you know where he is. If you verify that your kid is in a safe place such as at a friend's house with good parents, take a breath and relax. Ironically, your kid being on the lam may give you a needed break as well to do some thinking. Let him know that you love and miss him, and that he needs to check in periodically with you, but that if it's OK with his friend's parents, he can stay for a few days. Talk directly with those parents to be sure that the supervision pieces are all in place. Thank them, but understand you may be returning the favor one day.

The next thing you do is get that teakettle going again and review what's been happening in your house. Just like the non-violent protestor, your child is sending you a message. Try to figure it out. It's in there somewhere, between the outrageous demands for unchaperoned Mexican vacations and coming home at 3:00 A.M. It might be that you are too controlling, or that your own needs are getting played out on your kid, or any one of a million reasons. Try to reframe the weekend warrior as a peaceful demonstrator desperately searching for a non-violent way of making a point about something that's very important to him.

One variation of the weekend warrior is the child who takes off with the appearance of never coming back, but who leaves a trail of clues that Inspector Clouseau couldn't miss. She wants you to call and find her. Often, she'll call you just to say don't bother trying to find me at the bus station downtown in the second concourse level over by the candy machines. This is just another message-sending mechanism.

Regardless of the type of retreating your kid does, if you can discover her point and show respect and support for that concern, you're on your way to healing and your kid is on her way home. But at all costs, avoid focusing on your child's retreat as a crime that deserves punishment. If you threaten your kid with reprisals or dare her to really run away, you might lose her to the third class of runaways. You don't want this to happen. These can be the forever kind.

The third group of kids who run away are the serious ones who are in serious trouble. These kids represent the small minority of fleeing children, but they are at the greatest risk. These are the kids who truly intend to never come home. They leave no trail and head for high-risk environments where all kinds of predators await them. Often, these kids are running from brutal or extremely rigid homes where they feel they are never listened to or negotiated with, and thus have no options left. Kids with no options are easy prey to the perverts, pushers, and pimps of the world.

I intentionally frighten you here because an astounding number of these kids were thrown or dared out of their homes and told things such as "You don't have the guts to run away," or "It's my way or the highway," or "Get the hell out and don't ever come back." DON'T

DO THIS. If you're that out of control in a fight, walk away now. You will accomplish nothing good and maybe a whole lot bad by continuing a heated exchange. I've known parents who feel it is OK to say these things to their child, but would never dream of leaving loaded firearms around their teen. Yet to me, the risk is similar. Remember, you're dealing with an impulsive, brain-challenged human being who lives in a very dangerous world. The last thing you want to do is provoke this crazy person to act crazier.

CRITICAL DOs	CRITICAL DON'Ts
◆ Stay calm	◆ Snap out
◆ Determine the type of runaway your child is	◆ Do nothing
◆ Locate your child or call the cops	◆ Immediately call the cops if she's safe
◆ Find and respect your kid's message	◆ Punish her for running away
◆ Lovingly ask that she stay home	◆ Throw your kid out or dare her to leave
◆ Inoculate	◆ Mandate

School Achievement

If there is one area of parenting where we all become shortsighted, it is that long-sighted goal of educating our children. As parents, we become obsessed with that report card, scanning every score and nuance looking for more things to whack our kids over the head with. Much is said about excessive athletic pressures brought to bear on some kids, but the hidden pressure-cooker is that grade competition that we so lovingly inflict on our children. "What," you exclaim indignantly, "could possibly be wrong with demanding academic excellence?" "Nothing," I reply, "as long as you don't get the grades and lose the kid." Let me turn your competitive zeal against you for a moment.

Long-term, high-level academic achievement is a marathon run, not a sprint. It is an event best mastered by kids who possess qualities like self-awareness (identity), emotional resilience (identity), positive out-look (identity), persistence (identity), and self-directedness (identity). In other words, it's a game for folks who have consolidated their iden-tities. If you think back to our discussions of identity-building, you'll recall how one good way to impair that identity process is to either over- or under-control your kid. The magic is in the balance.

When you have those high school achievement discussions, you must bring this information to mind. You must weigh whether the "A" in physics is worth the price you may have to pay. If you have to choose between getting the "A" and damaging your relationship with your child by yelling and threatening, or letting your kid get a "C" and hav-ing her learn a lot about herself in the process, you have one tough decision to make. But if you're asking me, go for the "C," with condi-tions. That "C" might be the grade that gets her through postgraduate biochemistry. How?

Think of what you've learned about building your child's identity. Remember, you want to strike a balance with your kid by providing a safe zone within which she can find out who she is. With school issues, this means that she *must* attend and she *must* pass, but it *must* be up to her to decide to strive for excellence. This is so for a number of rea-sons. First, as with religion, this is something, ultimately, you can't force. You can compel excellence for a period of time, but you'll use up all of that vital parental respect ammo which you must save for the life-threatening fights. Second, if you review that list of characteristics that breed long-term academic success, you'll see that building those qualities is done with that dispassionate engagement approach. Your kid learns to make good decisions when you allow her to sometimes make bad ones. Scary, isn't it?

Third, incessantly grinding your child down for the sake of grades will not instill the life-long love of learning that characterizes people who achieve long-term academic success. More likely, your kid will come to hate school and everything associated with it if you become the prison warden. This is a function of how most adolescents view the concept of secondary education.

To most kids, school is a weird abstraction created by adults for rea-sons no one can seem to explain to them very well. Teens can make powerful arguments about the irrelevance of what they are taught in school based on studies that suggest that most of what you learned in high school, you've forgotten due to its irrelevance to your life. (Quick: What's the gross national product of Bulgaria?)

You might want to steal my rap to your kid when he complains to me that school is boring and irrelevant. I tell him that school is actually irrelevant and boring. He laughs and asks, "What's the point?" I say the point is that it's a game. The game is to do well so you can go to more school and then get a cool job. He says he can get a cool job without school. I pull out data that shows that cool jobs are grabbed by people who learn the discipline of learning irrelevant and boring stuff. He starts to rethink what school means.

Why would I speak so cynically about education, something I prize? Because that cynical view reflects the reality for your kid, at least at the moment, and by first respecting his position, you can then jump into that adolescent thinking to try to sway him a bit. Plus, you sidestep endless, pointless, and rage-producing arguments about the relevance of schoolwork. After I agree with them that school is stupid, most of the kids I see amend their positions to admit that some of it actually is interesting. "Oh, yeah?" I ask with amazement, "You actually like math? No! You're lying! I hated math. Wow! Maybe you're like a scientist-type person or something. You must be like those engineers who work at NASA. Now that looks like a cool job."

In other words, don't entirely bail out of the school stuff by any means. Remain dispassionate to keep the lines of communication open, but don't be afraid to tinker a bit. Keep the discussions going on what he thinks cool jobs would be, and what kinds of academic dues they may require. Offer (don't inflict) any and all assistance to help him do well, such as computers, tutoring, or study skill programs. Ask him if he'd like to be bribed. Setting up a rewards program can often be enough incentive to help him deal with the frustrations of learning stupid stuff. The "learning for its own sake" ethic may develop later as a part of his own identity as he experiences the exhilaration of rising to the challenge of academic excellence.

CRITICAL DOs	CRITICAL DON'Ts
◆ Dispassionately monitor school performance	◆ Become uninvolved
◆ Agree that school is boring	◆ Argue that it's relevant

- Offer supports and bribes for excellence
- Mandate minimal performance goals

- Hammer for excellence

- Accept failure

School Attendance

The short version here is to say that any issues of school attendance should be addressed by getting expert help yesterday. An unwillingness to go to school can represent a bunch of different problems that have to be carefully sorted out before you can respond effectively. Equate your kid's refusal to go to school without a good explanation with your own refusal to go to work, and you have a sense of the significance of this problem. Something big is going on. Immediately call your school to see if they have response teams to help you deal with school avoidance problems.

Why the urgency? The more school days your kid misses, the more difficult it is to eventually get her back in. So while you're waiting for the shrink appointment, use any measure you can to get her face in the place.

Discussing and negotiating are your first courses of action. See if there is an identifiable problem that can be worked through. If your kid says she's just burned out, try negotiating a planned mental-health day later in the week that maybe you could both spend playing hooky together. Planning and preparing for a day off is a lot different than letting fear dictate a course of action. Bribing is a good second option. Yes, it may establish a precedent that she'll try to use later, but most teens are strangely moral about not taking advantage in that way. The bribe may help her confront whatever monster awaits her at school.

Pushed to your last resort, let her know that you can't condone her ducking school and that you'll have to report her as truant because that's the law. Keep downplaying this hardball response, repeating that you really want to find another solution, but be dispassionately clear that going to school is non-negotiable.

Most important, remember that your kid is probably hurting really badly if he's drawing these kinds of lines in the sand. I tell you this not to encourage you to cave in, but to ask you to stay calm and avoid anger or ridicule. You could end up pouring acid on a wound you did-n't even know he had. He will understand and forgive your standing dispassionately firm about school attendance, but dumping more hurt on top of some secret pain might devastate him.

CRITICAL DOs	CRITICAL DON'Ts
◆ Get her to school at any cost	◆ Allow avoidance behaviors
◆ Get help immediately	◆ Assume that this is just a phase
◆ Realize she's hurting somewhere	◆ Use anger or sarcasm

Supervision

Do you know which hours of the day your adolescent has the greatest chance of becoming or getting someone pregnant? 3:00 P.M. to 5:00 P.M. We don't like to talk much about this, since in most American families, there are two working parents.

There's a research smokescreen that confuses this problem. Substantial studies have been done on the effects of working mothers on children. As we'll discuss shortly, virtually all of these studies show either positive or no differences from kids with stay-at-home moms. I realize that focusing on working *mothers* versus working *fathers* is a sexist concept, but such is the debate in our society and the research is done accordingly. The problem is that this reassuring research applies to younger children who are rarely left unsupervised by adults. Teenagers, by comparison, are typically left unsupervised by adults when parents are not around. And if the adolescent acting-out statistics for the three- to five-shift shock you, you should hear what goes down if your kid is left alone for two days.

The bottom line is that home alone, your 16-year-old might be more at risk than your 6-year-old. Leaving a young child alone at home raises a huge public outcry, sometimes among the same parents who think nothing of taking off for a weekend and leaving a brain-challenged, impulsive, hormonal, and curious adolescent home alone.

She can't be left unsupervised. She's crazy. She cannot handle the call of the wild that begins when she waves goodbye to Mom and Dad. I know that this is grossly unfair to all of those adolescents who don't go nuts when the cat's away. I also know that it is grossly unfair to all of those exhausted parents who need time away alone, but it only takes one small lapse of judgment in that already-tenuous teenage brain to lead to a catastrophe in your family.

We don't let exceptionally responsible 14-year-olds drive or 17-year-olds drink because their brains can't be relied on to consistently handle such responsibilities. So how do we justify leaving these children, even the exceptionally responsible ones, unsupervised for long periods of time?

I know it's impossible to supervise all the time. Do the best you can. Insist on after-school activities to fill in those pregnancy-happy hours. Bribe your kid to stay at the library in the afternoons to do his homework (*"It's a much better academic environment"*). Find a house sitter. Have your kid stay over at a friend's house when you are away. If you don't have coverage for a weekend, don't go away. She'll be gone in a couple of years and then you can run around as much as you like.

Are these measures in conflict with my mantra of inoculating your kid and letting him make decisions? Nope. Trust me, your teen will find plenty of wiggle room to be confronted with those scary identity-building decisions no matter how well you supervise. The purpose of these restrictions is to provide that safer space for his explorations. A weekend without adults somewhere in the vicinity is not a safe exploration—that's walking a wire without a net. He might make it across, but do you really want to find out?

CRITICAL DOs	CRITICAL DON'Ts
◆ Provide supervision 24/7	◆ Do *Home Alone 14*
◆ Put off your own needs for now	◆ Guess she'll be OK
◆ Remember she's still a child	◆ Think she has an adult brain

Working Parents

After having beaten you up about leaving your child unsupervised while you work, now let me tell you why working is OK and maybe even a good thing for your kids (provided you have that supervision for your child). For most families, having two parents working is not done as a fun option, but as an economic necessity. For single-parent families, there is no alternative. The increasingly popular portrayal of working moms as self-centered, neglectful women who choose to advance their own careers to pay for oceanfront vacation homes at the cost of their children's welfare is incredibly ignorant and insulting nonsense. In the vast majority of situations, that second income is used for such self-indulgent luxuries as food, tuition, and clothing. For some lucky mothers, working may be an option they choose, but it can benefit children in several ways.

The large, well-conducted studies have found no emotional differences between children of working moms and children of stay-at-home moms. Most of the other studies suggest that, in general, children of working mothers suffer no deficits and may gain a few plusses in areas like school achievement and self-reliance. Studies of single-parent moms show only familial benefits to working, which include financial security, higher morale, and higher self-esteem.

There is absolutely nothing wrong with choosing to stay at home and be a full-time parent if you can and, more important, *if this is who you are*. If you find this life fulfilling, challenging, and rewarding, do it, for you will do it well and become energized and uplifted by it. However, if you find yourself unhappy, depressed, and angry, think about whether or not this is the lifestyle for you. You might not be as effective a parent as you could be if you worked—and we are now confident that mothers who work do not harm their kids.

Many men and women find that they are much better parents if they work *and* parent. They find that work gives them a balance that keeps them feeling more positive, tolerant, and, ultimately, giving to their children. They report being more excited to see their children and more able to focus on their kids' needs.

The bottom line is that if you work, whether you have to or choose to, you are not harming your children. If you have the choice, choose according to who you are, because choosing to either stay at home or work because someone else tells you it's the right thing to do will increase the likelihood of harming your children by making their mother nuts.

Working Teenagers

Jobs are good for most kids. They teach them many lessons about responsibility, money management, discipline, tedium, socialization, and so on. Terrible jobs can be great antidotes to those discussions of the irrelevance of school. Chop onions for 10 hours and then tell me how stupid school is.

Once again, it's a question of priorities and balance. The priority must be school. That becomes Job Number One. If Job Number One is under control, we can discuss having a second job at the pizza parlor. If Job Number One slides, then Job Number Two goes.

Balance refers to the hourly demands. Jobs that take over 20 hours out of a school week tend to foster dropping out. Twelve to 13 hours seems to be the maximum that most kids can handle and still do well in school.

When you're getting relentlessly pounded to sign the working papers, don't forget to manipulate the situation to build increased responsibility like getting better grades, if needed, or perhaps, banking half of the earnings.

CRITICAL DOs	CRITICAL DON'Ts
◆ Allow jobs, with conditions	◆ Miss this growth opportunity
◆ Require schoolwork first	◆ Allow jobs to take precedence
◆ Agree to up to 13 hours per week	◆ Agree to 20 hours per week or more

This list of what-to-do-when could go on forever, but it won't here because, by now, you've gotten the essence of how to approach the thousands of other situations you will face. The principles are universal and simple: Strive to first build identity, then achievement. Respond to anger with calmness. Inoculate, don't mandate. Remember that your kid is nuts. Remember to laugh. And remember that this will all end one day.

Speaking of ending, we are leaving this chapter without addressing one other critical what-to-do situation that is so important, it will be the exclusive subject of the next chapter: teen privacy—how to balance respect issues with concerns for survival. Did I mention that parenting adolescents is hard?

Chapter 12

BALANCING SAFETY WITH PRIVACY:
WALKING THE RAZOR'S EDGE

I CAN GUESS the reason that you're not sleeping so well these days. You're tossing and turning, sighing and sitting up, laying back down in a huff, getting up in a huff, walking rapidly to your teenager's room, and stopping at the closed door. He's away at a sleepover. You angrily grab the knob, then suddenly release it like it was red hot and return to your bed muttering to yourself as you begin the whole cycle over again. If you have a teenager, you know this to be the "should I search his room?" insomnia.

What could cause this much distress? Weighing the pluses and minuses of searching through his drawers, reading his diary, checking his e-mail, pulling his bookbag apart, looking under his mattress, and, in general, giving your beloved child less trust, respect, and privacy than a judge might accord a known felon. How is it that the relationship between parent and child comes to this point?

Lana sat down heavily on the couch, staring at the floor. As she began speaking, the circles under her eyes and the stoop of her shoulders told me it had not been a good week for this mother of a 12-year-old boy. "I told you last week that I suspected Brian was doing drugs. He's so moody and angry with me all the time, and he's always in his room when he's not out. I know you suggested that I not search his things, but you don't understand what I'm going through." She looked up now to make her case. "Late one night, I watched a TV show about this poor man whose son died of a drug overdose in his own house. This father was saying how he'd been ignoring all the symptoms right under his nose and he pleaded for all the parents not to ignore the signs like he had." Lana became energized as she relived that night. "I thought of what you said, but it wasn't good enough. My son could die! Maybe tonight!

"So I snuck into Brian's room while he was sleeping and began going through his things. I saw that he was beginning to stir, so I quietly took his book bag back to my room to search it. There must have been 20 pounds of crap in there, but the worst thing I found were some crude jokes the kids were passing around. Then I found it. He had made a secret compartment in an inner pocket that no one could have found except me searching like I was. In it was an old yellow envelope with something inside. I knew it was drugs. My hands were shaking as I opened the envelope and dumped the contents. Out fell a picture and a small piece of cloth."

Lana lowered her head again as tears splashed onto her lap. In a shaking voice she explained, "The cloth was a corner of his old baby blanket that he slept with from birth until it disappeared sometime last year. And here's the picture."

Lana held her weeping face in one hand and held out the photo with the other. The creased and wrinkled picture was of a beautiful little boy about six years old resting peacefully in his mother's arms on a beach while watching the ocean. A much younger and much happier Lana was smiling adoringly at this precious little child that she obviously cherished. Why then was Lana so distraught now? Her voice startled me as she continued her explanation.

"That picture was from a special vacation we took together. We used to love going to the beach. As I sat there in amazement looking at this photograph of my six-year old, I heard a noise behind me. There stood my son with his face red with rage. I tried to explain, but he cut me off. At the knees. 'Nice, Mom,' was all he'd say, 'Really, really nice.' I tried to give him back his things, but he threw them at me saying he didn't want them anymore. Ever." Lana cried harder at her words now. "He didn't even yell. He just became cold. I've lost him forever. I can feel it. I cut the last tie between us."

As I watched her sob, I thought to myself that Lana's struggle over Brian's privacy was like balancing on the edge of a razor. Fall either way, and she could lose her kid. Staying still meant living with the cutting pain and fear.

That razor's edge waits for all of us. If you are thinking that you already know what you would do in Lana's place, lose those ideas now, because they can hurt you and your child. The fact is that you cannot prethink decisions like this until you get there. There are no easy answers to these dilemmas, and people who tell you there are should be ignored. The question of privacy is yet another one of those battles for which there should be parent medals. This struggle is agonizing, frightening, and often inconclusive, no matter how courageously you fight. I'm now going to take you through a few different points you must consider when making these decisions, but you alone have to make that call just like I do. No one else can do this for you or for me.

Why You Should Always Invade Her Privacy

Admit it. Whenever you're reading those newspaper accounts about teenage overdoses, school shootings, bombings, or suicides, don't you often shake your head and think, *How could those parents have not known? Didn't they ever look in his room, for God's sake? If they had, that kid would be alive today.*

And you'd be right. If people had rummaged through those kids' rooms, they would have found evidence of insanity waiting to happen. Guns, drugs, suicidal writings—all that stuff can be found in a good search. Kids sometimes leave these clues in obvious places as distress calls, secretly wanting them to be found.

It's the job of parents to look for these things—openly, if possible, or in secret searches, if need be. If it bothers the kids, well then, too bad! If they have nothing to hide, it shouldn't bother them. Given the times we live in and the fact that we now know they're brain-challenged, we *owe* it to our adolescents to invade their privacy if we think something is wrong. These are not adults. They cannot have the same rights of privacy as we do.

Strategically, it's smart to do, anyhow. If your kid knows that periodically you're going to look through his room, he's a lot less likely to think he can hide crazy things that can kill him.

Last, but not least, how could you live if you decided to respect your kid's privacy and not search her room the night before the morning you found her dead from the gunshot that jarred you awake? If the possible cost of not invading her privacy is the life of your child, how can there be any other decision? What other considerations could possibly outweigh survival?

Dad was clearly upset. You could see from his agitation that he had been whipping himself for some time. "You see," he began to explain, "when I was a teen, my room was like a sacred shrine for me. No one, I mean, no one, was allowed in without my permission. That room was my safety zone where I knew I could finally just be myself and not worry about what anyone else might think about me. It felt like I wouldn't have survived if I didn't have that space. So I just assumed that Cheryl felt the same, particularly since she was so depressed. I wanted to respect her privacy in her troubled times, and just being her stepfather instead of her father…" He didn't finish his last sentence, realizing that he was excusing himself, something he was not normally inclined to do, and something that seemed to disgust him.

"Anyway, all that is not the point. The point is that I blew it. I knew better all along. I just didn't want to see what was going on because it was so scary to consider. So I just pretended that things were OK. You want to know how I ended up searching her room? I decided to check for roof leaks in a heavy storm." Bruce laughed sadly at himself. "That was my excuse to get into her room when she wasn't there. The next thing I know, I'm going through her stuff. That's how I found it. A bag full of pills. At first, I thought that she was doing drugs, but her mother recognized them as the antidepressants she was supposed to have been taking these past three months. As I took out the crumpled note that was in the bag, I found myself hoping that she was only selling the drugs. In my head, Cheryl being a dope dealer seemed better than the truth that unfolded in my hands.

"In what she had intended to be her last words to us, Cheryl begged us to forgive her and to please know that there was nothing we could have done to save her, and to not feel guilty. My God, we came so close to losing her just because she was acting like a depressed teenager, believing that there was nothing else we could do to help her." While Bruce sat and shook his head at himself, I wondered what call I might have made if that were my kid. It made me shiver.

Why You Should Never Invade Her Privacy

Admit it. Whenever you're reading those newspaper accounts about teenage overdoses, school shootings, bombings, or suicides, don't you often shake your head and think, *How could those parents not have known? Didn't they ever look in his room, for God's sake? If they had, that kid would be alive today.*

And you'd be wrong, for that act of searching your child's room might contribute to crazy acting-out behaviors that could include suicide.

The factors that most contribute to catastrophic acts of adolescent insanity are a lack of connection to loved ones and poor identity. When kids who hate themselves are free-falling without loving parental bonds, evil incarnate comes sniffing around. One of the best ways I can suggest to put your child at risk is to shatter his sense of identity along with his love and respect for you by telling him that you don't trust him. Searching his room is calling him an untrustworthy liar. Going through his book bag sticks a knife into the heart of your relationship with your son and is a great way to make sex, drugs, and rock 'n roll look very attractive to him.

If you want to push him further down that road towards insanity, go ahead and pull his room apart. If you want to do a thorough job and make your kid really safe, you'd better strip-search him, too, since he might be hiding drugs in some body cavity. And maybe this should occur nightly, along with lockdowns. Isn't this where you're headed once you take that first step into his room? If not, where do you draw the line?

Let me give you some other reasons why you should never search. First, the odds are astronomically high against something really terrible going on that you could prevent with a search. Do you forbid your teen from flying, since airplanes do crash occasionally? Or do you decide that the good gained in accepting the risk is worthwhile?

Second, if your kid is going over the edge, your search won't do anything but drive him closer to the craziness. He'll learn to conceal things better, while he grows to hate you all the more for your actions. If you search and find nothing, you just gambled the farm away. And if you do find something, then what? When you confront him about that switchblade you found, I guarantee that all the screaming will be about your invasion of his privacy and not the contraband. Your behavior, not his, will become the focus of his future actions. Just as with the cops, any evidence you get in an "illegal" search will be useless in the "court" of your discussions with your child. Weapons are easily replaced. Trust is hard to buy on the street.

Third, you put a torch to any respect currency you had with your kid. That respect becomes *all the more important* when your child acts like he hates you. Don't make the common mistake of thinking that you have nothing to lose by searching just because he won't talk with you anymore. *The fact that he's furious with you doesn't mean he disrespects you.* And that precious respect may be the very lifeline that's keeping him safe at the moment.

When you search, you shred your child's respect for you by denigrating your own values. You teach him that all that talking you did about trust and boundaries is just so much jive to be disregarded if you are upset about something. You prove that these principles are arbitrary, to be tossed aside whenever you feel like it. You also diminish yourself in his eyes by appearing panicked, out of control, and weak.

Fourth, the odds are that whatever you find (if anything) will be very low-level threat indicators, some of which you'll wish you had never found.

> "I know I shouldn't have done this, but I just had to see if he was doing drugs. I didn't find drugs, but I did find a pornographic movie that I confronted him with. He was livid. He marched out on me, went upstairs, and brought back a dirty movie belonging to me that I thought he would never find. He threw it at my feet and stomped out. That was eight days ago, and he hasn't spoken to me since."

Even if your kid is hiding his first six-pack of Miller, what is the greater good here? Do you want that six-pack at the cost of your child's respect, or would you rather have your kid feeling bad because he lied to you about taking that beer? Knowing that you held to your values of trusting his word and not searching his room when he betrayed your trust will make him feel guilty. This is good. Don't forget the therapeutic value of feeling guilty. Perhaps he will never own up to that beer heist, but maybe he will dislike feeling guilty so much that he won't betray your trust again when the stakes are a lot higher. In letting your kid take advantage of your trust, maybe he'll learn a lot about how hard trust is to earn, how precious it really is, and how easily it is destroyed.

Now that I've presented both sides to you, what is my first position on the privacy issue? You must absolutely invade their privacy, except in those situations where you should never invade their privacy, unless it is a time when you have an obligation to invade their privacy, which is usually never, but frequently often. Any questions?

My second position is that you must make your decision to search or not to search based on rational versus reactive emotional factors. In other words, you get to lose sleep on many nights wrestling with this one. Understand that invading your kid's privacy is a terribly risky and damaging business that must have an outcome worth the cost, a last-ditch tactic to be used only in life-threatening situations. Just like the cops, you have to have probable cause to violate your child's rights or this action will blow up in your face.

What constitutes parental probable cause? Hard evidence of life-threatening behaviors. What constitutes hard evidence? That's your call, but I'd be inclined to pick locks if I saw signs of possible suicidal thinking (see Chapter 5) or *unusual* amounts of anger or aggressiveness. A complete withdrawal from the family lasting longer than a couple of days might get me thinking, also.

What does not constitute hard evidence? Probably the reason that you just broke into her diary, and are now so sorry that you did because you read a lot of things you wish you hadn't (don't worry—90 percent of that stuff she wrote probably never happened). Privacy also serves to protect relationships, not just to conceal scary behavior. Study after study proves that the best protective action you can take as a parent is to keep your lines of communication open with your kid. Feeling relatively close to your child will greatly reduce your sleepless nights since you will have a sense of whether or not she's OK. Adolescents who report being able to confide in a parent are much less likely to engage in high-risk behaviors. So the best privacy policy is to work very hard at keeping connected to your kid with all of the training you've had in this book so that you don't need a privacy policy. Respect and trust are the best craziness-prevention tools we'll ever have.

In summary, in making the privacy calls, you are truly juggling the lily of trust with the chain saw of insanity, hoping that your kid doesn't get hurt. And you thought achieving Middle East peace was tough.

Now That You've Irresponsibly Disregarded
My Excellent Advice. . .

. . .and done what I'd probably have done—given in to panic and violated her privacy for a dumb reason—you have to move quickly to minimize the damages.

First, seek her out and *apologize* for doing the search *before she finds out,* and even if there's a chance she won't find out. Remember that old line you used to lay on her all the time about how you'll be less upset if she admits to doing something wrong versus lying about it and getting caught later? Well, what goes around comes around, and now it's your turn to do the right thing. You're going to apologize *even if you found evidence that she was doing something wrong.* Why?

First, you're going to apologize because you broke the laws of trust and respect, and there is no excuse for that—for either you or your child. Finding contraband does not, does not, does not justify your actions. Finding the contraband is a separate issue you need to take up with her later. First, plead guilty to the charge of violating her privacy. You want her to understand that, even though you screwed up, these principles of trust and respect must be universally held, not conveniently used. You want her to see you applying the same standard to yourself that you apply to her.

The second reason you're going to apologize *in advance of being caught* is to clear the air as much as possible so that you can then address subsequent critical issues *in later separate discussions*—like how your relationship could have deteriorated to the point that you would get so crazy that you felt you had to search his things. If he demands an explanation for what you did, plead insanity. Tell him that this is no excuse, but that you've gotten out of control from worry and love for him.

The other follow-up talk the two of you need to have is about the contraband that you found. If your kid keeps diverting to the issue of your search, keep pleading guilty as charged, and discuss what consequences might be appropriate for *your own* inappropriate actions. Don't hook his crime to yours as a justification, or you'll get nowhere in your talk.

Hold off on the discussion about the consequences for his behavior until the furor over your betrayal dies down. Then if his protests keep recurring, dispassionately note that you guys have dealt with your failure and now it's time to talk about his.

But remember, however successfully you recover from the betrayal, nine times out of ten, you could have done more good by not searching (unless you have good reason to believe something imminently life-threatening is afoot). Sometimes, you just end up looking really stupid—and not just to your kid.

My psychologist friend Marty was talking too fast. Something big had happened today between him and his newly inherited 15-year-old stepdaughter Lauren. "I just couldn't take this anymore. Lauren has been so damn obnoxious towards me that she must be doing some kind of chemicals. She's insane—screaming, tantrumming, and throwing things. Michael, this can't just be adolescence."

He paused to catch his breath. "Anyway, while she was at school, I searched her room. Hidden way down behind her chest in her closet, underneath piles of old clothes and dolls, I found red unmarked pills in a plastic bag. I looked them up in my drug reference book and found nothing like them. I ran them to the pharmacist who said he'd never seen anything like this, but perhaps these were some street form of methamphetamine. He told me to take them to the police to get them lab-tested.

"I didn't want her to get arrested, so I called our physician. He told me that he heard that street reds are sometimes encapsulated in sugar and asked me if the pills were sweet. He said amphetamine couldn't hurt me if I let one dissolve in my mouth a little bit, but he warned me that they might be anything, and he said to take them to the cops for analysis. So I hung up, thought for a bit, and then decided I just had to know now. I got one of the pills and placed it on my tongue for a minute. At first, I tasted nothing, but then an incredibly bitter odor seemed to envelop my whole head. I ran to the sink and spit out the pill. My mouth was all red. It looked like most of the pill had dissolved already. Suddenly, I had a raging headache and felt nauseous. My head started spinning. It felt like I was poisoned. I wondered if this was LSD or something.

"After a few hours, when I could move again without my head splitting apart, Lauren came home. When I walked into her room she saw I was sick and asked me what was wrong. I yelled, 'PLENTY!' but

I had to stop yelling because my head felt like it had a bayonet in it.

"I said, 'Lauren, this is really, really serious. If you just tell me the truth, I promise I won't call the cops or ground you or anything. But I've got to know the truth.' I handed her the bag of reds and said, 'What are these?'

"Lauren stared at them for a moment and seemed to be genuinely perplexed. Then with a slow, sarcastic smile she said, 'Those are pills for my dolly.' I said, 'OK, Lauren, if you're going to be like that, I have no choice but to tell your mother.' She wasn't fazed at all. You know what she said? She said, 'Well, Marty, a man's gotta do what a man's gotta do. Tell my mom. See what she says.' As I left her room, she yelled after me, 'AND MAYBE YOU SHOULD CALL THE COPS, TOO!'

"When Kate got home, I gave her the pills and told her the story. She was devastated. She wasn't even listening to me fully until I got to the part about Lauren mocking me by saying that the pills were her doll's. Kate stared at me quizzically for a minute, just like Lauren had. Then that same stupid grin I got from Lauren was now on Kate's face—except she started to laugh and said, 'Marty, I think those pills are her dolly's.' Hearing that, I decided I must be hallucinating from the drugs, as I watched Kate look closely at the pill bag while she continued to laugh.

"Kate said, 'These are pills that came with some weird doll she got when she was six or seven. Her father was always buying her gifts that were inappropriate for a young child. The pills came with a warning that they were toxic, so I put the doll away and forgot about it. I don't know how these ended up in her closet.'"

Marty paused to rub his throbbing temples, and then, in a defeated voice he continued. "So I asked Kate why in God's name a doll would come with drugs. Kate got hysterical now. She could barely talk, she was laughing so hard, and all the while my head was pounding. All I could make out was her saying 'diaper rash, diaper rash,' and 'how could you be so dumb.' Turns out these poison pills are for mixing with water and feeding to this stupid doll that then gets a rash on its freakin' ass."

Now I was the one trying not to laugh, but this was just too funny. Marty was not happy. "I could have died from the God-knows-what that was in those pills, and everybody's yukkin' it up." Marty's forlorn puppy-dog face moved my giggling into laughter. To see this normally brilliant, perfectly controlled psychologist acting like Jackie Gleason was too much to bear. "Marty," I gasped, "those pills are truly amazing. They were meant for the doll's ass but they made one out of you."

Marty's pride and head were both still in pain. "Mikey, you go right ahead and laugh, funny guy. Enjoy yourself at my expense. Just remember that you've got kids. And your day is coming, my man. Your day is coming."

That quieted me a bit. You don't believe in karma, do you?

I share my friend's tale of grief with you for two reasons. One, I couldn't pass up an opportunity like this to embarrass him further, and two, I wanted to underscore the tremendous torment parents feel, whether professionally trained or not, when wrestling with that terrible decision about violating their kid's privacy. This is not easy.

And while we're talking of things that are not easy, it's time to move on to the riot-control section of your training. This next adolescent ordeal will place more demands on your skills, discipline, and character than any other experience you may share with your child: responding to his rage.

Chapter 13

SURVIVING YOUR KID'S RAGE

WELCOME TO PARRIS ISLAND for parents, cadets. Get those seat belts back on, but take comfort in knowing that parenting will not get any tougher than this.

The experience of teenage rage is so traumatic and, potentially, so physically dangerous that this training is vital for you to have, even if you are so blessed as to never need it. But don't be smug and think that you'll never face this problem. Those PFA (Protection From Abuse) orders that wives obtain against abusive husbands are now becoming commonplace in juvenile courts—not requested by kids against kids, but requested by parents as *protection from abuse by their own children, and, specifically, from their children's rage episodes.* We haven't seen this level of rage from adolescents ever before, and as parents, we're responding with outdated training that actually worsens the rage. If you're wondering exactly what I mean by rage versus anger, then you've not seen rage, because subtle it isn't.

What Rage Is

Rage is purple faces, popping neck veins, and clenched fists. Rage is vile, hurtful, spit-punctuated, screaming words that leave bleeding, emotional wounds. It is a hell-spawned tornado blasting a path of unthinkable emotional destruction through your once-loving home. Rage is the forest fire of a child that becomes a conflagration when fanned by the winds of a parent's fury. It can be shoves, slaps, and punches exchanged between two people who once, without pause, would lay down their lives for each other.

In the end, rage becomes a quiet, whimpering sadness, a consuming vision of a bleak landscape forever changed by the storm. It dies late at night with the solitary, soft, choking sobs of the wounded parents and children who believe in their hearts that a wonderful loving innocence has been lost forever. Those bonds can be lost forever if you don't rise up with love and true strength to meet this greatest of parent challenges—and, for this, you need training.

First, you need to understand the science of rage so that you can depersonalize this behavior as much as possible. Often, your kid's rage has nothing to do with you directly. You might just have been in the wrong place at the wrong time with the wrong training. Teenage rage is an emotional car wreck and a physiological runaway train. In other words, it is a bad emotional accident your kid has because he's not ready to drive. He's nuts, remember?

Three aspects of adolescent rage have contributed to its popularity as a contemporary phenomenon. First, adolescence is a time of tremendous tumult, which can present overwhelming pain and fear to many kids (see Chapter 1). As is true for many of us grownups, teens often find that it feels safer to express pain and fear by screaming, rather than by becoming vulnerable and wimpishly admitting to these scary feelings. Second, the physiological and physical changes of adolescence encourage these out-of-control bloodlettings. Your kid is wrestling with brain-wiring challenges, aggressive hormonal surges, oppositional behavior impulses, and a powerful new body, all of which encourage acting out—versus talking out—anger.

Finally, we've raised these fragile creatures in a rage-based culture that honors violence and aggression. So when you are in a routine confrontation with your kid, all of these powerful rivers can swirl together in your child's misfiring brain, whispering "you've got to fight the powers that be."

Given these factors, is her rage really so unthinkable? And is it really as personal as it feels? Think long and hard about this. To maintain your balance, you need to believe that she's just nuts when she puts that emotional spear in your gut because the fallout from a rage episode can devastate a parent-child relationship if you are not clear about its potential impact.

The Impact of Rage

Ever had food poisoning? You know, one of those rally-to-die experiences where you seem to empty your insides out all over the place from every orifice of your being? Your kid tells me that raging is like that for him. It leaves him shaking, weak, and scared, terrified by his own demonic voice saying words he never really thinks—like calling Mom an f'ng whore or suggesting that Dad perform certain sexual acts illegal in some states.

Your child is left horrifically embarrassed to the point where he doesn't want to talk about what happened, what he said, if he meant it, or even to acknowledge that it occurred. He's frightened to think that this might be who he is. He'd rather just act like it never went down. This is a little tough on parents, who don't sleep at all the night of a rage episode, mulling their child's words endlessly in their heads and prepping for the conversation he now refuses to have. The damage to parents can go far beyond last night. It can reach back decades of nights to old, forgotten nightmares.

Claudia sat stone still, rock hard with her care-worn hands clenched tight as if restraining some terrible animal within. Her husband tried to hold her hand softly, but she seemed not to know he was even in the room with her. "In my entire life, I've had one physical fight," she intoned, "and that was when I was seven years old and got pushed into the thorn bushes. After that, I had to learn not to get angry or my father would beat me. My being angry was a beating offense. He made a point out of raising welts on me with a hose once a week, sometimes more. He was what he used to call a 'strict-for-your-own-good father.'

"Last night, my daughter Christine was at me again, relentlessly needling, badgering, mocking, you know, just with words. But this time she escalated into screaming and calling me an f'ng bitch. Inside me, my accelerator pedal suddenly jammed. I rushed her, had my hands on her throat and bounced her head off of the wall before I even realized I had moved." Mom spoke even more carefully now with a voice that quivered. "I think maybe I have to go away. I saw the terror in my daughter's eyes that I worked so hard to leave behind me. This just cannot be me. I cannot become that person. I felt a rage I had taught myself not to feel when I was 10. And that was for my father. Now I feel insane again. I feel like I might hurt her. Even if I don't hurt her, I don't know that I can forgive her for making me feel this way again."

Like Christine did with Claudia, our kids can find and tap our own sometimes secret rage, and it does some nasty things. First, it can reinforce rage as part of our kids' expanding brain by modeling that behavior and teaching that this is how to handle conflict. Second, it can make us hate our own children for making us feel and act so horribly. Sometimes, we can even hear our own old tormenters in our kids' screaming voices. Third, when we hate our children, they know it and they sense our withdrawal of love, which, in turn, throws more logs on the fires of adolescent rage.

The fourth effect is the loss of parental control, and this leads to more rage episodes. Raging at a raging child is like using gasoline to put out a bonfire. In the good old days of fear-based parenting, parental rage could often overwhelm the teen's fury, but today's teenagers have been born and bred in a rage culture, and they are very fluent in that language. They can get a lot crazier than you can.

The final effect is perhaps the most devastating one. After you've lost it on your child, he feels a sadness, a despondency in seeing you that far out of control. He doesn't see rage as power. He knows it to be the armor of the insecure and the weak. He needs you to teach him something much more vital to his survival: the tolerant, quiet, and loving self-control of true strength. Strength so powerful that it can withstand the withering blast of adolescent insanity without raging back.

Your strength gives her hope that, because she is your child, she can become better than she is now. She can learn that rage does not have to consume everything good in its path, that there are things that are much stronger that, in the end, win out. What you must show her is the love of a parent.

Rage Prevention

Preventing rage from ever happening is really work for a decade ago. The best prevention efforts begin the day you bring your child home for the first time. But like giving up cigarettes, it's never too late to begin, because you can only help make things better.

The vaccination against teenage rage is a mix of goals and tasks you might want to work on. We've already talked about these tasks and how to accomplish them. The antirage list includes building qualities in your child like autonomy, respect, self-esteem, and identity, and creating family processes of power sharing and good communication skills.

If you enjoy adolescent rage, then try over- or under-controlling your kid, being rigid, cold, demeaning, and unavailable. That should about do it. And the quick-mix recipe for adolescent rage has only one ingredient: corporal punishment. If you're still relying on hitting and it seems to be working because he hasn't hit you back yet, get help now. I promise you that there is a fuse ticking inside his head. Please don't wait for that click just before the bomb goes off. Sometimes, the pieces can't be put back together.

The Rage-Response System: Where Winning Feels a Lot Like Losing

In the face of true rage from your kid, the first thing to do is decide not to do all those things that feel so right to you in the moment, like screaming back, tearfully pleading, or punching her lights out. The second thing to do is switch your control center from your heart to your head: Become that dispassionate cop—this time, a cop at a political protest verging on becoming a riot.

A protester (your kid) gets in a rookie cop's face (yours) and starts screaming profanities and daring the cop to do something about it. If the cop swings or even screams back, the riot's on. If the cop keeps his cool and keeps talking calmly, the protester eventually runs out of steam and moves on. If you ask that rookie cop what he felt accepting all of that abuse from the protester, he'll say it was the hardest thing he's had to do so far, that he felt rage and impotence in following his training. As you replay the videotape of that exchange for the cop, he is amazed to see how calm and strong he looked by keeping his cool. He also sees how he defused a potentially explosive situation by doing what he had been trained to do, and not doing what he felt.

Welcome to adolescent parenting, where winning feels a lot like losing. The cop's first job in a near-riot situation is the same as yours in a rage event: to defuse the potential violence.

Become that dispassionate cop. As your kid starts screaming, talk more quietly, and with very few words in very short sentences. Let your child hear her own out-of-control voice echoing off the walls. Don't let her off the hook by screaming back. This only allows her to focus on your craziness instead of hers, and it makes her behavior seem normal in comparison with yours. Confront her with the insanity of her own behavior by isolating and contrasting it with your own quiet responses.

Dispassionately refuse to talk to her if she continues to rage, and try to withdraw from the room. Don't try to handle an entire rage episode on the spot. There are many parts to this process, including eventual discussion and consequences, but that's tomorrow's work. Your immediate goal is to help your kid safely get his internal control back. Keeping a secret sense of humor helps, too, by maintaining a distance from your child and seeing that the banana in front of you shouldn't be taken too seriously at the moment. This distancing from the rage is critical to maintaining your cool. If you think fighting is hard, staying dispassionate with a raging adolescent is incredibly tough, but also incredibly more effective. Let me show you what I mean.

Child screaming: "F— YOU AND — ALL YOUR F—ING RULES. I F—ING HATE YOUR F—I NG GUTS. I WISH YOU WERE F—ING DEAD."

Quiet dispassionate parent response: "I'm sorry you feel that way." (Thought to self: *He's so well-spoken. I think his lisp is almost gone.*)

Child screaming: "YEAH? WELL, F— YOUR PSYCHOLOGICAL BULLSHIT, TOO! YOU'RE NOTHING BUT A F—ING JOKE!"

Even quieter dispassionate parent response: "Is that really the way you want to talk to me?" (Thought to self: *How much did I pay for Bradley's book?*)

Child screaming even louder: "F—IN' 'A' IT IS!"

Dispassionate parent response with a sigh: "OK." Parent withdraws from the room, thinking, *Another jewel of quality time with Johnny.*

If your child follows you and makes aggressive physical contact with you, look him straight in the eyes and quietly tell him, *one time,* that if the pushing continues, you must call the police. If it persists, make the 911 call without further warnings. DO NOT GET PHYSICAL IN RETURN. Leave the house, if you must. If he demands that you rescind that call, refuse, dispassionately saying, "I love you too much to have violence between us. If *we're* this far gone, *we* need emergency help." The flashing red lights in the driveway are embarrassing, but you must make this dramatic statement to your child that if the family (not just your child) resorts to violence to settle differences, then it is truly out of control and needs outside help. If he calms down and asks for an explanation, repeat that you love him too much to have violence in his home, and that under *no circumstances* is violence acceptable. It is simply never, ever OK.

Implicit in this response is the obvious fact that if the violence continues, your son may have to leave your house. *But don't say this to him.* The cops will explain this for you. Your position is that you are always searching for ways to keep him in your home, short of accepting violence, because you love him.

If you are able to withdraw without further confrontation, congratulations! Believe it or not (and I know you don't), you've won! Your kid was unsuccessful in his attempt to get you nuts, too. This not only helps him regain control, but also teaches him a huge lesson in what being tough is really about. Don't fall into the trap of thinking that a quiet, nonviolent response to rage looks like weakness to your kid. Remember, which cop seems truly stronger to you, the angry one or the dispassionate one?

MORE TIPS FOR DEFLECTING ADOLESCENT RAGE

Here are more suggestions for defusing your child's rage, and keeping your relationship intact:

1. *View rages as seizures.*

Think of her brain challenges, and it may help you not to take this personally. Picture her as having an epileptic seizure. Don't get physical, just provide a safe space to let her vomit the poison out. Depersonalize the behavior. She really doesn't mean those terrible things she says.

2. *Distance yourself quickly and dispassionately from the insanity.*

It's very contagious. Get away emotionally and physically, if need be. Don't get hooked by rageful provocations. ANY OTHER RESPONSE IS REINFORCING and encourages repeat performances.

3. *Let him bolt out the door.*

Running out is preferable to a possible physical confrontation. Allowing him to go is not weakness, and he will not interpret it as such. Maybe he gets out when you want him in, but when he comes home he knows there will be a consequence. Most raging kids calm quickly when they get to the sidewalk.

4. *Quickly think ahead four years.*

Try to regain your calmness and perspective by picturing her driving away to college or off into the service. It won't be very long now, perhaps only four Thanksgivings. And as you wave goodbye, how will you feel then about having done what you're about to do tonight? Don't plant regrets. That crop always gets harvested.

5. *Don't do too much.*

Just safely containing the rage is a job well done. The follow-up system (which we'll discuss shortly) must wait until later. Just let it be for now. The response system is much too important to risk torching with smoldering rage ashes that can re-ignite in a flash. Provide a substantial time period between the rage event and your follow-up response.

6. *If rages repeat, get help NOW!*

Repeated rages are screeching smoke detectors. Somewhere there is a fire. Don't go looking for it. Call for help. Delaying might allow for a catastrophe. The system described here is designed only for the infrequent rages that many kids manifest. Repeated rages, particularly where there is physical contact, are extremely serious symptoms that must be evaluated by an expert.

So there you go. You now know what you should do under fire, but you won't know how you will actually react until the shooting starts. If you're like most of us, you'll find these strategies are very easy to talk about and very hard to do. Facing your first rage may cause you to forget all of your training and just react with your gut—but that's OK, because if you stay with it, you'll find that your rage-containment skills will get better each time you're tested.

Jenny was obviously proud of herself as she sat down, something very different from past sessions. As the single mother of a raging 14-year-old son, she had a very tough time using the rage-response system, feeling that she was being too weak with her son. "My ex-husband would have knocked Michael out 10 times by now. I know you've told me repeatedly that my son was looking for someone to take charge of him, but I couldn't see that staying calm while he went nuts was a way of taking charge. It just seemed too wimpy to me. That's why I'd keep losing it and screaming back at him."

Jenny paused and smiled with feigned smugness. "Well, guess what happened last night? Last night, Michael phones in at his 10:00 P.M. curfew and says, 'I'm staying over at Jeremy's house.' He doesn't ask, he tells me like I'm his secretary. So I first thought of my training and I responded *dispassionately.*" Jenny rolled her eyes and emphasized this word I had pounded her with for weeks. "*Dispassionately* I said, 'Sorry, Michael, but our rule is that you must request overnights by the night before. I want you home by 10:30. We can talk about sleeping over tomorrow night.' Michael went nutso on the phone, screaming, 'I HATE YOUR F—ING RULES! I HATE YOUR F—ING RULES! YOU'RE NOTHING BUT AN IGNORANT BITCH!'

"There I was at my usual crossroads, fighting back the urge to get nutso too while trying to keep my discipline of training. This time, I won the fight within me. As quietly as I could, and in a monotone voice, I said, 'Michael, you must be in at 10:30.' Before I could say I was getting off the phone because he was screaming, he cut me off by screaming, "WELL, I'M NOT COMING. SO WHAT ARE YOU GONNA DO, CALL THE F—ING COPS ON ME?'"

Jenny sat forward now as she narrated with confidence for the first time since I had met her. "Somehow in getting past that old crossroads where I always lost it before, I felt empowered, like I was finally in charge of myself. Like my lunatic son no longer had control of me. It almost seemed easy. I could see what to do now without thinking hard. My response was a reflex. 'No threats, Michael, I'm just telling you that you need to be in by 10:30. You can't stay over tonight. I'm getting off the phone now. I love you, and I'm sorry you're so upset.' As I hung up the phone, I heard him screeching that he was not coming home a minute before 11:00. I almost laughed. It was like he was three years old again. Suddenly, I was no longer scared of him. Still worried, but no longer so terribly scared. It felt very strange and very good.

"Anyway, Michael walked in at 10:50. I was amazed! I decided it was best not to make an issue of the missed curfew. This next part you won't believe. Without a word from me, he started doing his chores that he neglected to do that day. He worked until midnight.

"And here's the final thing you won't believe. Even after he called me those names, I was calm enough to remember that I still loved him even if he was nuts, and how hard it was for him having a son-of-a-bitch absentee father. I went and asked if I could hug him, and told him I knew how much guts it took for him to come home and then do his chores. I told him that I was proud of him and that I loved him." Jenny paused to emphasize her next words. "He let me hug him for the first time in a year. He never said he was sorry, but I knew he was. He showed me the best he could. The rest will come.

"He let me hug him," she repeated. "He let me hug him."

The Rage Follow-Up Response System: Repairing the Damage and Growing with Your Child

As painful as an adolescent rage experience can be, it can also produce many positives that you must take the time to gather. Ironically, all of this pain provides powerful opportunities for growth if you can use as much discipline with the follow-up as you did for the initial rage response.

View rage events as a distinctly two-step process. The rage event itself is the hurricane. There's not much to do except ride it out safely and minimize the damage. Fighting with raging storms is pointless. Fighting with raging teens can be dangerous. So view your role as the Red Cross, not the Marines. Go in after the storm has passed to follow up. Here is where you do your fighting against the insanity. It's the only place you can do any good.

The critical follow-up response is designed to do two things: to repair the damage to the structure of your relationship, and to do this is in a way that makes the house even stronger than it was before the storm. The goal here is to *teach*, not to punish. The teaching is how the follow-up can strengthen your relationship. Handling this part well can reduce the ferocity and duration of subsequent storms, but handling it well is probably the last thing on your mind just after a rage episode. So be sure to provide for a substantial cooling-off period before attempting to reconnect with your kid, for your sake as much as your child's, because if you are anything like me, your gut reflex after a verbal assault is to get revenge, not to give instruction. If you were familiar with fear-based motivation as a child, then you probably feel like you have a score to settle with your kid. It's important to admit this to yourself because then you know you are not quite ready for the additional hard work ahead. If your kid is approaching you for a peace conference and you're still hurting, thank her for approaching you, but tell her you need a little more time to gather your thoughts.

If the suggestion that your terrorist teen wants to reconnect more than you seems absurd, try to remember that his rage is typically a cover for pain and vulnerability. Adolescents with those feelings usually want to feel better, not more alone. They are still children. Generally, you can bet that the height of the rage marks the depth of the pain. If you can rise above your own fury at his actions and understand this paradox about your kid, you will hold a tremendous advantage over him—but this is a very hard thing to believe until you've seen it for yourself.

Eva looked like she had been on the emotional roller-coaster ride of the century. She had. Her teenage son had raged the night before. "I was sure my child was gone forever. The things he said, the threats he made—it was absolutely horrific. He made it very clear that he was leaving for good and that he truly, truly hated me.

"I cried myself to sleep, picturing court hearings, group homes, and fistfights with my own son. Suddenly, I jolted awake to the smell of something burning! I thought, 'Oh my God! He wants to kill all of us!' I leapt out of bed to see where he started the fire to burn down the house, and stepped on a plate of sort-of-scrambled eggs, accompanied by very black toast. My 'homicidal' son had left me breakfast in bed, a first for him.

"One of us is nuts and should be put away. I hope it's not him because I need the rest. What in God's name is he trying to say to me?"

Like Eva's child, your kid will likely be trying to say she's sorry, but she's all twisted up with a hundred other emotions that you need to begin to unravel so they don't explode like that ever again. To do that, your first task after the fire is out is to reconnect.

RECONNECTING

Your relationship with your kid is never more precarious than after a terrible fight. Oddly enough, how you handle this post-rage phase is actually much more critical to your future with your child than how you did during the battle the night before. More than ever, go in using your training, not your gut.

◆ *Go in as that dispassionate cop.*
Using all of that dispassionate cop training, approach your child slowly and ask if it's OK to talk. If he says no, ask for a definite time when it will be OK. If he sets a time, honor that, but if he won't respond, ask him to please just listen for 60 seconds. Tell him that you love him, that nothing can ever change that. Tell him that you can see that the two of you need to talk to be sure you never again have a night like last night, and you'll be back later for that talk. Honor his request not to push it right now. He might still be smoldering.

◆ *Sidestep all of last night's insults.*
Your job here is to reconnect, not to restart the battle. Don't rub her nose in her failure to control her outrageous behavior and words. Going there would only invite another round. You'll do no good. But if you can find the strength to rise above her craziness, she will love and respect you for it. If it helps you to maintain your discipline, know that in counseling sessions, she tells me in guilt-stricken detail every horrible word she said to you. If you did a decent containment job with the initial rage episode and left her with her own insane words ringing in her head, she is painfully aware of what she did. You really don't need to go back there.

◆ *Offer, but don't require, a hug.*
If he says no, honor this, but let him know that you miss him right now and when he's ready, you've got a hug waiting for him. Tell him you will

honor his wishes. Try not to become discouraged or angry by a refusal. He might still be so jumbled up inside that he can't be crowded right now. Here, again, he will see you setting aside your own needs as a sign of strength. This will earn his love and respect for now and later may buy a hug. If he is able to accept a hug, you're ready for phase two of the follow-up: the growth.

GROWING WITH YOUR CHILD

Check the connectedness ice carefully. Be sure it is thick enough to support the weight of the two of you having a direct talk about what happened. If you feel connected enough, go for it, but shock the cynicism out of your child by doing the unexpected.

◆ *Model, don't mandate.*
What she expects to hear is the rap sheet of her offenses and punishments. She's expecting to hear you demand "how could you" explanations for saying things she can't quite believe she said, let alone explain. She's becoming deaf as she prepares for the lengthy lecture and demands for an apology she thinks must be coming. Do none of that. Instead, catch her brain incredibly off-guard and open to you by astounding her with an unimaginable response: *Talk solely about your contribution to the rage event,* not hers.

◆ *Talk about what you learned.*
Focus on the mistakes you made, the things you regret saying, or maybe find fault with yourself in not understanding how wired-up she was that day. Tell her what you learned in this event and what you would do differently the next time.

◆ *Talk about what you felt.*
Speak openly about how gut-wrenching that episode was for you. Tell her about the dark, scary feelings that rage brings on for you, and how that uncontrolled emotion can make you say things you don't mean. Perhaps share a tale or two of your own childhood experiences of being crazy.

Why would you speak only of your own part in that rage episode? To teach her by modeling how we learn from our mistakes. Your child doesn't know how to recover from an emotional bloodletting like rage. She's likely a huge emotional knot inside, a bundle of a hundred twisted emotions that she has no idea how to unravel. Teach her by doing it yourself in front of her. Let her observe and ask questions. Put the spotlight on yourself, not on her. This will lower her defenses so that some real learning can occur.

What about consequences? Shouldn't she be punished for the things she said and did? Yes and no. If walls got punched out, yes, the puncher must repair them. You might want to make this a joint project so that you can teach her how to repair the gypsum that your grandson may put his hand through one day. If her rage terrified her little brother, yes, she owes him an apology and an explanation. In all of these things, try not to issue "you'd better" orders. Instead, pose questions like "What needs to be done about that wall?" and "What needs to be done about your little brother?" See if she can come to her own decisions about consequences.

But *never, ever* demand an apology for the damage she caused you. Show her strength and control like she never knew existed. Don't fish for an apology. If one gets offered, graciously wave it off, saying, "Forget about it—it's OK." Find the love to step right past her wounding of you without losing a stride. I know this sounds impossible, but in raising adolescents, we are often called on to do the undoable. If refusing to make her crawl to you with an apology feels weak, then feel again. Mercy is not a weakness that encourages her to snap out again. It is a rare and wonderful grace that will humble and awe her and make her want to be like you—and respect you.

Let her know that a power exists in her life that is so strong that the frightening impulses she feels and the terrible things she says cannot overwhelm it. Let her know that the beacon of your love rises above the thrashing, raging seas of adolescent storms to guide her home just when she seems most lost.

Be her parent.

Chapter 14
DRUGS: THE DOs AND THE DON'Ts

Arianne had the look of a righteous mother who was spiritually beaten down, like the victim of schoolyard teasing. She looked like she finally found the courage to make a stand, but picked the wrong bully to fight. She had learned a terrible truth about making stands with bullies: The bigger they are, the harder they hit. She also learned that, sometimes, the true act of courage is in not taking a stand.

She began to speak apologetically of her feelings about her 12-year-old daughter, Kelly, who was acting out. "I know that every week I come into these counseling sessions convinced that I should drug test Kelly, and every week I leave deciding not to do that, but the indicators were always there. Everyone kept telling me it was obvious that she was doing drugs. Could everybody be wrong? My father-in-law kept yelling that I've got to take a stand with her. I thought maybe he's right. I never knew what to tell him. What if I was wrong for not testing her? I just didn't know anymore and I felt like I had to do something.

"The other night, during a fight with my daughter, I shouted, 'I know you're doing drugs. I recognize all of the symptoms. I'm not stupid, you know!' 'Fine,' Kelly screamed, 'take me for a drug test. Right now!' I used to use that bluff with my own father when I was high at one in the morning. I wasn't about to be as dumb as he was. So I finally took a stand. I took her.

"There we were at 2:00 A.M. sitting in the hospital emergency room. I was already thinking that maybe this was a bad idea, but it was too late. It was humiliating for both of us, but particularly for Kel. She sat staring without saying a word to anyone. I could feel her hatred towards me growing larger the longer we sat.

"Finally, the nurse came back and motioned me out of my daughter's earshot. 'Kelly is clean,' she said quietly. 'Not even marijuana traces, which can last for weeks after a use.' Then she asked if Kelly had any warning that I was going to test her. My answer was no. I guess there are ways to fool the test, but Kelly couldn't have used any.

"The worst part of this was my reaction when I heard the good news that Kelly was not on drugs. I was disappointed. I know this doesn't make any sense, but in one way a positive test result would have been good. Then I could at least feel like there's a reason that would explain Kelly's behavior to everyone. I think I wouldn't feel so helpless. Isn't that a horrible thing for a mother to say?"

Arianne sat and shook her head at herself and then continued. "That nurse saw my eyes fill up when she told me the good news. I started to cry right there in the hall. This stranger put her arm around me and told me that she understood. She said, 'This is your first teenager, right?' Turns out she raised three teens. She said, 'Honey, don't try and fix it all. You'll just get crazy and old before your time. Just try and keep everybody alive for now. The rest usually sorts itself out.' For some reason what she said helped."

God, fate, or Mother Nature must have a tendency to overdo. We know this to be true because of what you are going through with your kid. As if adolescence alone isn't a rough enough parenting challenge, you now get to spend more sleepless nights agonizing over another issue: whether or not she's doing "drugs," *a term that must include using alcohol, which is the drug that most often kills our children* (see Chapter 2). This issue of unprecedented levels of teen drug use provides another charming twist to contemporary adolescent parenting.

There are several aspects to this sleep-depriving agony. The first has to do with our terror at the thought of losing a child to an overdose or drug-related accident. That's the lightning-bolt picture that keeps searing through your tortured brain when he's two hours late and you're silly enough to try to at least pretend to sleep. The second part of the agony focuses on how in the world you are supposed to differentiate the symptoms of drug use from the symptoms of normal adolescence, which happen to be amazingly similar.

The third part of the agony is wrestling with the thousands of strategies that are thrown at you by friends and family on what to do about your suspicions that she's doing drugs. It's usually about dawn when it dawns on you that there's precious little you can do anyway, or so it seems. And for some of us, that terrible, helpless feeling can begin to kill our love for our child, or at least it feels that way.

Bob tried to keep calm, but panic and exhaustion quavered in his quiet voice and white-washed the knuckles of his clenched fists. His wife, Rose, turned towards him, sensing that he was about to say something important, something not good. "I've been up all night thinking about Sandra (their 15-year-old daughter)," he began. "I haven't even told Rose about this, but I've come to a decision. I want Sandra out of the house."

Rose was staggered by his words. "What are you saying?" she asked incredulously. Bob refused to look at her as he continued. "We're not able to help Sandy, at least I'm not. She keeps using grass, at least I think she is. I mean I'm pretty sure she is...I don't know what I mean. That's why she has to go." Rose looked at him as if he were crazy. "What is your point? LOOK AT ME!" she yelled. " This is our child you're talking about."

Bob glanced at her, but couldn't hold her gaze. He shifted and sighed, saying, "That's my point. That I don't know what I mean, I don't know what to do or say or anything. I feel completely helpless and out of control. Dr. Bradley, you've got to put her away somewhere. There must be some program, some therapy, some medication they can force her to take that can help her stop screwing up her life. I know that we can't or that I can't help her. I WANT HER SOMEWHERE WHERE THEY CAN FIX HER," he yelled, "I WANT HER OUT OF OUR HOUSE!" Then Bob looked even sadder for having lost control and telling the ugly truth.

Rose stared at him, stunned and speechless. It felt like their home was collapsing in my office. "Bob," I began, "if Sandy's not willing to go, you can't just stick her somewhere. The law doesn't work like that. She's not in any imminent danger as far as we know, so a judge would probably not grant a commitment order, and besides..."

Rose stood up, interrupted me, and finished my sentence better than I could. "BESIDES," she emphasized, "WE are her PARENTS, Bob. Her mother and her father. Who else do you think could have more impact to help her through this? Dr. Bradley? A bunch of strangers in a hospital? Some pill? For God's sake, listen to what you're saying. YOU and I, Bob, only YOU and I can give her what she needs. Do you think that throwing her out will help her to get better?" Bob was frighteningly resolute. "Then, Rose, Sandra is doomed because I've got nothing left inside for her."

Bob turned to me imploringly as if I might support him in his position. I just shook my head. Thinking clinically, I knew that Rose was correct. Thinking personally, I knew that I would have been a better liar than Bob. I would have been too ashamed to voice those ugly feelings that I just as easily could have had about my own child. I felt bad for Rose. I felt horrible for Bob. Rose still knew who she was. Bob had lost himself.

I warned you that your teen might take you to places you don't want to go. This issue of drugs (including alcohol) is one of them. There may not be any other adolescent struggle you face that will confront you with so many terrible feelings, both about your kid and yourself.

Both Rose and Bob were telling the truth. Bob felt that he had already lost his daughter to drugs, and he was right. The person he needed Sandra to be was gone. He had lost his feelings of connectedness, of bonding with his daughter, at least for the moment. Throwing out the remaining dysfunctional shell of his child seemed appropriate to him.

Rose was right, too. Nobody—no drug, no therapy, no hospital—can do what you can for your struggling teen.

So here we parents are, once again trying to do the impossible, but backwards and in high heels—this time, in trying to decide if our kid is doing drugs. Just who is that person who writes those drug articles about teenagers in all of those magazines? You know, the one who can so maddeningly and authoritatively imply how stupid you must be not to see that your kid is doing drugs. This is the same writer who tells you to *just talk* to your kid—the kid who would often request that you send a telegram, rather than tell him in person that the house is on fire.

Well, here's where I become that infuriating writer, telling you that you must somehow see if your kid is doing drugs and that you must talk with her. The difference is that now you've had some pretty rigorous training for that second part, the "must talk" part, and you have skills to keep you from hitting the bottom, like Bob did. Use them, because the odds are that your kid is doing drugs to some extent. Chapter 2 lays out the scary drug statistics, but the only one you need for now is that the vast majority of adolescents do drugs to some degree before they leave high school. The exposure is certainly there. The training you've had in this book is even more critical for dealing with drugs than for dealing with any other issue. Inoculate your kid, don't mandate the evil away. To do this well in the drug game, you need more specialized training to build on what you've gotten so far.

So get out your yellow highlighter. We're about to take a tour of the why (kids do drugs), the what (drugs they use and what the symptoms are), and the how (they use them). And, oh yeah, I almost forgot: the what-you-can-do-about-this.

Why They Do Drugs

Adolescents do drugs for a thousand different reasons, and your kid usually can't come up with one that makes any sense to you. So don't look at this list as rational (they're crazy, remember?), just view it as another insight into the insanity of adolescence.

The first reason kids do drugs, which applies to all the reasons that follow, is impulsivity. Your kid's brain doesn't work so well when it comes to things like judgment and decision making (see Chapter 1). Often, your teen will tell me that one night he said, "Screw it," and went out and got high.

That fits nicely with reason number two: angst. All that upheaval and turmoil of adolescence is nicely anesthetized by drugs like alcohol. How frequently have you experienced some stress, turned to a companion, and said, "Whew! That was tough. Wanna get a beer?" And you're supposed to be a grownup who has skills at handling frustration and stress. This is brand new to your child.

Being cool ranks way up there for a lot of kids, particularly for kids who are not so cool to begin with. Taking on the role of a drug user can give a kid with a poor sense of self an instant personality, and give her things to talk about and to share with other kids whose approval she desperately needs.

Another reason for drug use is the reactive side of identity exploration, you know, the part where they do things you don't do just because you don't do them—just to see what it's like not to be you. Most often, this will be the primary reason we smell marijuana on our child's clothing. This is also why you must be very disciplined in your handling of that event. If you use your training, your child's drug use will likely stay at that experimentation stage, but if you lose your cool and let your rage do your parenting, you stand a good chance of contributing to her increased use.

You can also look to yourself as another powerful explanation for your kid's use. If you use, your kid will, too. Spare yourself the "but she's only 15 years old" whine. You know that your kid does not see these age distinctions as you do, and she powerfully models your behavior. If you do drugs (a list that includes alcohol), you are sanctioning them as an appropriate activity for your child. The 1999 National Household Drug Abuse survey turned up an amazing statistic reflecting the enormous power your behavior and attitudes toward drug-related issues have for helping or hurting your child. Households with parents who strongly disapprove of even cigarette smoking were *four times less likely* to have teens who used marijuana in the prior month than kids from homes where the parents neither approved nor disapproved of smoking.

The final and deadly reason that he uses drugs is to solve personal problems. Issues like shyness, depression, and anxiety seem to magically improve after a few hits of whatever. The deadly part is that the chemicals work so well, but for so short a time that he needs more and more of them.

The list of justifications for drug use can go on and on. If you are reading that list and asking what you can do about those problems, you've asked a great question that you can't answer without more data, such as what drugs a kid might use and what the symptoms might be.

Common Drugs and Their Symptoms

Here are the most common drugs your kid is exposed to and their symptoms:

Alcohol: I don't have to tell you what this drug is because you know it so well. And that is precisely why it is the true nightmare drug of today's adolescent culture. Reread Chapter 2 if you're tempted to skip over this section since "alcohol is not really a drug, right?" More than half of the 20 million alcoholics who are citizens of this nation learned their art as teenagers. These numbers make all of the following drug discussions seem silly by comparison.

The good news is that you probably know the symptoms of alcohol use very well, such as sudden, unexplained giddiness or glumness; slurred speech; poor memory; vomiting; and uncoordinated movements such as an unsteady walk. Don't forget that what a kid might call "a few beers" can kill. Alcohol can stop your kid's breathing. Toxic levels are usually indicated by loss of consciousness and coma, so if your kid staggers in and collapses, he may not be harmlessly "sleeping it off." He could be dying.

If you are in doubt, get him to the hospital. I know you think this is silly; after all, you've been drunk and you're not dead, right? Take him anyway. If you guessed right and this was "just a drunk," you'll nevertheless impress your kid with your stand on alcohol as he gets his stomach pumped. Keep in mind that another thing that's changed since your day is how kids drink. Teens today love binge drinking or "running shots." They take in huge, often near-lethal, amounts of alcohol in short time periods for fun. They have even developed innovative techniques such as vodka-laden gelatin cubes to help poison themselves more effectively by overcoming their innate distaste for booze. What we used to call brain food has become food for disordered brains. And there's always room for Jell-O.

Amphetamines: The term amphetamines actually describes a whole group of drugs, often called speed, that has similar effects on kids. The drugs might be stolen "legal" drugs, such as diet pills or the psychostimulants we use widely for ADD/ADHD (see Chapter 5). There are also a whole bunch of street-manufactured versions, such as a particularly nasty one known as "ice," due to its crystalline appearance when magnified. "Ice" is an almost completely pure (and thus wildly powerful) stimulant that can be smoked.

Kids on amphetamines can have all sorts of symptoms that include super-high energy levels, nonstop talking, restlessness, grandiose thinking, and impaired judgment. You might also see repetitive behaviors, unreasonable emotional sensitivity, and rapid anger and willingness to fight.

If you're seeing these extreme behaviors, get to the hospital—not only to potentially save the life of your child, but also to have a drug test done to find out which class of drug he's using, something important to know as you proceed. If your kid becomes combative, call the cops. DO NOT PHYSICALLY ENGAGE HIM. He may become aggressive to an uncontrollable degree that you've not seen before, and that you may not be able to contain.

Cannabis (marijuana, hashish): If you think you're an expert on this section as well, there are two reasons why you should take a minute and read this, just to be sure. The first is that your kid has a 66 percent probability of experimenting with this drug before age 18, and second, *this is not the same drug you may have once known so well.* The primary active part of the cannabis plant is a chemical called tetrahydrocannabinol or THC. It's usually smoked, although sometimes it's eaten. If you smoked in the 60s and 70s, you were doing a drug that was 1 to 5 percent THC. The cannabis of today commonly runs to *three times that dose of THC.* There's a new brand of cannabis now becoming available called "Dank" that offers mega doses of THC at twice the price, kind of the champagne of the Cheech and Chong crowd.

If you are an ex-grass user, you may be desensitized to your kid using cannabis since you smoked a lot in your day and you're "OK." Unless you're a pothead now, what she's smoking ain't what you smoked, and we really don't know the long-term effects of this new drug. A lot of parents of adolescents used to laugh at the old *Dragnet* episodes, with their apocalyptic warnings about grass. Now you might be sitting there laughing at my apocalyptic warnings. DON'T DO THIS.

We are now beginning to see some very disquieting preliminary research that suggests the dumb old warnings about grass might now be true with the new THC levels. Among other effects, cannabis may provide a gateway to other drug use, and it may reduce achievement motivation in adolescents who, by nature, are underachievers. We may have chicken-littled ourselves into a cannabis corner with our kids.

If your daughter is high on cannabis, she'll be mildly euphoric and her memory and concentration will be impaired. If she's really whacked on Dank, she can look drunk without the booze odor. Particularly in light of our new and improved cannabis, smoking and driving should be viewed and responded to as seriously as drinking and driving.

Cocaine: The symptoms of cocaine use in your kid are similar to those of amphetamine use, with the added telltale sign of pupils dilated out towards his ears. And, no, hay fever doesn't do that. Cocaine was a rare adolescent problem in your day when kids were comparatively poor. Ironically, kids are not as poor these days and coke has become a "blue light special" with many dealers—it's cheap. It's a particular bargain in its deadliest form, called crack cocaine, which is smoked rather than snorted. Crack is immediately and powerfully addicting.

Enough cocaine can cause coma, along with heart and lung problems. It can be a killer.

Hallucinogens (LSD, ecstasy, DMT, MDMA): This category encompasses a wide array of different drugs, some of which may be familiar to you, like LSD (lysergic acid diethylamide), mescaline, and ecstasy (a mix of amphetamine and mescaline). Many other forms continually appear on the adolescent drug market like new cars. The common symptoms of hallucinogen use include hallucinations, anxiety, paranoia, sweating, dilation of pupils, tremors, and palpitations. Many kids on hallucinogens look to parents like they're having nervous breakdowns, with the kid crying and screaming, "I'm losing my mind!" Just as with the music, these popular 60s drugs are seeing a resurgence of popularity among adolescents.

Opioids (heroin, codeine, and morphine): Of the opioid choices, heroin is the surprising rage of the contemporary adolescent drug culture. Once usually injected (and thus unattractive to many drug-involved teens), heroin has become "new and improved" for the new millennium in a form so pure it can be snorted. Somehow, a dangerous myth has evolved in some adolescent circles that heroin is only addicting if injected, but not if snorted. WRONG!

If your kid is doing heroin, he'll show constricted pupils (unless he's overdosed—then his pupils will be wide open), unusual apathy (to a point where an onrushing train won't upset him), slurred speech, and, possibly nodding, as if he's about to fall asleep. He could become comatose on you. Any doubts, call 911.

Phencyclidines (PCP, Hog, Tranq, and Angel Dust): These drugs are all variants of surgical anesthetics that became street drugs in the 60s. They can be smoked, eaten, or snorted, and they create a hallucinogeniclike dissociation from reality, sometimes with an aggressive twist. Adolescents on low doses may become dizzy and nauseous, have slurred speech, and exhibit unusual apathy. Medium doses produce the hallucinogenic-type effects of weird thinking and strange sensory perceptions. Highly-dosed kids on these drugs become belligerent, unpredictable, and willing to fight over nothing. If sufficiently dosed, they can become dangerous raging bulls with unusual levels of physical strength and undeterred by pain. DO NOT PHYSICALLY ENGAGE A KID LIKE THIS.

How Drugs Are Used

Knowing that a kid is "doing drugs" is like saying you are "doing cigarettes." How much of a problem that behavior represents depends on the specifics of the use, such as how much you use, why you use, and how great a price your use costs you in terms of life impact.

The softest brush with drug use would be *experimentation,* typically with alcohol and cannabis. This phase is marked by low-level use that, typically, many parents aren't even aware is happening. There may be no changes in your kid's behavior. This usually is a party-type activity that occurs with friends at sleepovers or weekend hangouts. The bad news is that your kid does not consider this type of drug use to be "doing drugs." He refers to this as "partying." The good news is that for most kids, drug use stays at this level for marijuana and alcohol, although too many graduate to the next level of use, called *misuse.*

The misuse phase is marked by significant changes in drug frequency, setting, and choices. Now she may start to use on most weekdays, use alone, and use harder drugs like amphetamines, opiates, and hallucinogens. The kids call this "doing drugs" or "doing pills." Here, you stand a much greater chance of actually seeing your kid under the influence of a drug with the consequent strange behaviors specific to that drug. You'll also likely see overall behavior changes like rapid mood swings, school dysfunction, and old friends who mysteriously stop calling. If help does not arrive, misuse can deteriorate into *drug abuse.*

In the abuse phase, things start to really come apart. Almost all of your kid's behaviors become a function of the chemicals. Truancy, fighting, stealing, even drug dealing can begin, along with wild, withdrawal-based mood swings from the highest highs to the darkest lows. Suicide becomes a huge risk here. And, yes, this can worsen into something called *dependency.*

Dependency is the bottom. A drug-dependent child lives for no other purpose than to stay high, 24/7. Anything goes. Muggings, prostitution, self-mutilation, contaminated needles—whatever it takes to get high on whatever it takes to get high. This is the portrait of the full-blown addict. Not a picture you ever want to see.

If those stages sound like a ladder to hell, you're exactly right. That's what addiction is: a step-by-step progression from "one hit ain't gonna hurt" to madness. Most kids stay on that top rung and are fortunate enough to be able to laugh at our antidrug paranoia. But sorting out which kids are going to slide down that ladder into the clutches of evil is tough work. We do know that certain factors appear in the backgrounds of most adolescent addicts—like a family history of addiction, poor self-concept, distant and overcontrolling or permissive parents, and poor social skills.

We suspect that having a family history of substance abuse creates an unchangeable *predisposition* towards addiction, but a predisposition alone does not *cause* a kid to become an addict. It takes a whole bunch of factors to create a drug abuser. As it turns out, most of the other factors that are associated with drug abuse *can* be changed. Addiction can be avoided. *And the factors that can be changed to avoid addiction can be changed best by you, both in the short term and in the long term.*

What to Do: Short-Term Strategies for When You Suspect Drug Use

You must sometimes walk an excruciating tightrope on drug issues with kids. On the one hand, you need to subtly monitor them for use indicators. These may include chronic eye redness and runny nose; dilated or constricted pupils; radical mood shifts; major changes in sleeping, eating, personal hygiene, school, or social functioning; contact avoidance; sudden secretive activity; sudden weight changes; missing money; and missing possessions. However, you could argue that many of the characteristics on this list are, at times, common to teenagers who don't do drugs, so be very careful. Don't ever aggressively accuse, even with some cause, unless it appears to be a crisis situation. If you only suspect experimentation, first raise concerns dispassionately (getting tired of that word yet?) so that you can gradually build the case if the behavior continues ("*Jim, I'm not demanding that you tell me if you do drugs.*

I am demanding that you hear me say that I love you and I'm worried to death about you. I worry that things are not going well for you, and that drugs might begin to seem real attractive to you. Please be very careful. If I can help, please let me know.").

Never aggressively confront your kid while he's under the influence. If he walks in high or drunk, he's in no shape to have an important discussion. Just let him know that you know, and that you will meet with him tomorrow on the use issue. Evaluate whether or not he needs to go to the emergency room, regardless of what drug you think he's used (remember that alcohol is a poison, enough of which can kill your child).

If he seems to be worsening, breathing irregularly, hallucinating, sleeping too deeply, being wildly active, getting aggressive, talking or laughing uncontrollably, having a seizure, or if his pupils are dilated or constricted, make the trip to the hospital. Chances are it's unnecessary, but do you want to gamble? Besides, it really shocks the heck out of your kid and helps drive home the point that this is not a game (ever had your stomach pumped?). Minimally, the docs will usually do a drug screening (identification), which will help you to decide your next step.

If all you have are suspicions, keep your cool. You don't want to be aggressive and provide your kid with more justification to do drugs by hammering her unfairly (see Chapter 12). Try to keep in mind that a one-event drug use is not a catastrophe, and, in a weird way, it can be a good thing. It offers you a real-world opportunity to address the inevitable issue of drug use with your child in a context that can be much more effective than lecturing to a nonuser. If you can be dispassionate, you might help your child use that one-time experience to decide that maybe drugs are not for her.

But being dispassionate does not mean that you tolerate use. Ever. You must maintain the line that no use is acceptable. To you, drug use must indicate levels of irresponsibility that preclude adolescent privileges of driving, extended curfews, sleepovers, and so on. Any drug use exception that you make raises the possibility of the next exception. These exceptions might end with your daughter injecting heroin between her toes. If your kid tells you that you're naive and nuts because all her friends and all their parents do grass, agree with her. Tell her that, most likely, you are nuts and you definitely are naive, but that you love her too much to not fight with her over drug use, or anything else that you believe can hurt her. Let her know you won't give up. This is one battle you must fight to the end. Here's where you use all that respect and power ammunition I kept telling you to save.

This is also one issue for which you definitely want to get professional help. The potential risks involved in today's drug scene do not warrant just hoping for the best. Ask an adolescent expert to perform a risk assessment for your kid. If the drug use is life-threatening, rules of confidentiality don't apply, and the expert will have to inform you even if your kid refuses to tell you himself. If the behavior is less than life-threatening, your therapist may have to respect your child's wish for confidentiality, but at least you'll have involved a neutral third party who will both provide therapy and monitor as best she can. Although there are no guarantees, it's a much safer path.

Be very, very careful about forcing drug testing. Reread Chapter 12 slowly before making him pee in a cup. If you only suspect minimal use, you might cause a lot more harm than good in testing. If the test comes back positive for cannabis, what exactly will change? You probably were pretty sure he was smoking some grass, anyway. If you somehow got your kid into a rehab (which is very unlikely if he's just experimenting), the rehab folks will drop him back on your doorstep in a week or two, and suggest that you work on the core issues of respect, autonomy, responsibility, and positive identity-building. In other words, you would be back where you started, except now your kid really hates you and has been thoroughly immersed in a concentrated drug culture called rehab.

Don't be in too much of a hurry to rush your kid straight into a drug rehab. We are seeing a growing body of research that strongly suggests that we can seriously worsen a variety of adolescent problems by treating them in therapy groups with other offenders. The effect might be like sending Sally to druggie graduate school. Any decision concerning rehab should be made in conjunction with an expert who has performed an assessment to weigh the risk/benefit factors of a rehab. If your child is heavily involved with life-threatening drugs, rehab is the only choice. Short of that, stop and think.

What to Do: Long-Term Strategies that Begin at Birth

If you asked me for the best strategy to drug-proof your kid, I'd tell you to reread this book. When you've worked with kids as long as I have, you get a little arrogant in making secret predictions in your head that you never share with your clients because you're not supposed to be doing this to avoid contaminating your work. Those predictions are about what the eventual outcome will be for a particular drug-involved kid. I figure my prediction batting average runs about 80 to 90 percent. I'm not brilliant, I'm just observant.

Those predictions for success or failure leap across the coffee table at me when I meet Mom and Dad, and see them interact with their child. Whenever I see that elusive balance of nurturing, firmness, respect, and emotional control in the parents, I have to work not to get too complacent about their kid. Almost always, those parental skills mean that child is home free. Oh, he'll get bumped and bruised a little, and Mom and Dad will get scared a lot, but they'll all survive pretty well. They walk in the door with all of the ingredients for success.

Those parents already know that the best antidrug tactic we know of is helping your kid make his own decision not to use. This "inoculation" will best protect him out in the world where fear of parental rage not only becomes impotent, it also becomes motivation to do drugs. These parents instinctively use all of those tedious, time-consuming, and emotionally demanding respect- and identity-building techniques you've now been trained in.

So don't get hopeless about the drugs, get angry—at the *drugs,* not at your kid. She's just crazy, remember? Then use that anger to fuel your discipline to use your skills. Separate the child you love from those scary behaviors you hate, and talk to her in just those terms. You are her best and only hope—because you are the one who loves her.

CRITICAL DOs

- Go to the hospital if safety is in doubt
- Set a drug-free example with yourself
- Set zero-tolerance rules for drugs
- Monitor for drug symptoms, quietly
- Confront symptoms dispassionately

CRITICAL DON'Ts

- Assume she'll just sleep it off (she might be dying)
- Be hypocritical (he'll eat you alive)
- Negotiate "what's OK" or "when it's OK" to use
- Randomly accuse as a test
- Ignore clear indicators of use (they won't go away)

- Look for local help
  (school intervention teams,
  county task forces, etc.)

- Obtain a risk assessment
  from an expert

- Let family pride keep you
  from getting help
  (this stuff can kill)

- Rush off to rehab unless your
  kid is out of control (there's
  no magic there and it can
  worsen the situation)

Since we're already feeling sad about the loss of innocence implicit in our kids' brushes with drugs, we might as well push on to that last loss-of-innocence topic: sex.

Turn the page and let's get it over with.

Chapter 15

SEX AND DATING:
WHAT YOU NEED TO KNOW

As I was writing this book, I had to laugh when I realized that I had put off the subject of sex to the very end. You don't suppose my Irish-Catholic training had anything to do with this, do you? Has your training had any effect on you?

The day had finally arrived. Being twelfth graders in 1969 meant that we would get the (cough, cough), you know, (sex) talk. In what must have been an act of divine intervention motivated by a great sense of satire, Father Murray somehow was picked to give us "the talk." This was the same "Lotta Yuks" Father Murray who once gave me detention for innocently saying "*Merry* Christmas, Father *Murray*."

Anyhow, Father Murray marched into our classroom with cheeks blazing red enough to stop traffic. He clutched a pile of papers so tightly to his chest that it seemed as if he was trying to keep the evil words contained within from leaping off the pages and infecting our hormonal brains like an alien plague. His jaw muscles kept working furiously, and he fussed nonstop with his collar, as if he felt a noose slowly tightening around his neck. Man, was he ever angry.

When he appeared, this room full of rowdy boys went into an absolute dead silence like we were all suspended in deep space. I think some of us stopped breathing because it made too much noise. The problem is that the more you scare 17-year-olds out of laughing, the more intense that urge becomes, building like a giant tsunami. We could all feel it coming.

Father Murray walked over to close the classroom doors and slowly lowered the shades, something that was only done for showing movies.

Ray Bulgosi whispered, "He's gonna show a porno." This was a very bad thing for Ray to say because the palpable tension in the room was about at the level you might expect if we were defusing a ticking nuclear device. The joke caused strange squeaking noises to scatter across the floor, sort of like the creaking of a wooden ship at anchor. This, of course, was the sound of cartilage tearing away from rib cages as forty 17-year-old, near-hysterical boys attempted not to laugh. Father Murray knew this noise and wheeled about with matador speed to try to catch the joker or jokees, if he could. He didn't even issue one threat. He just burned holes through our souls with a demonic stare that blazed out of those Clark Kent glasses he wore. This was truly a unique situation.

Another reason it was very bad that Ray Bulgosi made that joke was it meant that Ray was headed into one of his uncontrollable kamikaze runs, where his sense of humor would fly way ahead of his instinct for self-preservation. We had seen this before and it wasn't pretty.

Father Murray ferociously launched into his lecture. The only problem was that whenever he came to a, shall we say, controversial word, he would pause to leave that word unsaid, instead raising his eyes off of his text to look at us and say, "And you know what that word is." For example, he would say, "...and the female genitalia, which is called the, and you know what that word is, receives the male genitalia, which is called the, and you know what that word is." This was just too funny to endure—at least for Ray.

Father Murray started to get more comfortable, and then daring. Tiring of having said "and you know what that word is" for the millionth time, he turned, perhaps not coincidentally, to Ray, who was hanging onto his suicidal urges by the thinnest of threads. He asked, "Mr. Bulgosi, would you please tell us what that word is that describes the female genitalia?"

That scene went into slow motion in my eyes as 39 heads swiveled as one to see Ray's mouth form and sound the word "c_ _ t" right in Father Murray's exploding face. As Father Murray rushed at him, Ray apparently decided that they can only hang you once. "Snatch?" he offered alternatively.

The room went nuts. Murray went for Ray's throat, and the two of them toppled backwards over a desk as the rest of us screamed laughter like I've never heard since. A friend of mine who was in the room next door said the screaming sounded like the "baying of the hounds of hell." The baying only worsened when Father Murray bellowed out the most horrible punishment his rage-contorted brain could summon. Ray's punishment would be that he "MUST SIT IN THE GIRL'S SEX-ED CLASSES FOR THE REST OF THIS WEEK." We screamed with laughter until we couldn't breathe.

I share this ridiculous but true story to remind you of the ridiculous but true baggage that many of us carry into talks about sex. As silly as Father Murray looked to me back then, today I find myself hesitating at certain words with my own fatherly sex talks. These discussions can be very hard to get through. They are also absolutely critical, so fire up your nerve.

Chapter 2 pummels you with all of the scary statistics about teen sex that show that sexual activity is at record high levels and is becoming a function that is void of emotion. Reread that chapter to increase your panic and help you pay attention here. But there is one hopeful statistic. Research shows a steady decline in the number of adolescent births over the past 10 years to a record low for the past few decades. While everybody is claiming credit for this, the objective view holds that this good news is the result of both safe sex *and* abstinence practices—which, in turn, suggests that the real credit goes to all of those embarrassed parents who engage their teenagers in meaningful discussions about sex. The encouraging bottom line is that if you talk skillfully to adolescents, they will listen. So here are some tips on talking well.

Dr. B's Disclaimer

Before we proceed, here's my disclaimer. As I talk about these sexual issues, note that I speak *only* as a psychologist, not as a religious or moral ethicist. Many of the things I say are OK psychologically, but may not be OK according to your religious or moral views, or even my own. It is not my job to comment on those aspects of sexual behavior. That's your job, so note that when I say something is harmless or normal, I do not mean to denigrate your religious or moral views, which might be in sharp contrast. View the data I am going to give you as the "science" part, over which you must impose your own personal views.

"The Talk"

The first thing you need to know is that "The Talk" should really be an ongoing dialogue of a thousand minitalks. All of the suggestions I'm about to give should be spread out over many discussions. Look for all kinds of excuses to talk about sexual issues—like movies you watch together, incidents that happen with peers, or (a favorite tactic of mine) those lyrics on his CDs.

Next, you *have to have these talks*. Contrary to the popular myth, most research suggests that talking with kids about sex tends to postpone the first intercourse and tends to make sexual activity lower-risk. Did I just see you wince because you don't want me to talk about minimizing risk, you just want me to eliminate it entirely by finding a way for your kid not to have sex? Well, I wince, too, so if you have any ideas on how to enforce abstinence, please send them to me. I keep asking my daughter if she'd like to consider convent life until she's 30. She just laughs. She thinks I'm kidding.

So my fallback plan must be the same as yours. We have to keep talking, because the fact is that half of our kids have intercourse between 15 and 19 years of age, and far too many have it much earlier than that. Is this too young? Of course it is, but it is the way it is, and we must deal with it. You don't want to be giving a psychologist the intake information that Paula had to give about her daughter.

Paula narrated her daughter's story with frightened eyes. I didn't fully understand her look until she got to the end of the story. "My daughter was really crushed by this last relationship. I don't think Carina was ever really in love like this before. I think it was more than just being sexually involved. For a month now, she's retreated to her room, hardly eats anything, and often won't get up in the morning. It's like she's lost her will to live. When you see her, you'll know what I mean." "I'm sorry," I interrupted, looking incredulously at the intake sheet, "but how old did you say your daughter is? My intake form, I think, says 13?" Mom nodded. "She was 12 when her first sexual relationship crashed."

When I recovered as gracefully as I could, I asked Paula, "What does Carina say about having such involved relationships at such a young age?" Paula shifted uncomfortably. "I'm not sure how she feels because we have a really hard time talking about sex, you know? And she gets all the information she needs from school, doesn't she? Don't they teach kids about this? And besides, she never comes to ask me anything, so what could I possibly tell her that she'd actually listen to?"

Here are a few tips for "The Talk" that you might find useful:

1. *You first.*

Don't wait for your kid to come to you with questions. This isn't Leave It to Beaver. Sex is just too tough for most kids to talk to parents about in general—plus, she may be scared that you'll go nuts if she asks specific questions, and that you'll ask her some specific questions (like if she's doing it). Set the tone by chatting one-way, if needed, without any interrogation questions, so that she relaxes and listens.

2. *Have short chats, not marathons.*

Let your kid set the pace for these talks. All kids, parents, and relationships are different, and each must find the formula that works best, but most kids prefer the shorter bursts. Watch for the signs that tell you when he's had enough, and let it go for now.

3. *Help her decide to postpone sex; don't demand it.*

If you mandate no sex, the conversation is over and your kid's oppositional, unstable, and impulsive brain says, "sex is for me." Use your training. Dispassionately help her consider all of the issues in sex decisions. This is also known as identity building.

4. *Don't be afraid to state the obvious.*

Abstinence for adolescents is clearly the best policy. Sex with deeply committed adult love is the best policy. Even kids who have had intercourse say this. Parents are often afraid of appearing uncool by stating these "dinosaur" positions. You're not supposed to be cool. You're supposed to be a dinosaur. You're supposed to be her parent. But convincingly arguing your abstinence position is not the same as forbidding her to have sex. Telling her that you love her and that this is what you believe is best for her is not only fine, it is critical. Yelling or threatening is not OK and actually greatly weakens your influence over your kid.

5. Do those dumb role-plays.

Your daughter tells me that it is actually helpful to have practiced responses to those age-old lines like, "If you loved me, you'd have sex with me." What may seem to be a silly, old sales pitch to you may seem like a unique argument to a brain-dysfunctioned and hormonal girl hearing this for the first time. Don't assume anything.

6. Tell him what sex is to girls.

Most girls see sex as emotional intimacy, exclusive commitment, and love. Many girls have been trained to try to mime the boys' version of the sex game (to have the boys say that they're cool), but they get emotionally crippled in the process of attempting to have depersonalized sex (see Chapter 2). Ask him if he is willing to be that cruel, even to a girl who claims she doesn't care about emotion in sex.

7. Tell her what sex is to boys.

For most boys, sex is conquest and physical release. Many develop strong emotional attachments as well, but the basic boys versus girls sex game has changed little since you played.

8. Don't forget the pregnancy and disease risks.

Amazingly to parents, the research shows that kids are listening to these warnings if they are presented dispassionately. Once you start to preach, you'd better find the choir because your kid will be gone. When you talk pregnancy, ask (without naming names) if he knows someone who got pregnant and either aborted or delivered. Ask him to tell you the story about what happened and how those kids felt. Put faces on the statistics to drive home the agonizing emotional pain of teen pregnancy.

9. Discuss contraception.

First, reread my disclaimer. If contraception is a religious prohibition to you, then you must decide what to do here. All I can tell you is that the research shows that discussions of contraception tend to postpone a kid's first intercourse, as well as reduce her high-risk behaviors, when they are presented in a balanced fashion and include information about pregnancy, disease, and abstinence.

10. *Discuss homosexuality.*

Psychologically speaking, homosexuality is a fact of human existence. It is not a disease or a disorder. It may be unacceptable to you by virtue of your religious beliefs, but that is a separate issue apart from the psychology of homosexuality. The science of sexuality shows that homosexuality is nothing more than an alternative form of sexual expression.

Many critics of homosexuality like to claim that both the American Psychological Association and the American Psychiatric Association were politically strong-armed into dropping their previous position that gay people were somehow sick. The fact is that 25 years ago these prestigious associations were simply suffering from the same uninformed and fear-based bigotry against homosexuality that afflicts many of the rest of us: It seems weird, so it must be a disease. The revisions in the positions of these associations were actually courageous victories of science over ignorance. When we combine fear and misinformation with significant differences among people, we often end up with an explosive and dangerous mix. Such is the way with homosexuality.

So the primary purpose of the talk here is to try to counter some of the unthinking rejection, loathing, and hatred that much of our society vents upon homosexuals. This evil has become condensed and even more lethal among our teens. *"Gay" has now become the most common adolescent adjective to describe anything that is loathsome in your kid's life* ("Man, this test is really gay").

What is your handle, your pigeonhole descriptor? Baptist, Jewish, black, white? How would it feel to hear a good friend talking to someone else and saying "That tax plan sucks. It's really (Baptist, Jewish, black, white)"? If it would seem hateful and ignorant to you, you've got the picture. This is precisely the daily experience of adolescents who think that they might be gay.

Tom winced as if I had just drilled his tooth without numbing it. He repeated my question as if to frame its lunacy: "Have I ever thought of coming out of the closet with my friends? Only all of the time! Don't you think that I'm in agony living secretly as a homosexual? But do you have any idea what it's like to be 16 years old and gay? I don't know where you grew up, but I'm not kidding when I say that, if word got out about me, there's a good chance I'd be dead before my senior prom. I play football and nobody messes with me now. The team protects its own, you know what I'm sayin'? But, man, if the kids ever knew I was gay, I'd be hunted down like a mad dog by the skinheads and no one would lift a freakin' finger to help. No one would even call 911. Just another dead fag, right?"

Tom paused to collect himself. He took a deep breath and then he quietly continued. "That's not the worst part, you know? I could, like, handle the skins, I think. I'd be scared, but you know what? Those red-suspendered assholes are not what I fear the most. They couldn't scare me enough to make me live like this. The thing that would make me really want to die is the look I know I'd see on my friends' faces when I told them who I really am." This tough boy's eyes began to mist. "We're really tight, you know? We're like brothers. Most of us come from bad times and bad homes. We're all the family most of us got." Tom got up and walked to my pictures of my wife and kids. "So when you ask me that question, you think about whether you'd ever say anything that would make you lose your family. And not just lose them like in a car wreck, but have them walk away from you like you were some dangerous, sicko pervert or something. So tell me, Doc, what would you do?"

You have to have this talk with your child about homosexuality for three people. The first is your kid. He might be gay. Although the odds are against your kid being homosexual, we know that a large percentage of our society is gay. We can't reliably fix that number, because openly admitting to being gay in America is like standing up at a Ku Klux Klan rally, taking off your sheet, revealing your African heritage, and saying, "Hey, who's for a couple beers after the meet?" Most of us wear the sheet of heterosexuality in this society, and we turn and stare at the courageous homosexual who takes off his cover. Could you do this? I've thought a lot about it and I don't think I could. My sheet would stay on and I'd lead a life of tortured silence and pretense. I don't want this for my kid. How about you?

So have the talk for your kid's sake. Even if she's not gay, she may be agonizing over a sort-of sexual attraction she's having towards another female. Sexuality can be a very vague process in adolescence, with both heterosexual and homosexual attractions occurring until that aspect of identity resolves itself. Don't let your kid get all tied up in secret knots because she's terrified to say the word "homosexual." These bigotry-based secret sexual crises are where we do psychological damage to kids.

The second person for whom you need to have the homosexuality talk with your child is your kid's friend. The odds are that your child knows kids who are gay, whether they admit to it or not. How do you want those friends to be treated by your child? What, exactly, do you want those fine-sounding words of tolerance and respect to mean when your kid faces fine human beings who are his friends who happen to have sexual differences? Intolerance and bigotry are heirlooms we hand down to generations that follow us.

Finally, have the talk for you. Knowing that I'd never take off my heterosexual sheet makes me worry about my kid being gay and being as practical-minded (or as scared) as I am, and not telling me that he is homosexual. That would mark the end of our intimate relationship and that would about kill me. How about you?

If your kid confides that he is pretty sure he is gay, do all of you a favor and think about getting some expert help. The issues involved here are so emotionally laden and potentially explosive that an expert can more safely ease the way. But be sure that when you raise this option of counseling with your kid, you underscore the fact that the need for the expert is a function of a disease of society, not of his sexual orientation.

That's about all you need for "The Talk," except the nerve. Now that you're thoroughly pan-fried on the sex issues, why don't we jump right into the fire and talk about dating?

Dating

Teens manifest tremendous variety in the dating world. Some kids are practically engaged in seventh grade, while others don't date anyone twice until college. The early sexualizing of children (see Chapter 2) has had some scary effects on many teen subcultures. Some groups of kids decide it is cool to pair off in "intense" relationships at the ages of 12 and 13. Dating can become another area in which kids fight out issues of autonomy and rebellion with parents. You don't want this, because the concept of teen dating has radically changed over the past 10 years with ominous sexual and emotional implications (see Chapter 2).

However, adolescent dating can also become another place for your kid to safely grow and develop an identity that will help strengthen him with wisdom for the more serious relationships that are around the corner. Whether dating becomes an identity-builder or a battleground is mostly up to you. The formula for success is for you to focus on maintaining your relationship with your kid and not becoming obsessed with demands and mandates. Here are a few tips:

1. *Negotiate rules in advance of relationships.*

After she's met Mr. Wonderful is not a good time to agree on a minimum dating age if she doesn't make the cutoff. Look at what happened with Romeo and Juliet. Set jointly agreed-upon rules before love strikes so that she can factor that restriction into her decision about intensifying a relationship. That minimum age is best negotiated between you and your kid, but when pressed, most experts suggest 14 as the minimum age for real dates (I, personally, am looking for research to support 33, but haven't found any yet).

2. *Discuss relationships in advance of relationships.*

In case you haven't noticed, relationships are hard. They're a lot of work and they make your stomach hurt. You should have these discussions with your kid before his stomach starts to hurt. Ask him for stories of peers (without names) who have gotten seriously involved with someone. Usually your kid has watched a friend go through that first real relationship agony. Try to dispassionately remove the aura of romance from the coupling behavior. Look for opportunities to help him decide what kinds of limits he would like to set for dating in order to maintain balance in his teenage life. DON'T LECTURE!

3. *Stay neutral and connected.*

Once the game is afoot, keep your frosty. Nothing cements true love for a teen like the forbidding rantings of parents. Once upon a time, back in those days of fear-based parenting, you could rant and rave and maybe win. No more. Keep cool so you can keep the lines of communication open into your kid's brain, which is now doubly insane. If you're worried about the intensity of the romance, say so dispassionately. Try engaging your 13-year-old future daughter-in-law at family outings so that Junior can see her in a more realistic light. What seems to be the love of your life in a forbidden nighttime encounter can look more like just plain old white bread when viewed at a family picnic.

4. Don't laugh off the love of 12-year-olds.

Another interesting bit of research shows high levels of emotional devastation in both adolescent girls *and boys* when intense relationships fail, as they are bound to do. Getting dumped at 12 may feel worse than getting dumped at 32, because at 12 you don't have the emotional strength of identity to carry you through. I won't terrify you again with the statistics on adolescent depression and suicide if you promise to remember that you must be there to support that crushed 12-year-old as if this were a friend's marriage failing. Your kid will cycle through the pain much quicker than your friend will, but relatively speaking, your kid's pain is just as bad and just as potentially harmful.

5. After the divorce, have another talk.

Whether your kid seems fine or devastated after the relationship ends, take her out for a few Slurpees. Get her to talk about what she's learned and how this experience shapes her future thinking. The idea here is to put another brick in that wall of identity she's building that can strengthen her for the next round. Remember that the wise parent skillfully does this by asking questions and only offering advice if requested.

Pregnancy

If pregnancy hits, get help fast. Teenage pregnancy is a car wreck with bleeding victims who are facing potentially permanent disabilities. This is a time for crisis intervention and for stemming the bleeding, not for lecturing, punishing, or even teaching. Both you and your daughter will, most likely, need outside decision-making help, since the two of you will be panicked, and this is precisely the time you need to think most clearly. Go make that call.

The next thing you need to do is ignore your own knee-jerk mandate reactions (*"you are having an abortion!"* or *"you will deliver this baby!"*). You might, ultimately, end up at those positions anyhow, but you'll mangle your daughter's life in the process. *She must be involved in the decisions.* Part of that involvement is giving her and yourself some facts before you all decide what to do, such as:

1. *Teen marriages and teen parenting don't work.*

Eighty percent of teen marriages disintegrate within two years, throwing girls and babies into the streets or back into parents' homes. Most teen mothers never complete high school, and then they struggle to reach even poverty levels of subsistence, ultimately earning half in their lifetimes what older mothers earn. Picture this life for both your child and grandchild.

2. *One in five teenage fathers contributes financial support towards their baby.*

And this one "stand-up" guy disappears within a year. Don't rely on the bravado-based, meaningless commitments of teenage fathers. They have no idea what they're talking about when they promise to support their baby. These parents are children, and they're nuts. Mom is on her own.

3. *Half of those stand-up teenage fathers who cohabit with mom and child never make it to high school graduation themselves.*

So even if the father has the exceptionally rare adolescent moxie to stick it out, he's headed for the same poverty train that awaits single teen moms.

4. *In the past 10 years, we've thrown 64 percent more children into foster homes.*

This is a human tragedy. As an ex-foster father, I note this not to knock foster parents (the good ones are the Green Berets of the parenting world, doing work that is far too tough for me), but I've looked helplessly into the terrified faces of screaming babies who didn't know where they were and what happened to their mom. You don't want this for any child.

So sort out the facts carefully. Have a series of minitalks reviewing all of the options. If your daughter is headed down a path that looks life-ending, get her to meet people who have tried the single teen mom route. Pose questions, not mandates, based on the statistics I presented, and ask how she'll deal with these issues.

The last stat you should know going into these teen pregnancy talks is that 9 out of 10 adolescents admit that they cannot handle the rigors of parenting—so she probably knows this somewhere inside. Use dispassionate questions to get at this wisdom. Your anger will push it away and create oppositional urges. Stay cool.

So there! We had the talk and it wasn't so bad, was it? And I didn't even have to pull down the shades. As you consider what to do with the shades in your own sex talks with your kid, keep two final points in mind. First, while many things are very different in your kid's sexual world, luckily, many things are also the same, particularly regarding what constitutes healthy sexual functioning. Those words like commitment and love still hold true as universal ideals, even in these scary days. So that makes you an expert. Don't forget to calmly advance your own beliefs in these discussions with your kid. I can almost guarantee that she'll listen if you talk directly from your heart without threats or mandates.

Second, don't make the mistake of thinking that talking about sex increases the odds of it happening too early. It's quite the opposite. Frequent, respect-based minitalks tend to cause teens to put off sexual activity. As with suicide, here's another "S" word that you want to use a lot to reduce the odds of it visiting your home.

Chapter 16

GETTING HELP

M AKING THE DECISION to get professional help can be hard. Then comes the harder part: sorting out a dozen questions, including what type of expert you need, what credentials they should have, how you know who's good, how you decide between types of therapy, how you get your kid there without shackles, whether your insurance will cover this, and whether you should consider medications. These issues can be confusing and discouraging at a time when holy hell may be breaking loose in your home, and you and your partner's joint decision-making skills aren't exactly at an all-time high. So read this chapter now, even if you don't need help at the moment, and you'll be more ready if you ever do.

Where Do You Start?

There are two overall categories of expert help for adolescent issues: public institutions or agencies, and private practitioners. Your first step is to decide between these two categories. That decision depends on the types of problems you're seeing; your best guess as to how your kid will react to each category type; and the availability, affordability, and quality of these services.

Public sources of help are typically free or low-cost and include schools, religious institutions, local government-assistance programs, public mental health centers, and social service agencies. The quality of services and the credentials of the staff in these places can vary dramatically. Some are excellent and some are a waste of time.

Your first stop for academic problems should be your child's school.

Many districts have outstanding adolescent support and treatment programs that parents often don't know exist. Even if the problem is not school-related, your kid's school counselor or teacher can usually guide you further in making appropriate choices. They deal with adolescent problems daily and are often very knowledgeable about youth help programs. The down side is that many kids don't want their school to know of any personal problems they're having at home. I have had more than one teen complain bitterly about how their privacy was not respected by school personnel who shared their stories with other school staff without permission. Be sure to get a commitment of confidentiality from any school professional you consult.

Religious organizations often have programs to help teens. These may be of particular value if the issues involve religious conflicts and you are concerned that a nonreligious professional may not be as sensitive to your particular faith. But keep in mind that your child might be better off seeing a clinician not affiliated with any religion because this person will not have a vested interest in keeping a lamb in the flock.

Your phone book will list all of the various government and social service agencies in your area, some of which are dedicated to specific adolescent issues like drugs, sex, or aggression problems. Try asking friends, neighbors, and religious leaders for their input on these choices. Check at work to see if you have some type of employee assistance program that might offer some low- or no-cost help.

Your other source of help is the private practitioner. There are several different types of therapists, which we'll describe shortly. But whether you go public or private, all of the guidelines discussed in this chapter apply to your choice of expert. Don't be bashful about asking important questions to determine the appropriateness of the professional you're considering. If anyone thinks you're being too pushy, call the next person on your list. This is *your child* you are talking about entrusting to someone else, whether you pay privately or the service is publicly funded. Pick an adolescent mental health professional with at least the same amount of scrutiny you would a pediatric surgeon. If you don't like something, move on to someone else.

But before wasting your time calling the private practitioner nerds, call your insurance company. You may be in for a shock.

Does Your Insurance Cover This?

Your insurance probably does not cover these costs, at least not in the way you think. Most HMOs or managed care policies insist that you seek mental health services only with providers they "approve." The approval process is not a rating of expertise—it is a business deal. The insurance companies often control the number and frequency of sessions these providers can give, and it is in the insurance company's interest to keep the sessions (and their costs) to a minimum. They also typically pay less to their "approved" experts than the going hourly rate for private services. For example, most adolescent psychologists I know charge $85 per hour and up. I've seen managed care programs that, ultimately, pay $20 per hour to the practitioner.

Other insurance companies seem to take an entirely different view of the importance of providing good coverage and many provide excellent programs. One company executive told me how their own studies proved that providing high-quality mental health coverage saved the company money in reduced physical illness claims. So the answer to the insurance question is that it depends on your particular insurer. Call them and ask questions that include:

◆ Who decides what services my kid needs? The parents and the expert, or the company?
◆ Do I have to see only the company's contracted providers or can I choose my own? If I must see the company's providers, can I see a list of adolescent specialists from which to choose?
◆ Is there a deductible or co-pay for services?
◆ What limits are there on costs or number of sessions?

I hate to be so mercenary this early in the discussion, but quality mental health services are not cheap, and you don't need the added stress of unexpected bills. You also don't have time to waste checking out providers you may not even be allowed to see. So check out these insurance matters before you start your expert selection process.

What Type of Expert Do You Need?

As if you didn't already have enough to do since you've decided to get help, now you're confronted with a bunch of confusing titles and credentials that probably have little meaning to you, but the distinctions can be very critical in your decision-making process. Let's take a look at the kinds of folks you might see as treatment professionals, both in public agencies and in private practice.

Counselor, Therapist, or Psychotherapist: These are catch-all labels that describe lots of mental health professionals. People who identify themselves this way might have several degrees and licenses, or they may have none at all. You need to ask these experts what degrees, licenses, or other credentials they have that demonstrate an objective evaluation of their competence. Most insurers will not cover services provided by practitioners without substantial credentials, such as a state license.

All of the experts I'm about to describe must meet rigid and demanding requirements such as mandatory education, internship, residency, state licensing, regulation and examination, and ongoing training. These requirements help confused parents know that experts holding these kinds of credentials have demonstrated some levels of competency to third-party evaluators.

Psychologist: In most states, the title of psychologist can only be legally claimed by someone who has completed a doctoral-level degree at a university that requires a supervised internship or residency. In past years some psychologists fulfilled these requirements with a master's degree. Psychologists do not prescribe medications at this time in most settings, although many are trained in psychopharmacology (medications used to treat psychological disorders).

Psychiatrist: A psychiatrist is a medical doctor who fulfills additional specialty training in the field of mental health in a supervised training residency. A psychiatrist can prescribe medications and is particularly appropriate to treat illnesses that have medical components.

Psychiatric Nurse: In many states, licensed nurses can obtain additional training, supervision, and degrees to become certified to provide mental health services. In some states, they may prescribe medications, although usually in collaboration with a psychiatrist.

Licensed Clinical Social Worker: Most states offer licensing programs to social workers who are specifically trained to provide mental health services. These practitioners are called Licensed Clinical Social Workers. They do not prescribe medications, although many are trained in psychopharmacology.

Don't be shy about verifying the credentials of the experts you interview. They've all worked hard to get those pieces of paper hanging on their walls and should not be offended by verification requests. I have worked with clients who spent years in treatment with a well-known local "psychiatrist" who turned out not to be a psychiatrist or any type of credentialed professional at all. Since then, I fully understand clients who insist on seeing my pieces of paper.

Which Expert Do You Pick?

Within those expert classifications I have just described are all kinds of further subspecialties. You're looking for folks who are skilled at *and who like* working with adolescents. These clinicians are a different breed. "Normal" mental health practitioners often shake their heads at us adolescent treatment types like we're a little crazy. I'm not sure exactly why that is—are you?

Anyway, as you phone around, don't get upset if you find mental health professionals who refuse to take your adolescent's case and refer you to someone else. It's nothing personal. It's just that they know how nuts your kid can be and that this is not their cup of tea. You want to find practitioners who enjoy things like wild, roller-coaster rides and working with teens. These people are usually well known to your local schools and religious institutions. Also, lay down that silly pride and ask your friends if they know of someone. You'll be amazed at how many parents of teenagers will rattle off names to you without missing a beat.

Now that you've narrowed your field of choices, interview a couple of people. Go with your kid if she's willing, or alone if she's not for now (more on this later). See what the person looks like, how she talks, how her office feels, and so on. Ask her about the types of therapy she might use and how they work. Some use open-ended, nondirective styles where they say little or nothing to your kid. Others are highly directive and do lots of talking. Most are in the middle. These factors are important for you to know because you know your child and you are in the best position to guess if your kid will "click" with the expert. And that "click" is really, really important.

If you are thinking that shopping for a shrink is a lot like buying a pair of shoes, you're right on the money. You and your kid are going to spend a lot of time in those shoes, so they'd better fit. If someone doesn't fit for you and your child, go home and start working with your list again. Nothing good is likely to happen if you force the issue and see someone who just doesn't fit well with your family.

A controversy rages as we speak about which types of psychological therapies work best. Oversimplifying the issue, it's pretty much a debate between those who believe that the *type* of therapy determines success, and those who believe that success is a function of the *relationship* between the therapist and the client. The truth is probably that success is a combination of the two, and it can vary according to the type of problem being treated. Unless you want to study treatment efficacy models (a *great* sleep aid), the part of the success equation that you can evaluate is the relationship part. And when it comes to working with adolescents, the relationship part is far more important than the style or type of therapy.

So try on the shoes. See what you and your kid think about the expert. It's probably the best predictor for success. Don't feel shy about doing this. Good practitioners will welcome your request to interview them to see how they fit for you. We know that who we are as people cannot be right for everybody. Remember that we work for you. We're not your boss; we're your consultant. We're not your priest; we're your mechanic. We're trained in repairing the machinery of adolescence.

If you and your kid are going to be able to listen, you have to feel comfortable and confident in your expert, or nothing good will happen. Your kid has to feel like he can talk with and trust the clinician. You have to feel confidence in her abilities because she may be helping you make some very difficult calls.

Avoid blisters. Try on your experts.

How to Get Your Kid There: Controversial Kid Tricks

It is the unusual adolescent who initially thinks that going to see a shrink is a good idea, particularly if this idea crops up in the midst of a battle between the two of you. Teens are typically secretive about their personal lives, and inviting a stranger into their business seems very weird. They are also used to getting yelled at by adults, so he may think of this idea just as your way of calling for reinforcements. Kids also know better than anyone else that they're nuts. They see, feel, and hear firsthand all of those wacky impulses, radical mood swings, and strange thoughts emanating from their roiling brains. The thought of exposing all of this insanity to a stranger may seem very frightening—and it is.

The reality is that seeing a therapist is very hard to do, even for adults, let alone crazy teenagers. Keep this in mind as you raise the possibility to your kid. Don't initially demand that she go for treatment. Rather, softly raise the idea that you and she might benefit from seeing someone. Don't push for an immediate answer; just ask that she mull this over. Tell her you are going to start checking out some possible options and ask if any of her friends know of someone they liked seeing. Although you may end up seeing any type of mental health professional, use the softer word "counseling" for now, since she is familiar with this concept from school. Try to initially avoid using the word "psychologist," "psychiatrist," or "therapist," since your kid may hear this as *One Flew Over the Cuckoo's Nest* time. As you zero in on a specialist, you can interchange the words (*"Dr. Bradley is a psychologist who has been suggested for our counseling"*).

If your child seems open to the idea of "counseling," involve her in the selection process. Ask if she has a preference for a female or male professional. Try to give her as much power and control as possible so that she feels invested in the process.

If she's dug in and resistant to the idea, don't push. If she ultimately sees therapy as a punishment, you're probably dooming the process to failure. If you can, be patient. She might need some time to become comfortable with the concept. She might tell a friend about your ridiculous idea and that friend might respond that her life got so much better after she saw a counselor.

If the situation is not too urgent, you might use this first discussion to lay the groundwork for a later decision. Tell him you understand his reluctance and that you're not anxious to go either, but you think it might help. Perhaps suggest that you all see how you do over the next month and that if things are still tough, maybe then you'll discuss this again.

If the situation seems urgent and she's still refusing help, you might want to try a few controversial kid tricks. These are last resorts, less-than-ideal manipulations to get your kid into the office.

Before you employ any of these tricks, announce to your teen that, even if he won't go for now, you think that you must be doing some things that contribute to the tension, so you are going alone. But underscore that you want him to join you whenever he's willing. Then start the selection and screening process I described earlier. This becomes even more important if your kid is resistant, because if you use a controversial kid trick, you want to be sure you've got a very compatible therapist lined up. If you take a resistant kid to a clunker of a clinician, you've set back your cause considerably.

Trick #1: Set a field of options before your child, but tell him that he must pick one. This way, he'll feel some control, but within a set of boundaries to which he must conform: "Bobby, living like this is terrible for all of us, so let's see if we can make it better. We need help. This is a problem that involves all of us. I've made an appointment with a counselor. Please just see him once. If you hate him, we'll try another to find someone you like. Remember, Bobby, whatever you tell him, he'll have to keep secret." The concept of confidentiality can sometimes seem cool to an adolescent. Your expert will fill you both in on exactly how confidentiality works, but, essentially, unless your kid is in a life-threatening situation, the clinician will keep your child's secrets.

Trick #2: If Trick #1 bites the dust, you might become more devious and go to the macho manipulation. It runs something like this: "Bobby, why won't you go with me? I know it's scary, but what exactly are you afraid of?" Bobby rises off the couch: "I ain't afraid of nothing!" Parent: "Good. Then go one time and I'll stop bugging you. Deal?"

Trick #3: If Trick #2 goes down in flames, try: "Hey, Bobby, how does 10 bucks sound?" As lousy as this seems, if your situation is urgent and your kid is resistant, pull out all the stops.

Trick #4: If bribing doesn't work, you might have to impose limitations: "Bobby, if you're so set on not going then I guess that's it. But I'm worried that some of the things you've been doing can hurt you, so until both of us can get some counseling, I'm afraid I've got to cut your curfew back." After Bobby goes nuts, you dispassionately reply, "Sorry, but I'm out of options. I have to keep you safe, but I also want to respect your opinions. What do you suggest we do?"

These tricks are slow steps away from ideally involving your child voluntarily in treatment, each exacting a cost by diminishing the chances for successfully engaging your kid. But desperate times call for such measures, and adolescent clinicians are skilled at engaging resistant kids who get drafted into treatment. Even if he refuses to go back for a second visit, you've probably helped set the stage for successful engagement down the road. He saw that the expert is not scary or demeaning, and that it was kind of cool to be able to say whatever he felt and know that it would never be repeated.

Emergencies

Emergencies are those get-to-the-safe-place-now situations. These are not really treatment options, although they may evolve that way. These are actions to keep everyone alive. Emergencies include suicidal activities or threats, assaults or serious threats of assault, panic or anxiety attacks, drug overdoses, and psychotic behaviors.

In such situations, use your dispassionate cop training to effect calm at any cost. No parenting, no rule enforcement, no nothing except bringing things back from the brink. Talk quietly, slowly, and in short sentences. Keep your hands down. Try to get agreement from your kid to go voluntarily with you for help. If not, call 911 without pause.

Head for the nearest emergency room. The hospital is there to keep everybody safe, but not much more, so keep your expectations low. The staff there will do a preliminary assessment to decide what the next step might be. This takes time, so plan on being out for a while. They might suggest psychiatric hospitalization, which may mean transferring your kid to a specialized hospital or to a hospital that is covered by your insurance. If this is the case, *insist* that your kid go to an adolescent treatment facility. Fight with the insurance company if you must, but don't allow your kid to be hospitalized with adult psychiatric patients. This whole process will be difficult enough for your child. Hanging out with adult patients is not helpful. Seeing other adolescents who have troubles can be therapeutic. Kids love to hang out with other kids, even if it's in the hospital.

The other option the emergency room staff may suggest is to release your kid with medications, which is also an option that might be raised by your nonemergency clinician. You want to think about this issue of giving drugs to your kid now before your mind goes blank as you sit and stare at your expert after she says, "I think that maybe we should consider the option of a medication for Bobby. Ms. Jones? Ms. Jones? Did you hear me?"

Medicating Teens

The treatments for many mental disorders often bring parents to that terrible sleep-destroying decision of medicating their child. The chemicals used for these sorts of problems are called psychotropic medications, meaning that they try to help change bad behaviors, thoughts, or even perceptions of reality by changing the way a kid's mind functions. Sounds pretty scary? Well, it is. It also sounds a lot like why kids do illegal drugs, doesn't it? And aren't kids stealing and using these same legal drugs illegally? Yes, they are.

So how on earth can someone sit there and tell you to hand your kid dangerous chemicals that can change her at her very core? Because before most clinicians suggest that you go down that path, they will carefully weigh those very real medication risks against the terrible pain in which your child may be drowning. But raising the prospect of medicating a child takes us to the core of a very passionate contemporary debate having to do with drugging kids. And that debate is often erroneously framed by the public as a philosophical dispute between psychologists who believe only in drug-free therapy and psychiatrists who believe only in drug therapy. This dispute doesn't exist.

Treating serious psychological disorders often requires both therapy and medication. Psychologists and psychiatrists recognize this and collaborate very well, but many parents are biased against the use of medications. Frequently, parents view psychologists as occasionally weird, sometimes ineffective, but at worst, harmless agents to their kids. In other words, low risk. They feel less threatened by potentially bad therapy than by potentially good medications. These parents may alternatively view a psychiatrist who prescribes medication as a borderline pusher, as a maniacal pill-dispenser who sees chemicals as the cure to the world's ills and who cares little about the potential implications of medicating children. Lousy therapy, some parents reason, may just waste our time and money, but the chemicals might kill our kid.

The truth is that bad therapy can maim and kill just like bad chemicals. There's a popular radio psychologist whose "therapies" are so frightening and professionally embarrassing that a colleague of mine jokes that now when asked at parties what he does for a living, he replies, "Assistant Head Cashier at the local 7/11." Talk therapy is not always benign.

And I've yet to meet one of these monster psychiatrists the radio psychologist likes to talk about. Just like the occasional scary psychologists, I'm sure they exist, but the child psychiatrists I've known for over 27 years are serious, competent, and caring physicians who worry a lot about the kids they see, and are typically conservative in handing out pills.

In the mental health debates, all sides unanimously agree that we clearly overmedicate in this nation. We do so love our drugs. But those joined hands become unclasped when we try to determine exactly who is being overmedicated. It gets complex. As a culture, do we use too many drugs? Yes. Should this fact have any bearing on your decision to medicate your kid? Oddly enough, no.

The answer to this dilemma is for you to have those sleepless nights wrestling with issues *that only pertain to your individual child*. You can't be swayed in your thoughts by what a radio psychologist says about psychiatrists and drugs any more than by what your neighbor says about how to bring peace to the Middle East. These are global views of cultural issues that are irrelevant to your problem. Your problem is local and specific, so you must directly pick the brain of every expert who has firsthand knowledge of your kid so that you can ultimately decide what is best. This is your job, Mom and Dad; it's what you signed on for. There are no easy answers, but let me make a few points that might help.

The first one is simple. If you're a drug bigot, your child's in trouble. Whether you are a pro- or anti-drug bigot, you're not helping your kid.

"My daughter Christina suffers from mood disorder. She's all bubbly one day, down the next, and shrieking at me on the third. My neighbor said my daughter has bipolar disorder, which she knows about because her aunt has it, and I got a doctor on the Net to put her on a drug for that. Now she just sleeps all the time, and her schoolwork is nowhere. I think she's really got ADHD too. We're starting another drug tonight, but the Net doctor says we have to see a psychologist also, or he won't prescribe any more for us. Shouldn't we just wait and see if the drug works before starting therapy? My husband and I just can't stand her ups and downs."

These runaway pill folks are an obvious problem. The other bigots can more subtly hurt their kids, but just as much.

"Dr. Bradley, you are the third psychologist we've seen, and we're here since we were told that you don't believe in using drugs with kids. The other two doctors we saw tried to send us to psychiatrists for pills. As a family, we are strongly antidrug. We work very hard at keeping a healthy lifestyle for our family. We're willing to do anything to help Ronnie, but we will not poison him with chemicals that just drug away his problems. That's no kind of solution, is it?"

Virtually all research shows that many mental disorders respond best to a combination of medication and therapy, so having preset drug opinions etched in stone does not help. You need to research as much as you can any suggested medication, and thoroughly interrogate the professionals you're working with. You want to know as much as possible about how these meds work, what they do, what they don't do, and how they differ from street drugs. This will help you deal with the second part of this dilemma: how to respond to the tricky questions that are raised when you medicate your kid.

So, Dad, Prozac Is OK, But I Can't Smoke Grass?

I can feel you flinching at this one. Don't feel bad. I start squirming too when I hear this from one of my medicated adolescent clients. It's bad enough we have to face that question from an adolescence-challenged kid who sees illegal drugs every day. What makes this query so much worse is that it is one heck of a question for us grownups to answer, even to ourselves.

How *do* we justify handing out these mood-altering, reality-changing, energizing, or de-energizing powders to kids whose rooms we search for drugs? Thanks to all of his drug education, biology, and chemistry classes, your son may mount an impressive argument that he'd be better off just smoking dope than taking your pills. Even worse, his local connection (drug dealer) at school stocks the same dope you purchase at the pharmacy. And sometimes you pay more.

Last year, 20 percent of our college students reported illegally using Ritalin (a stimulant used for ADHD treatment) for studying and for fun. Our nation alone uses *85 percent* of the world's supply of Ritalin. Your new-millennium adolescent has an understandably blurry view of the distinction between illegal drugs and legal medications.

So what should you say to convince your kid to take the med, but not sound like you're endorsing a Cheech and Chong lifestyle? First, read all the street drug information you'll find in Chapters 2 and 14 of this book. Then borrow some of the responses I've leaned on with moderate success in fielding this question from your kid.

First, depending on the medication, I try to make the argument that the legal pills don't change him into someone else, they really just allow him to be who he truly is. These meds cannot make him do anything, but can allow him more choices to make as he wishes. I talk about legal meds as leveling the playing field so that his brain can operate as efficiently as someone else's, but that what he does after that is totally up to him and not the drug. For example, I'll suggest that no drug can make him do his homework, but the Ritalin provides him with the option of doing it, if he wants to.

I'll tell her that the antidepressant won't make her sing "happy, happy, joy, joy," but it can help her begin to do the things she used to love to do, and that getting back to her life is, ultimately, what counteracts depression. The drug is just the tool to help her do what she needs to do.

I'll argue with your kid that those illegal drugs are just temporary escape hatches, and dangerous ones to boot. What they do is to generally make him too stupid to care about anything, and they'll only do that while he's under the influence. Once the high wears off, he's back to ground zero or worse. I tell your kid that the street drugs shut down his life, while the prescriptions can open up doors. I argue that the dope can end his life with finality and the prescription can finally start it.

Second, when she tells me that her street drugs can do the same things, I try to impress her with my Physicians' Desk Reference (PDR). I let her hold that massive book and look up the drug that her psychiatrist wants her to take. I ask her if she thinks her connection has tested out her street drugs as thoroughly, and what quality control measures the pusher employs. I also ask her to name kids she knows of who got messed up with street drugs. Then I ask for a list of the kids who got messed up taking legal medication as prescribed. The score usually ends up about 10 to zip. I also ask her to think of the last person she saw really stoned on illegal drugs and if that drooling, zombie-look attracts boys.

Third, if she's like a lot of kids who fight the idea of taking medication out of a sense of autonomy and the need for control, I'll suggest a trial use. I'll say that although this drug that her parents and psychiatrist want her to take may well be all the terrible things she thinks, what would be the harm in trying it for a while? If she gives it a chance and doesn't like the way she feels, she can always stop later. And besides, maybe if she is willing to try, Dad might be willing to reconsider the tricolored buzz haircut request.

The final dilemma of the medication issue has to do with who holds the pills: you or your kid. We have loud yelling matches at shrink barbecues over this point. Some psychiatrists say it's the kid's life and choice, and, therefore, they have to medicate themselves and take on that responsibility. Others call that crazy and dangerous, and say that the parents have to monitor these potentially harmful substances. I punt and say it's a complicated decision that depends on the kid's age, problem, maturity level, and the nature of the relationship between parent and child.

The bottom line with medications is that there is no clear bottom line. There are only risks and benefits, which you must weigh. The only truly wrong decision you can make is one based on fear or prejudice. The experts can only offer you their views. The ultimate call must be yours. Wade into the complexity.

So in summary, if you think that maybe you need expert help, it is very likely that you do. Delaying often just makes the problem that much more difficult to treat, so err on the side of safety. What parents frequently anticipate to be the most difficult part of getting help, involving a stranger in their personal lives, turns out to be a fear that evaporates in the waiting room. Almost every parent says that they were so relieved after that feared initial session that they were sorry they waited so long to get help. So gather up your courage and make that call if and when you need to. This is just another one of those headaches you get paid to have as a parent.

Speaking of headaches, your training is complete. Almost. The hard part is done. Now that you've pictured your child in all of those terrible scenarios I've been describing, let's move on to our final chapter to see what happened to those kids who had all those terrible problems, and to those parents who lost all of that sleep. Aren't you dying to find out?

Chapter 17

EPILOGUES: COMING HOME

THE GREATEST GIFT OF AGE is perspective. As we get older we are better able to look back at the events of our lives and see them more clearly. Only perspective gives us true understanding, because when we're busy living an event, we often understand very little about it. We think that being in the middle of an experience enables us to know everything there is to know about the experience, but this is an illusion. Being there makes us part of the experience, but we don't necessarily understand it. Perspective comes later. Perspective is what I think we recognize as wisdom—and you only get it by living and then looking back and reflecting.

Nowhere is this more true than in the world of parenting adolescents. When we're engaged in adolescent battles, just trying to keep everybody alive, we get caught up in the immediate events and think of them as representing forever. This happens because adolescents are so grownup-looking and grownup-sounding that it's very easy to forget that they are just large, brain-dysfunctioned children on their journey to adulthood. The things they passionately embrace are just for today, they're not forever. When parenting teenagers, mistakenly viewing what they are today as representing forever can be very depressing and lead to panic in parents—which, in turn, leads to more insanity in kids.

So in the name of perspective, we're going to cheat Mother Nature a bit and give you some wisdom of age before your time. We're going to play Ebenezer Scrooge and visit with the ghost of your child's future by sharing the end stories of other parents who earned their wisdom the hard way, and then requested that I share it with you. They hope these chapters of their kids' lives will help you keep your cool in dealing with your own child. Calmness is a precious commodity for parents of adolescents.

Many of the folks I've worked with have asked me how I stay so calm when their kid is talking crazy, screaming, or storming out of my office. Actually, it's pretty easy to be Clint Eastwood when the banana isn't your own kid, but an added calming effect is my 27 years of working with teens. In that time, I've seen so many good endings to adolescent stories that the wild middle chapters don't concern me as much as they used to. The statistical fact is that the overwhelming majority of teens have relatively short-lived storms of insanity that, if handled well, transition into the smooth seas of well-adjusted and productive young adulthoods. But statistics are only convincing to cold clinicians who deal with the truths of large, impersonal numbers. Overwhelming probabilities of success don't mean much to terrified parents dealing with the reality of their own crazy kid. Parents of teenagers put much more faith in true stories with names and faces. So take these epilogues as gifts to you from your predecessors.

The veteran parents of adolescents that I know have a lot to say and seem anxious to share their wisdom with others. But the kids, now young adults, say strangely little about their own insane days, perhaps out of discomfort with their embarrassing proximity to the recent past. Many seem to have expunged these bad memories. I see it in their eyes when I softly reference some past terrible time and they squint as if searching for a distant 40-year-old event, saying, "Oh yeah, I think I remember that." It's an odd but clear message: Just let it go. The veteran kids don't have much advice to offer you.

But the parents will talk all night about their experiences, like folks who went on the scariest ride at the park and left exhilarated, as if surprised by their survival. And the people they want most to talk with are all those queasy-looking parents getting strapped in for the next ride. That's you.

"Dr. Bradley? Dr. Bradley? That is you! How are you?" I was shaken out of my mindless staring, waiting my turn at the deli counter, when a familiar face appeared in front of mine. It was Donna. Two years earlier, we had concluded 18 months of working together with her teenage son who had been truant, raging at home, and using drugs to a dangerous extent. Being a parent as well as a psychologist, I'm always reluctant to ask the "whatever happened to?" questions, since I don't want to force someone to relive bad times. But Donna was bursting to tell me.

"Aren't you going to ask whatever happened with Sean?" Before I could explain my awkwardness with the question, she told me. "Sean's in the Marines now. He's doing great! You would never recognize him. When I think of what we went through…" Donna shivered and left that thought unfinished but picked up another. "Before he left, I almost called you. He was sitting there filling out his paperwork and two of the questions asked if he had ever been in mental health treatment and if he had ever done any drugs. He answered 'NO' to both. When I told him he can't lie on these forms he looked at me like I was crazy and asked what I meant.

"I thought he had a stroke or something. How could he have forgotten those days? When he realized what I was referring to, Sean said, 'Mom, they don't care about anything that long ago. That junk doesn't mean anything. That was two years ago! That was another life.' Another life, he says. At the time, it felt like the ending of mine."

Donna then asked me whatever happened with other kids whose parents she would chat with while sitting in my reception area. She withdrew her own question, citing confidentiality, but added, "I feel like I've left some school that hasn't got any reunions. I wish I could say some things to those poor parents who sit there so scared in your waiting room." I told her about this book, took out my pen, tore off a piece of paper, and said, "Shoot."

Donna got very serious. Then she said, "I'd like to tell them to try to remember when their teenager was a baby and got real sick in the middle of the night. That's the worst, you know, because babies can't tell you what's wrong and you can't comfort them. It's so horrible. Here's this screaming child you love so much and you're so helpless. You feel like you're not doing any good, like maybe you're hurting your kid by not knowing and at the same time you hate him for making you feel like that. It just tears you apart inside.

"But you survive. And the next time it happens, it's a little bit better because you know it will end, and you'll probably be fine. That next time you don't hate your kid so much, so you do a better job of helping them as best you can.

"Tell parents it's the same way when the kid's a teenager. They've got to ride it out and try not to hate their kid. He's just gonna be sick for a while." Donna stopped there and shrugged her shoulders. "Is that OK?" she asked. Very OK, Donna.

Reggie also had something on his mind that he wanted to pass along to you.

Reggie phoned in from his car to the talk radio show I was doing. I immediately recognized his distinctive Southern drawl, even though it had been years since we last spoke as we finished working with his adolescent daughter. He made a good point about the issue of drug searches that we had been discussing on the show when I asked if he'd feel comfortable telling the audience what he would do differently if he had to relive his bad days with his teen. I had forgotten how funny he was. He didn't miss a beat.

"I'D STOP BEING SO GODDAMNED MAD ALL THE TIME!" he yelled into his phone. Then he explained the truth in his humor. "Being pissed off at your kid all the while you're trying to make things better with her is like the Three Stooges trying to move the piano. Everybody's pushing against everybody else, gettin' madder 'n madder, and the piano ain't goin' nowhere, except back and forth, back and forth. Once I learned to stay cool, we started moving that piano. So if I was startin' over, I'd learn how to handle my temper first before I'd ever put a hand on that piano or tried to work with my kid. The day I stopped being a tough guy was the day I learned how to be strong. That's when my kid started coming back to me."

Mitchell also had a thought he wanted to share with you.

He stood by himself in the back of the auditorium where I was addressing a crowd of high school parents about working with difficult teens. When I finally realized who this man was whose nodding and sympathetic grinning increased with each distraught parent's question, I introduced Mitchell to the crowd as another adolescent expert who might have some thoughts for us. He laughed and then freely shared that he had worked with me for two years with his own troubled daughter. He briefly summarized their struggles a bit and then proudly noted that she was doing a Peace Corps tour in Russia. The crowd spontaneously began applauding this wonderful news, as if celebrating the possibility that maybe some of their own kids might survive the madness. Mitchell was embarrassed by the applause. "Thanks," he said, "but I didn't come here to brag about my kid. I'm not exactly sure why I'm here." He paused and walked down the aisle.

"But if I came here to tell you folks something, it would be this: I'd like for you all to not feel so alone. When our kids get crazy, we're all so ashamed and so sure that we're the only ones going through this that we kind of fold in on ourselves. That was the worst part for my wife and me. We ended up withdrawing from our lives like we had something wrong with us. That didn't help us and it won't help you. Try to remember that it's your kid who's nuts, that it's temporary, that you'll survive, and that you are not alone. My regret is that I spent so much time creating mountains out of molehills. Well, maybe not molehills, maybe they were small volcanoes, but they weren't the nightmares that I was always so sure they would be. Don't waste so much time worrying over things that never happen. It uses up lots of energy you need to keep yourself calm. Have some faith in the parenting work you've done. It's more powerful than you think." The grateful crowd embarrassed Mitchell a second time with applause.

Finally, Linney dropped me a note that she wanted me to share with you about her daughter Sara, who was one of the most angry and combative adolescent girls I've ever known.

"Dear Dr. Bradley: I had to write to let you know how Sara is doing. I just got off the phone with her. She's completed her first year at college and made *honors*. I told you there were such things as miracles. You were right about how things usually work out OK. I only wish I could have believed you sooner and calmed down more. But that's a very hard thing to do.

Please show this letter to other scared parents. Tell them there truly is a heavenly afterlife: It's called postadolescence. Tell them what Sara was like so maybe they won't have to be as frightened as I was if their kid is aggressive. Being so scared only makes you less able to help your child. Learning to see my daughter as terrified, instead of terrifying, was my turning point.

And sit down for this one. Guess what she's decided she wants to be? A PSYCHOLOGIST! The girl who kicked over your coffee table three years ago wants to be a psychologist! She did ask me to say hi to you, and to tell you that she has decided she would be great at working with teenagers, since she UNDERSTANDS them. She UNDERSTANDS

THEM? I almost laughed out loud, but I've still got my discipline. I just told her that would be great, and that I was so proud of her.' "

And so, dear parents, there's your ghost of teenager future. It looks pretty good, from what I see. If we can all keep cool in these temporary sieges of adolescent insanity, and use our training and not our rage, we can survive—and even flourish—with our children.

As scary as the current state of adolescent parenting seems, we're really just in another societal pendulum swing. Our skills as parents will soon catch up to the rapid changes we've seen in the adolescent culture. I've also come to believe that after all is said and done, parents who love their kids will win out, for these are the parents who fight for their children. Sometimes clumsily, sometimes counterproductively, but they always try. This effort is not lost on their child, particularly as the kid ages a bit, and, dare I say it, matures? Time is on the side of loving parents, if they can just ride out the tempest.

It turns out that love is the magic, after all.

Most of the soldiers who go to war come home. And most of those who return do just fine. A few have a couple of scars, some have lingering bad dreams, but overall, they live and find happiness. The horrors, blessedly, happen to only a few.

So it is with parents of difficult adolescents. Just like diapers, this smelly phase will end, and the results of all that work, worry, and occasional terror will pay off in the form of a personable, well-adjusted young adult who wonders why you aged so much in the last five years. Don't tell her. She's forgotten all about this, anyway, and if you try to tell her, she'll just think you've developed a fondness for exaggeration in your golden years. But don't worry, you'll have your payback.

Amazingly, she'll have kids of her own one day. And then one quiet afternoon you'll have to sit her down, make her a cup of strong tea, gently take her hand, and dispassionately say, "Now, honey, I don't want you to get upset, but there's something you should know about Johnny now that he's turning 11..."

Good luck. Be well. Keep your sense of humor!

Also by Dr. Bradley

A must-read for your teenage children

If you've found *Yes, Your Teen Is Crazy!* helpful, be sure your kids read the companion book, *Yes, Your Parents Are Crazy! – A Teen Survival Guide*. Written in a language and format that teens can relate to, it offers guidance and understanding on all the important issues teens face every day.

◆ Winner of the National Parenting Center Seal of Approval
◆ Foreword by Clay Aiken
◆ Great cartoons by Randy Glasbergen
◆ Filled with real-life stories about teens

ISBN 0-936197-48-X
Available at most bookstores or at www.harborpress.com

SUGGESTED READING

Your teen is unique and you may want more information on topics that pertain more closely to your child's specific situation. The books listed here can be of great help.

Adolescent Development

◆ Hauser, Stuart T., Gil G. Noam, and Sally Isbell Powers. *Adolescents and Their Families: Paths of Ego Development.* New York: The Free Press, 1991.
◆ Pruitt, David (Ed.), American Academy of Child and Adolescent Psychiatry. *Your Adolescent: Emotional, Behavioral, and Cognitive Development from Early Adolescence through the Teen Years.* New York: Harper Collins, 1999.

Anger and Rage Issues

◆ Carter, William Lee. *The Angry Teenager: Why Teens Get So Angry, and How Parents Can Help Them Grow Through It.* Nashville, TN: Thomas Nelson, 1995.
◆ Creighton, Alan with Paul Kivel. *Helping Teens Stop Violence: A Practical Guide for Counselors, Educators, and Parents.* Alameda, CA: Hunter House, 1992.
◆ Greene, Ross W. *The Explosive Child.* New York: Harper Collins, 1998.

Depression and Suicide

◆ Fassler, David G. and Lynne S. Dumans. *Help Me, I'm Sad: Recognizing, Treating, and Preventing Childhood and Adolescent Depression.* New York: Penguin Books, 1998.

◆ Williams, Kate. *A Parent's Guide for Suicidal and Depressed Teens: Help for Recognizing If a Child Is in Crisis and What to Do About It.* Center City, MN: Hazelden Information and Educational Services, 1995.

Eating Disorders

◆ Berg, Frances M. *Children and Teens Afraid to Eat: Helping Youth in Today's Weight-Obsessed World.* Hettinger, ND: Healthy Weight Network, 1998.
◆ Jantz, Gregory L. *Hope, Help, and Healing for Eating Disorders: A New Approach to Treating Anorexia, Bulimia & Overeating.* Wheaton, IL: Harold Shaw, 1995.

Educational/Behavioral Concerns

◆ Ayers, Harry and Doula Nicholson. *Adolescent Problems: A Practical Guide for Parents and Teachers.* London: David Fulton Publishers, 1997.
◆ Cogen, Victor. *Boosting the Adolescent Underachiever: How Parents Can Change a "C" Student into an "A" Student.* Cambridge, MA: Perseus Publishing, 1992.

Medications

◆ Koplewicz, Harold S., M.D. *It's Nobody's Fault: New Hope and Help for Difficult Children and Their Parents.* New York: Times Books, 1996.
◆ Nathan, Peter E. and Jack M. Gorman (Eds.). *A Guide to Treatments that Work.* New York: Oxford University Press, 1998
◆ Wilens, Timothy E., M.D. *Straight Talk About Psychiatric Medications for Kids.* New York: Guilford Publications, 1998.

Parenting

◆ Bodenhamer, Gregory. *Parent in Control: Restore Order in Your Home and Create a Loving Relationship with Your Adolescent.* New York: Simon & Schuster, 1995.

◆ Fenwick, Elizabeth and Tony Smith. *Adolescence: The Survival Guide for Parents and Teenagers.* New York: DK Publishing, 1996.
◆ Gordon, Thomas. *Parent Effectiveness Training (P.E.T.): The Proven Program for Raising Responsible Children.* Pittsburgh: Three Rivers Press, 2000.

Sexual Issues

◆ Basso, Michael J. *The Underground Guide to Teenage Sexuality.* Minneapolis, MN: Fairview Press, 1997.
◆ Owens, Robert E. *Queer Kids: The Challenges and Promise for Lesbian, Gay, and Bisexual Youth.* Binghamton, NY: Haworth Press, 1998.
◆ Stone, Bob and Bob Palmer. *The Dating Dilemma: Handling Sexual Pressures.* Grand Rapids, MI: Baker Book House, 1990.
◆ Stoppard, Miriam. *Sex Ed: Growing Up, Relationships, and Sex.* New York: DK Publishing, 1997.

Substance Abuse

◆ Marlatt, G. Alan and Gary R. Vandenbos (Eds.). *Addictive Behaviors: Readings on Etiology, Prevention, and Treatment.* Washington, DC: American Psychological Association, 1997.

More Parenting Resources

◆ Visit Dr. Mike Bradley on the Internet at www.docmikebradley.com

Index

decision making, 177–78
dispassionate approach, 166–69
guidelines, 225–51
listening skills, 169–74
modeling behavior, 120–21
picking your battles, 206, 227–29
reinforcement, 115–20
strategies, 161–95
teamwork, 135, 140–43
"Ten Commandments of Parenting," 165–95
verbal techniques, 174–76, 183–86
See also rules
parents
affection, need for, 103–8
cool vs. uncool, 121–23
grieving for childhood, 103–12
identity loss, 192–94
influence of, 39, 46–48, 101–2
pride, 179–80
peer pressure, 39–50, 237–39
internal pressures, 45–46
positive influence of, 42–44
vs. parental influence, 39, 46–48
physical punishment, 124–28;
180–83
Physicians' Desk Reference (PDR),
317
piercings, 228
pregnancy, 302–4
Pribram, Dr. Karl, 7
pride, 179–80
privacy, 252–62
problem-solving strategies, 225–51
Protection From Abuse order (PFA),
29–30
psychiatric help
See therapy
psychopathic behavior, 69–70
psychotropic medications, 314
puberty, 25
punishment, 117, 218–24
See also physical punishment

R
Radford University, 7
rage, 263–76
follow-up response, 272–76

impact of, 265–66
physical confrontation, 269
prevention of, 266–67
responding to, 267–72
reinforcement, 115–20
religion, 239–41
respect
and rules, 211–12
of teen for parent, 128–33
Ritalin, 316
rules
amount of, 210–11
consequences, 218–24
contracts, 211–12
enforcing, 212–15, 218–24
limit setting, 213–15
making, 196–203
negotiating, 203–5, 207–12
and respect, 211–12
running away, 241–44
Rutgers University, 147

S
school
academic achievement, 244–47
attendance, 247–48
deaths in, 29
middle school, 41
shootings in, 32
sex, 24–28, 292–304
abstinence, 296
and academic performance, 27
childhood, 24–26
contraception, 297
and drug experimentation, 26
and ecstasy, 27
homosexuality, 298–300
intercourse statistics, 26
and peer pressure, 26–27
postponing, 296
pregnancy, 26, 297, 302–4
talking about, 295–300
single parenting, 148–52
"Six or Sixteen Syndrome," 11
societal change, 16, 18
sociopathic behavior, 69
suicide, 33–35, 85–88
and guns, 36